WHEELS
WITHIN
WHEELS

Dervla Murphy

WHEELS WITHIN WHEELS

New Haven and New York

TICKNOR & FIELDS

1980

In Memoriam
K. R. D.
F. J. M.
R. A. L.
G. C. K.

Copyright © 1979 by Dervla Murphy

First published in the USA in 1980 by
Ticknor & Fields

Published in Great Britain by
John Murray (Publishers) Ltd

Library of Congress Cataloging in Publication Data
Murphy, Dervla, 1931-
  Wheels within wheels.

  1. Murphy, Dervla, 1931- 2. Cyclists—
Ireland—Biography. I. Title.
G269.52.M87A34   1980   941.7082'2'0924 [B]
ISBN 0-89919-006-5   79-27095

Printed in the United States of America

V 10 9 8 7 6 5 4 3 2 1

1

At 7.45 on the morning of November 28, 1931, a young woman in the first stage of labour was handed by her husband into Lismore's only hackney-car. The couple were slowly driven east to Cappoquin along a narrow road, in those days pot-holed and muddy. It was a mild, still, moist morning. During the journey a pale dawn spread over the Blackwater valley, a place as lovely in winter as in summer—a good place to be born.

The woman had waist-length chestnut hair, wavy, glossy and thick. Her features were classically regular, her wide-set eyes dark blue, her complexion had never known—or needed—cosmetics. She had an athletic build, with shoulders too broad for feminine grace. On the previous day, impatient because the baby was a week late, she had walked fifteen miles.

At five foot six the husband was no taller than the wife. "Beauty and the Beast," his mother had observed objectively when the engagement was announced. But this was unfair. He was well proportioned and muscular, with thick black hair, dark brown eyes, a straight nose, an olive complexion—not handsome, yet striking enough in a quiet way. He was earnest though not humourless and firm in his convictions to the edge of intolerance. His manner was difficult and as an essentially lonely introvert he found it easier to listen than to talk. Even at the door of the maternity home he had no ready words of encouragement for his wife. "I'll pray for you," he assured her solemnly. Then he retreated into the hackney and asked the driver to drop him off at the County Library headquarters in Lismore. It was a Saturday and if he started work at nine o'clock instead of ten he could, with a clear conscience, knock off at twelve instead of one. Characteristically, he did not consider granting himself any compassionate leave in honour of the occasion.

This was before the Universal Telephone era and at 12.30 Dr White appeared at the library door. An archetypal G.P.— florid, white-haired, stately, kind—he was accustomed to dealing with son-hungry farmers. "Well now," he growled, "I don't know if I should congratulate you or not." (My father at once visualised some ghastly deformity.) "It's a daughter you have. Came at a quarter to twelve. Strong child." (This was also before the days of universal weighing; babies were either strong or weak.)

My father's reply is not recorded. But as he and my mother had been referring to me as 'Dervla' for the past eight months he perhaps felt no great disappointment. At once he set out to walk the four miles to Cappoquin, carrying a bulky parcel which a more practical man would have put in the hackney-car that morning. It contained the nine records of Beethoven's Choral Symphony. By the time we met I had suffered my first misadventure, a badly burned bottom caused by a burst hot-water bottle. (For more than thirty years the scar faithfully registered severe frosts.)

As a child, it delighted me to hear my mother describing the celebrations that followed. When a gramophone had been borrowed she and my father settled down to hold hands in the firelit dusk while Beethoven expressed their feelings about parenthood and I, in a cradle beside them, expressed mine about burnt bottoms. At that time childbirth was considered an illness and occasionally a nurse would look in and remark ineffectually that my mother was a *patient* and should be *resting*. Then Dr White himself arrived to end this unseemly gaiety. I had been lulled to sleep: but the moment Beethoven stopped I started. So the Murphys won that round, when my mother indicated that she found the 'Ode to Joy' a lot more restful than a howling infant.

Two days later I was christened in Cappoquin's parish church. At first the priest refused to baptise me, insisting peevishly that 'Dervla' was a pagan name and must be changed to something respectably Catholic like Mary or Brigid. My father, however, would not give in. He recalled that a sixth-century St Dervla was reputed to have lived in Co Wexford and that from Ireland the name had spead throughout Europe. Then he carefully explained, to an increasingly impatient curate, that Dearbhail meant True Desire in Gaelic and that the English, French and Latin versions were Dervla, Derval and Dervilla. Finally they compromised; my birth certificate names me as Dervilla Maria.

Although my mother's recovery was rapid we were not allowed home until December 12. Then my first journey took me through countryside that had scarcely changed since Thackeray described it in 1842: 'Beyond Cappoquin, the beautiful Blackwater river suddenly opened before us, and driving along it for three miles through some of the most beautiful rich country ever seen, we came to Lismore. Nothing certainly can be more magnificent than this drive. Parks and rocks covered with the grandest foliage; rich handsome seats of gentlemen in the midst of fair lawns and beautiful bright plantations and shrubberies; and at the end, the graceful spire of Lismore church, the prettiest I have seen in or, I think, out of Ireland. Nor in any country that I have visited have I seen a view more noble—it is too rich and peaceful to be what is called romantic, but lofty, large and *generous*, if the term may be used; the river and banks as fine as the Rhine; the castle not as large but as noble and picturesque as Warwick. As you pass the bridge, the banks stretch away on either side in amazing verdure, and the castle walks remind one somewhat of the dear old terrace of St Germains, with its groves, and long, grave avenues of trees.'

From that bridge it was about a quarter of a mile to my first home on the eastern edge of Lismore. There my parents had rented half a decaying mini-mansion. The other half was occupied by the owner, an obese, elderly, gossipy widow who always smelt of camphorated oil. Her habit of glancing through opened letters, and asking our maid what the Murphys were having for dinner, did not endear her to my mother. At this stage my parents were of enormous interest to the townspeople. And their odd status within the community was greatly to influence my childhood.

Forty years ago the Pale was still a psychological reality and my parents therefore ranked as 'foreigners' in Co Waterford. As far back as the genealogical eye could see both their families

3

were of the Dublin bourgeoisie, only rarely diluted by Huguenot, Scots Presbyterian and Italian-Jewish blood. Among their forbears were printers, ironmongers, doctors, linen weavers, civil servants, cabinet-makers, architects, silk-merchants, musicians, soldiers and sailors. There were no priests or nuns on either side that I ever heard of—unusual in Irish families—and the only known deviations from the bourgeoisie were an eighteenth-century Earl (of Belvedere) and a nineteeth-century kitchenmaid (of Rathmines).

Inevitably, then, my parents were without any ready-made social niche when they migrated south. On one side of a deep rural divide were the gentry and aristocracy, mainly Anglo-Irish and Protestant, and on the other were the farmers and tradesmen, mainly native Irish and Catholic. No true middle class had yet evolved—we missed out on the Industrial Revolution—and professional men were usually the sons either of impoverished gentry or of prosperous farmers. Such people tended to retain their inherited attitudes and interests which, on most points, did not coincide with the attitudes and interests of the young couple from Dublin.

When my parents arrived in Lismore on their wedding day—being too poor to afford even a week-end honeymoon—they found a build-up of suspicious resentment. The previous county librarian had been a popular local figure since the 1870s. He had recently reluctantly retired, leaving nine books fit to be circulated, and the townspeople were furious when an aloof young Dubliner was appointed to replace their beloved Mr Mills. A secure job with a salary of £250 a year had slipped from the grasp of some deserving local and they smelt political corruption. It mattered not to them that no local was qualified for the job, and what little they knew of my father they disliked. His family was conspicuously Republican—a black mark, not long after the Civil War, in a predominantly Redmondite town.

During that summer my parents often travelled together around the county setting up embryonic branch libraries in villages and rural schools. Sometimes they slept in the back of the small library motor-van to economise on petrol—thus saving money for the purchase of extra books—and twice the van was stoned after dark by hostile natives. No doubt wisely, my parents chose to ignore these demonstrations.

4

My father's temperamental reserve must have exacerbated the situation. It was impossible to entice him into a pub and this fact alone, in a society which quite often confuses virility with a capacity for strong drink, aroused the scorn of many local males. Teetotalism on religious grounds would of course have been understood, and in some circles admired, but it was soon known that at home my parents drank *wine* on special occasions, as when entertaining friends from outlandish places like France, Germany or Poland. (They had first met as adults in Poland, where my father was on a cycling tour and my mother on a walking tour. It was then almost twenty years since their last meeting at a children's party in Rathgar.)

As for my mother—she smoked oval Turkish cigarettes specially sent from Dublin, and drank China tea, and preferred her cheese to be smelly. Also, she discussed in mixed company such obscenities as breast-feeding, and walked alone for miles all over the countryside like a farmer's wife—except that she didn't have to—and instead of saying 'good-evening' like a decent Irishwoman she said 'good-afternoon' like the gentry. Worse still, she had had the misfortune innocently to refer to Lismore as a 'village' within days of her arrival, and this monstrous *faux pas*—Lismore has been a cathedral town since the seventh century—was at once misinterpreted as a typical example of urban condescension.

My parents' poverty rendered their eccentric bourgeois tastes even less acceptable. Many initially saw them as penniless upstarts who just because they came from Dublin thought they could impress Lismore with their high-falutin' ways. But there was a certain lack of logic here. No newcomers out to impress the natives would have travelled from Dublin on their wedding day in the cab of the lorry that contained all their worldly goods.

Those goods were a large golden collie named Kevin; a solid three-piece chesterfield suite which remains as good as new to this day, apart from superficial damage inflicted by countless generations of cats; a single bed which provoked ribald comments as it was being unloaded but which seems not to have impeded progress since I was born nine and a half months later; two trunks of clothes and blankets; one tea-chest of crockery and saucepans; one cardboard carton of stainless

5

steel cutlery; one tea-chest of records, and a gramophone; twelve tea-chests of books; fourteen handsomely framed Arundel prints and an original surrealistic painting, by a Hindu artist, of the source of the Ganges; one inlaid Benares brass coffee-table and two silver-rimmed Georgian beer tankards; two kitchen chairs and a kitchen table with a loose leg; one round mahogany dining-table and one very heavy black marble clock which suffered internal injuries on the journey and has never gone right since. This last item was a wedding present from our only rich relative, my mother's grand-aunt Harriet. Unluckily grand-aunt Harriet was mad as well as rich and when she died at the age of ninety-eight she left all her thousands to the Archbishop of Dublin.

On the domestic scene my mother was a cheerfully incompetent bride. Helping my father to pioneer a rural library service was more to her taste than cooking his meals so she engaged an efficient general maid named Nora and, before my birth, devoted most of her energy to working as an unpaid library assistant. Soon the unfriendly natives were being disarmed by the dedication of this young couple to the people of Co Waterford. Also—to be less sentimental—in small communities hostility soon wanes if it cannot be seen to be having an effect. And my parents—deeply in love, enthusiastically absorbed in their new task, willing to be on friendly terms with everybody yet preferring nature-worshipping walks to social gatherings—were not easy targets for those inclined to attempt ostracism.

A romantic approach to nature was one of the strongest bonds linking a couple who in most ways were utterly unlike. Few Dubliners would then have taken happily to life in the country. Now it is 'trendy' to move out of the city, but fashionable migrants are never completely divorced from urban life; they can and usually do select which amenities they wish to take with them. It was different in the '30s. Lismore is some 140 miles from Dublin and during the early years of their marriage my parents could not afford to run a car or even to pay train fares. There was no electricity in the town and of course there were no television or telephone links with the outside world. There were no theatres, cinemas, concert halls or restaurants within reach. Until they had saved enough to buy

6

a wireless—one which I still use every day—they were dependent for entertainment on their modest record collection. And they had no congenial companionship, apart from occasional guests who never stayed long and went away marvelling at the Murphys' capacity for enjoying life against such gruesome odds. But to my parents the odds were not at all gruesome. As Thackeray appreciated, West Waterford is extraordinarily beautiful—and that made up for all that they had left behind.

Two miles south of Lismore a wooded ridge—Ballinaspic—forms the watershed between the Bride and the Blackwater valleys. Standing on a certain gatepost on Ballinaspic's crest one can survey the whole sweep of West Waterford, and always I feel an intoxication of joy as my eye travels from the coast near Dungarvan to the Cork border near Macollop. There are profound differences between one's responses to familiar and unfamiliar landscapes. The incomparable grandeur of the Himalayas fills me with a mixture of exaltation and humility. But the beauty of the Blackwater valley is so much a part of me that it inspires an absurd pride—almost as though I had helped to make it, instead of the other way round.

Looking across that fertile valley from Ballinaspic one sees three mountain ranges. The Comeraghs, above the sea to the north-east, seem like the long, casual strokes of some dreamy painter's brush. The Knockmealdowns, directly overlooking Lismore, are gently curved and oddly symmetrical and display as many shades of blue-brown-purple as there are days in the year. And the Galtees—more distant, to the north-west—rise angular and stern above the lonely moors of Araglen. Opposite Ballinaspic, another long, heavily wooded ridge separates the lower slopes of the Knockmealdowns from the lushness at river-level and is marked by several deep glens, each contributing a noisy stream to the quiet width of the Blackwater. And south-east of Ballinaspic, amidst a calm glory of ancient woods and irregular little fields, one can glimpse the marriage of the Bride and the Blackwater—after the latter has abruptly turned south at Cappoquin.

Due north of Lismore a mountain pass forms the letter V against the sky and is known, with un-Irish prosaicness, as the Vee. Less than three hundred years ago wolves were hunted hereabouts and not much more than one hundred years ago evicted peasants were forced to settle on the barren uplands of Bally-saggart. More fortunate settlers arrived in 1832, a group of Cistercian monks who were presented with a mountain-side by Sir Richard Keane of Cappoquin. Ten years later Thackeray observed that 'the brethren have cultivated their barren mountain most successfully', and now the grey Abbey of Mount Mellery stands solitary and conspicuous against its background of blue hills—an echo of those ancient monasteries which once made known, throughout civilised Europe, the name of Lismore.

In the seventh century St Carthage founded a cathedral and college in Lismore and by the eighth century the place had become a university city where in time both King Alfred the Great and King John (while still Earl of Morton) were to study. In 1173 the 'famous and holy city' was ransacked by Raymond le Gros; and when King John replaced the razed college with a castle it, too, was destroyed. Soon, however, the local bishops had built another castle, which Sir Walter Raleigh eventually acquired. But Sir Walter was not a very competent landowner and in 1602 he gladly sold his castle, surrounded by a little property of 42,000 acres, to Richard Boyle, First Earl of Cork. Some two hundred years later an heiress of the Earl of Cork married a Cavendish and Lismore Castle is still owned by the Devonshire family. Thackeray observed: 'You hear praises of the Duke of Devonshire as a landlord wherever you go among his vast estates: it is a pity that, with such a noble residence as this, and with such a wonderful country round about it, his Grace should not inhabit it more.'

Between the sixteenth and twentieth centuries West Water-ford had to endure less than its share of Ireland's woes. The Villiers-Stuarts of Dromana and the Keanes of Cappoquin always lived on their estates and generally were compassionate landlords—while the Devonshires, though absentees, were not more than usually unscrupulous. Moreover, a local historian, Canon Power, noted that the region 'seems to have been largely cleared of its original Celtic stock on the conclusion of the Desmond wars and . . . the first earl of Cork was able to boast that he had "no Irishe tenant on his land" '.

This successful mini-plantation may partly explain a scarcity of Republicans in the area. Many local families had not been settled in West Waterford for as long as the main land-owning clans; and in the absence of inherited resentments—based on racial memories of conquest and land confiscation—unusually harmonious relations developed between landlords and tenants. But one has to grow up in a place to be aware of these nuances. My parents, looking in from outside, recognised none of the benefits that for centuries had been made available to both sides by West Waterford's feudal system. Judging the rural social scene by urban standards, they saw only arrogance and profiteering on the one side and spineless servility on the other. And nowhere a slot for themselves.

What sort of person would I now be had I grown up a typical Dubliner, regarding the countryside as something to be enjoyed in literature and avoided in life? But I simply cannot imagine myself as an urban animal. To me, city-dwellers are The Dispossessed, unfortunates who have been deprived of every creature's right to territory. There is a sense in which country folk, however impoverished, own their birthplace and all the land around it that can be covered in a long day's tramp—the natural, immemorial limit to the territory of a human being. Or perhaps it is that each region owns its people, exacting a special, subtle loyalty, a primitive devotion that antedates by tens of thousands of years the more contrived emotion of nationalism. Either way, there exists an element of *belonging* such as surely cannot be replaced or imitated by any relationship, however intense, between the city-dweller and his man-made surroundings.

2

During the first year of my life the steep climb up to Ballin-aspic was among my mother's favourite walks. ("Sure the creature must be mad entirely to be pushin' a pram up there!") Yet by November 1932 she could push me no further than the Main Street. Suddenly she had been attacked again by that rheumatoid arthritis which had first threatened her at the age of twenty. By my first birthday she could no longer walk without the aid of a stick and by my second she could no longer walk at all. On the 29th of that December she was twenty-six.

There was of course no cure. But doctors in various countries were doggedly experimenting and, escorted by her favourite brother, my mother went to England, Italy and Czechoslovakia for six months, pretending to hope yet sure, inwardly, that she would never walk again. She spent the whole of 1934 either abroad or in Dublin, leaving me to be looked after by Nora under the vague supervision of my father. In theory this abrupt and inexplicable disappearance of an adored mother, when I was at the crucial age of two years, should have damaged me for life. Perhaps it has, but I am never troubled by the scars. I was by nature adaptable, my routine was unbroken, Nora was devoted and sensible and my father was attentive in his didactic way. (A family legend, possibly apocryphal but very revealing, tells of his bewildered grief when I failed, at the age of two and a half, to assimilate the rules governing the solar system.)

In December 1934 my mother returned to Lismore as a complete cripple, unable even to walk from the sitting-room to the downstairs lavatory, or to wash or dress herself, or to brush her hair. Between them, my father and the steadfast Nora cared for her and for me.

Now there were major money worries. My mother's search for a cure had cost a great deal and my father was heavily in debt to numerous relatives. Both my parents found this deeply humiliating, innocent though they were of any imprudence or extravagance. My father was almost panic-stricken and it was my mother who calmly took up the challenge. Probably a practical crisis, and the discovery of her own unsuspected ability to manage money, helped her at this stage. She soon began to enjoy pound-stretching; I still have some of the little account books in which she neatly entered every penny spent on food, fuel, clothes, rent and so on. My father then happily returned to his natural money-ignoring state and for the rest of their married life my mother held the purse-strings.

By this time my parents had realised that they could have no more children, which for devout Roman Catholics meant resigning themselves to an unnaturally restricted marriage. In our sex-centred world, this may seem like the setting for a life-long nightmare. Having been thoroughly addled by popular pseudo-Freudian theories about libidos, repressions and fixations, we tend to forget that human beings are not animals. It would be ridiculous to suggest that the ending of their sexual relationship imposed no strain on my parents, but they certainly found it a lighter burden than we might think. Religious beliefs strong enough to make sexual taboos seem acceptable, as 'God's will', do not have to be merely negative; faith of that quality can generate the fortitude necessary for the contented observance of such taboos. Restrictions of personal liberty are destructive if accepted only through superstitious fear, but to both my parents the obeying of God's laws, as interpreted by the Holy Roman Catholic Church, was part of a rich and vigorous spiritual life. This area of their experience—I felt later on—put them in a mental and emotional world remote from my own, where they were equipped with an altogether different set of strengths and weaknesses.

Not long before her death, my mother told me that after getting into bed on their wedding night neither of my parents had known quite what to do next. So they went to sleep. In the 1970s it is hard to believe that two healthy, intelligent human beings, who were very much in love, could have devoted their wedding night exclusively to sleep. But perhaps they were not exceptional among their breed and generation. My mother had been curtly informed by her mother—who had borne seven children and endured countless miscarriages—that sexual intercourse was at all times painful and distasteful. And my father would certainly have considered any investigation of the subject, even in theory, to be grossly improper before marriage.

Sex apart, an inability to have more children was agonising for someone as intensely maternal as my mother. It also put me, at once, in danger. All the emotion and interest that should have been shared among half-a-dozen became mine only. By the time I was five most people considered me a peculiarly nasty child and mistook the reason why. In fact my mother was such a strict disciplinarian that throughout childhood and adolescence I remained healthily afraid of arousing her anger. But what she could not avoid—my being the sole object of her maternal concern—was the encouragement of a ruthless egotism. However, this trait was no doubt useful at the time as insulation against the adult suffering around me. Elizabeth Bowen once wrote, 'Perhaps children are sterner than grown-up people in their refusal to suffer, in their refusal, even, to feel at all.' My mother—reading *Bowen's Court*—once drew my attention to that remark. She did not comment on it, but I have since wondered if she meant it to comfort me. During childhood, I never stopped to sympathise with my parents' situation. Indeed, only when I became a mother myself did I appreciate how my own mother must have felt when she found herself unable to pick me up and hug me, and brush my hair, and tuck me up in bed.

After my parents' deaths I came upon the letters they had written to each other, almost daily, during their six-month engagement. On the whole these might have been written by any happy young couple to whom marriage promised nothing but fulfilment. My father hoped to found a model county library service and write novels; with my mother to inspire him he felt certain these must be masterpieces. For relaxation he looked forward to some deep-sea fishing and an expanding record collection. My mother hoped to have six children at two-year intervals (three of each, if possible, though she conceded this might be difficult to arrange) and to use them—one gathered, reading between the lines—as guinea-pigs on which to test her various theories about physical and mental health. She also hoped to find time to study in depth, under my father's guidance, the early schisms within the Christian Church—a subject of ineffable tedium to which she remained addicted all her life. She felt, too, that in her role as county librarian's wife she should initiate a Literary Debating Society (she had not yet visited the town) and perhaps a Music Society. For relaxation she looked forward to walking tours in West Cork and Kerry, presumably on her own while my father deep-sea fished and their systematically increasing offspring were being looked after by some capable Treasure. This correspondence had just one surprising feature. Neither of my penniless parents ever mentioned money, or promotion, or buying a house or a motor-car, or in any way planning financially for the future. Both seemed to assume that they would spend the rest of their lives in Lismore—my father wrote ecstatic descriptions of the surrounding countryside—and judging by these letters they were utterly without material ambition.

The few personal memories I retain from my first five years are mostly painful. Our house—or half-house—was separated from the road by a six-foot stone wall, sprouting valerian. When attempting to pick a bouquet for my mother at the age of three I fell and broke my nose. A few months later, driving with my father in the library van, I broke it again when he had to brake suddenly because of wandering cattle. I also remember being excited by the exotic springtime glory of the giant rhododendron tree which overshadowed our unkempt lawn. (I have seen none finer in Europe outside Kew, yet it was felled in 1972 because it took up too much space ...) Behind the house were a small yard, a large garden and an enormous orchard securely enclosed by ten-foot stone walls. Here my movements were unrestricted and my chief companion was Billy, a rotund black pony who grazed the orchard, gave me rides and pulled us around the countryside in a trap. (At this stage we had no dog; my mother's beloved Kevin had been stolen a few weeks after my birth.)

In the spring of 1935 it was decided that for character forming purposes I needed 'young friends'. My mother

13

therefore arranged various juvenile social occasions and my most vivid memory from this period is a feeling of fury when other children disrupted the elaborate fantasy-world I had created in the orchard.

For my fourth birthday party cousins and an imposing cake were imported from Dublin. But at three o'clock, when the local guests began to assemble, I was missing. Nora quickly traced me to a derelict shed, overgrown with briars, at the end of the garden. My detested beribboned party dress of salmon-pink silk—I can see it still—was torn and streaked with green mould stains, and my back, in every sense, was to the wall. "You should be ashamed of yourself!" fumed Nora. "Stuck out here all mucked up with that *gorgeous* dress *rooned* an' your visitors waitin' inside an' even your blood relations down from Dublin!"

My reply was to become a clan slogan. "I don't want any bloody relations," I replied succinctly. "I'm staying here."

Nora, it seems, was familiar with this impasse. Compromising desperately, she assured me that if I consented to grace the party with my presence I need not wear 'party clothes'; whereupon I meekly trotted indoors. One changes very little. I still dislike 'party clothes'.

In March 1936 our obese landlady died and my mother and I moved to Dublin for six months while my father was house-hunting. I stayed in turn with my mother and maternal grandmother and with my father's parents.

My mother's mother was known as Jeff to her face, for some entirely obscure reason, and as The Battle-axe behind her back for reasons not at all obscure. She was an exceedingly disagreeable women who spoiled me methodically by way of tormenting my mother. As I was not allowed sweets she offered me sweets at every hour of the day and night and was piqued when I spat them out because they felt and tasted unfamiliar. As my normal bedtime was six o'clock she reorganised the household to prevent my getting to bed before eight o'clock. As comics were frowned upon, lest they might impair my tender literary taste-buds (a paternal directive, this), she bought me a daily comic. And so it went on, a spiteful campaign in which I was the unwitting weapon and her daughter the helpless victim.

14

My mother dealt with the situation by telling me, "Different people have different views. While we are staying here we must respect your grandmother's views." Thus she evaded direct condemnation while making it clear that on our return home the usual disciplines would be reimposed. For a parent who values consistency there is nothing more provoking than the deliberate undermining of a child's régime. Yet my mother's self-control never cracked. No doubt this restraint further incensed Jeff, who enjoyed nothing more than a good fish-wifely brawl.

Much as I relished Jeff's spoiling I was never quite at ease in that semi-detached red-brick Victorian house. My mother's parents had lived in it all their troubled married life and it had bad vibes. Family opinion blamed Jeff for the fact that her husband—handsome, charming and warm-hearted—was an alcoholic; but this may have been unfair. She can have done nothing to help him control his drinking, but it is doubtful if even the happiest marriage could have saved him from the bottle.

There was an amount of instability in my grandfather's background. His own father—the son of a senior civil servant at Dublin Castle—had fallen in love with the kitchen-maid, got a chamber pot thrown at his head when the betrothal was announced and soon after emigrated to America with his unacceptable bride and the statutory shilling. Three years and three children later the young couple returned to Dublin, my great-grandfather having found the American way of life insufficiently civilised. For the rest of his life he practised civilisation by drinking too much port and collecting coins while his wife—an energetic and courageous woman—ran an Academy for (very) Young Ladies. As she had been illiterate on her wedding day her husband perhaps deserves some credit for having taken the trouble to teach her how to read and write. Mercifully, Providence spared her any more children after the return to Dublin.

At the age of fourteen my grandfather had to find a job and with wild illogic his father objected to his working as a messenger-boy for a firm of silk importers. It was perfectly in order for a wife to work eighteen hours a day to support an idle husband, but for a son and heir to run errands—no!

15

Unthinkable! This son and heir, however, did not intend to run errands for long. On his twenty-first birthday, after a two-year training course in Lyons, he was made assistant-manager of the Dublin branch of his firm. And three years later he was managing-director—a good catch, then, for my unendowed grandmother.

The trouble on her side was religion. Her mother, the daughter of a Scots Presbyterian cotton magnate, had come to Dublin on a holiday, fallen in love with a dashing Roman Catholic cabinet-maker—presumably when he was working in her host's house as they would scarcely have been moving in the same social circle—and urged him to emigrate to Edinburgh. This he devotedly did and a clandestine courtship ended with an elopement—in a snowstorm, it is said, but I suspect this of being a period embellishment.

My great-grandmother's dowry would have been substantial had she married suitably and no doubt adequate had she married a cabinet-maker of her own faith. As it was, the statutory shilling again had to suffice though she did not herself become a Catholic. Sadly, her disinterested love was ill-rewarded; at the age of thirty-four she was left a widow with seven young children. When she despairingly contacted her family they offered financial help on condition that her four Catholic sons be brought up as Presbyterians. She herself must have been a convinced Presbyterian or she would have adopted her beloved husband's faith. But on their wedding day they had agreed, as was then the custom, to bring up their sons as Catholics and their daughters as Presbyterians. She therefore declined her family's offer of help and set up as a sempstress to provide for her children.

Despite their aura of smelling-salts, Victorian women were a gallant lot—often widowed young, never helped by the state, without formal training yet indomitably resourceful when obliged to support innumerable children. In this case three boys and a girl died young of the tuberculosis that had killed their father. But my great-grandmother survived into her eighties and was affectionately remembered by my mother as a tall, thin, gracious old lady with an ineradicable Scottish accent. Regularly on Sunday afternoons she read the bible to her restive Catholic grandchildren before providing lavish teas at which they could eat their fill of home-made short-bread and oatcakes and honey.

My mother and her siblings were not often allowed to eat their fill. Even when my grandfather was earning £3,000 a year—which in those far days meant affluence—my grandmother obsessively rationed the children's food. Avaricious and covetous by nature, she could not forgive her own mother for having put honour before wealth. (I have always uncharitably suspected her of becoming a Catholic simply to spite my loyally Presbyterian great-grandmother.) And her sadistic withholding of plentiful food from hungry children was probably a way of taking her revenge on her husband for his generosity (admittedly not always prudent) towards less well-off friends and relatives.

Jeff had a tight-lipped aversion to gaiety and pleasure, however innocent. As a very small child I became aware of her total lack of humour though I could not then have defined what so often made me uncomfortable in her presence. I also became aware of the animosity she felt towards my mother, which possibly explains an odd little incident which occurred in the autumn of 1936.

Jeff wore a wig, having been afflicted by total baldness as a girl, and though it was a most superior wig it did not deceive me. Sitting on her lap one afternoon I looked into the garden and saw her black Persian cat—strangely named Zog, after the King of Albania—stalking a bird under an apple tree. Then suddenly I knew that I was about to be very wicked. I remember thinking that there should be a choice—surely I need not be wicked—yet the compulsion to hurt Jeff was so overwhelming that it seemed to leave no choice. I turned and touched the wig and observed, "That's not real hair." And as I spoke I was so appalled by my cruelty that I began to shake all over.

Both my parents were present, sitting side by side in the background, and at once I glanced towards them. Yes, they had heard. My father looked grieved and my mother wrathful as she murmured something in his ear. Obediently he stood up, carried me out to the hall, reprimanded me sorrowfully and smacked me once very gently on the bottom. This was my first and last domestic experience of corporal punishment—if that is the right term for a chastisement that was virtually indistinguishable from a caress.

When we returned to the sitting-room Zog had caught his prey and was devouring it on the window-sill. Jeff cuddled and consoled me exaggeratedly while upbraiding my parents for treating their little innocent so harshly. I had never before heard grown-ups disagreeing openly about child-control and was fascinated by the new vistas of adult fallibility thus opened up.

Not long after this I nearly joined the angels by drinking half a bottle of neat whiskey. Had I gone on a similar binge in Lismore I would almost certainly have died. As it was, an ambulance rushed me to hospital where I recovered with a speed that ominously foreshadowed an infinite capacity for strong liquor. But the most significant aspect of my adventure was lost on me at the time. I had come upon this half-bottle not in the sideboard, amongst the genteel decanters of sherry and port, but at the bottom of my grandmother's wardrobe.

Given Jeff's views on sex, as transmitted to my mother, she must have been an insipid bedmate. It is therefore not surprising that my grandfather quietly maintained a second establishment in Paris, where his business took him with convenient regularity. Not long before his death he told my mother that five children had been born of this union—obviously his true marriage, in every sense but the legal.

At the age of forty-nine my grandfather was 'requested to resign' because of his hard drinking. My mother then had to return from Munich, where she had just begun to train as a singer. Her two elder brothers had already completed their education, but the younger boys had to be transferred from their Jesuit college to a free day-school. Then the Ford had to be sold, the servants dismissed, the telephone disconnected and the silver pawned. My grandfather could afford to go to Paris only very occasionally—when his mistress sent him the fare—and he was continually exposed to his wife's contempt. A proud man, he felt his degradation keenly. No one then thought of alcoholism as a disease and he was very conscious of being despised. He drank even harder and borrowed more and more frantically. Meanwhile the family was being kept by his port-sodden father, who had recently inherited a comfortable income from one of the sisters amongst whom his patrimony had been divided when he embraced his kitchen-maid.

My grandfather was declared bankrupt two years after his dismissal—or 'resignation', as the nicer members of his family chose to call it. A year later his father died and on the way back from the funeral he paused to light his pipe, sat unsteadily on a wall by the Royal Canal, toppled over, struck his head on a stone and was drowned in eighteen inches of water. Very strangely, for the spot was nowhere near their home, my mother chanced to be passing and witnessed his body being lifted onto the pavement. He was already dead. But for the first ghastly, absurd moment what most upset her was the stench of the slimy weeds that clung to the corpse's impeccable morning-suit. Even when bankrupt her father had remained something of a dandy.

My mother and he had been exceptionally close—hence Jeff's dislike of her daughter—and I heard him spoken of so often during my childhood that I now find it hard to believe I never knew him. Obviously father and daughter were very alike though luckily my mother's penchant for gracious living was tempered by an awareness that one cannot live both honestly and graciously on a few hundred pounds a year.

For both our sakes, my mother preferred me to spend more time with my paternal grandparents than with herself and Jeff. A fifteen-minute tram-ride took me from Kenilworth Park to Charleston Avenue so I could still see my mother almost daily. But though the spatial distance between the two households was slight the spiritual distance was vast.

At Charleston Avenue there was poverty, too, but it was happy-go-lucky rather than gloomy and self-pitying. The house was shabby, dark, damp and cramped—yet comfortable. It might have seemed less cramped had there been fewer tottering piles of books on every flat surface. The uninitiated sometimes hinted that a week spent tidily arranging these volumes would make life less inconvenient—not to say perilous—for all concerned. But the initiated knew that the volumes were already arranged to my grandfather's satisfaction and that from amidst the seeming chaos he could at a moment's notice produce any required work, whether on the Birds of Patagonia, the History of Printing in North Africa or the Bogotrid Sect of Tenth-Century Bulgaria. I remember that all ornithological tomes were stacked high on the first four steps of the second flight of stairs. Lord Brougham (Collected Works of) towered beside the lavatory and countless volumes of scriptural commentary had to be removed from the bed in the spare room before I could lie down.

I loved that spare room. Narrow corridors between piles of desiccated books led to the two beds and even before I could read I got high on the pungent mustiness of ancient volumes. On summer evenings I used to slip out of bed and move cautiously about the room, picking up and stroking and glancing through volume after volume, pleased if I found illustrations but not bored if I didn't. To see and touch and smell those books filled me with content, with feelings of joy and security and richness. And also—even at four and a half—with ambition.

I perfectly understood my grandfather's triumph when, at the end of a long day in the second-hand bookshops on the quays, he came trudging home hidden behind a pile of bargains. This, as far as he and I were concerned, was what life was all about. Therefore I have always relished The Tale of Pappa's Trousers.

Once upon a time Granny gave her spouse enough cash to buy himself a very necessary pair of everyday trousers. (For obvious reasons he was not normally entrusted with such large sums of money.) Wearing his Sunday suit, because he had nothing else fit to wear, he set off for wherever the cheapest men's clothing was to be had. But unluckily his route took him onto the quays and there he chanced to notice the ten-volume 1840 edition of Sismondi's *Histoire des Républiques Italiennes*, elegantly bound and without a blemish. It cost considerably more than he had in his pocket, but he judged it to be a bargain and acted with a decisiveness that had it been otherwise directed might have made him a rich man. Nearby was a second-hand clothes shop where he quickly flogged his Sunday suit and bought threadbare trousers for a few shillings. The substantial balance, added to his original allowance, just about paid for Sismondi and his tram fare home. He arrived at Charleston Avenue in a state of advanced euphoria. But as he was also in his shirt-sleeves, and very nearly indecently exposed, it is not surprising that his wife failed to appreciate the *Histoire des Républiques Italiennes* in ten vols.

Not that my grandmother could afford to criticise Pappa's obsession: her own was no less uncontrollable and, at least to me, a good deal less understandable. She played bridge, almost literally without ceasing. Naturally I found this a bore, yet I do not remember regarding as abnormal the fact that she and her cronies ate, drank and slept according to the fall of the cards. They might be retiring as I crept downstairs at 7 a.m. to play beneath the overgrown laurel bushes in the back garden. Or they might be in full cry at lunch-time, in which case Pappa and I would quietly settle down to a snack of bread and very ripe Stilton. (So ripe that it had been bought at half-price.) It was not uncommon for the cronies to sleep on divans in the sitting-room, lest their departures and returns might waste time.

Who cooked and washed up? (it was evident that nobody cleaned). I can recall no maid or daily, yet neither do I remember ever going hungry. However, the permanent state of the dining-table proved the subordinate rôle played by food in this household. It was a large table and my memory is of one sordid, crumby corner grudgingly left clear of books and journals and sheaves of notes written in Pappa's tiny, precise hand.

Pappa—when not delivering philosophy lectures at University College Dublin—was generally understood to be writing A Book. Its subject, however, was never disclosed. My guess would be that he started several books on diverse subjects and finished none of them for lack of mental stamina—or possibly for lack of physical stamina. As a captured Old IRA volunteer, he had been on hunger strike in England for six weeks during 1918, in a bid to have his status as a political prisoner recognised, and this effort at the age of forty-eight had permanently damaged his health. During the same period his wife had also been 'inside', as a leader of the women volunteers, Cumann na mBan, and a boundless nationalistic fervour was the couple's only obvious common trait. Yet they were very happy together, each amiably tolerating the other's foibles, and they gave my mother a taste of easy-going affection such as she had never enjoyed in her own home.

The flavour of that affection is well conveyed by the letter which Pappa wrote to my father for his twenty-first birthday, which was celebrated in Bedford jail. (My father had been sentenced to three years for concealing weapons and ammunition in his back garden.)

18 Garville Ave.,
Rathgar,
Dublin.
15 Dec. 1921

A Fearguis, a Mic mo Croide,

Many very happy returns of your birthday, my darling boy! Fondest love and congratulations and thousands of kisses from your mother. May God bless and protect and inspire you: may he fill your heart with his wisdom, his love and his comfort. Connie, Kathleen, Conn and Auntie join with us, your loving parents, in wishing you joy on your coming of age and hoping you will have a long and happy life.

I can scarcely realize that on tomorrow it will be twenty-one years from that joyous Sunday noon when I first heard your infant voice and held you as a tender babe in my arms —my first little son! Well, thank God, your conduct and character since that happy morning have never caused me a moment's anxiety—on the contrary, my love and trust and hope and pride in you have increased from year to year and today these thoughts and feelings are a source of the greatest joy and thankfulness. I think it right to tell you this, so that you may read it on the day when you are standing on the threshold of young manhood.

As I write this, An Dail is sitting to determine the most momentous question which had ever been considered by an assembly of Irishmen—shall the Treaty be ratified or not. I tried to put the best face on it for you in my last letter, but we cannot conceal the fact that it was a profound disappointment to most of us; and the more we look at it, the less we like it. It has one very big advantage and two very decided drawbacks. In the first place it provides for the withdrawal of the army of occupation from four-fifths of Ireland and enables us to set up our own army of defence, at least

40,000 strong, in the district thus evacuated—all this is to the good. But, we have not got a Republic and an absolutely sovereign state for four-fifths of Ireland—and we have got nothing at all for Ireland as a whole. We have not got a united Ireland—the Treaty recognizes and sanctions partition. The President, Cathal Brugha and Austin Stack are opposed to ratification and many regard the Treaty as tantamount to a betrayal.

It is uncertain therefore whether it will be ratified or not; or whether there will be an appeal to the country. Until ratification takes place, it is unlikely that the sentenced political prisoners will be released and consequently you may have to eat your Christmas dinner yet again in an English prison. But keep a stout heart. No matter what happens our position is greatly improved. It is difficult to know which to pray for—rejection or ratification; there is so much to be said both ways now. You must, accordingly, abate the ardour of your first enthusiasm: mine has cooled very rapidly.

Perhaps you had best spend a week in London and have a look round. You may not get the chance again for a long time. It will be interesting in the future to look back upon what London was like when it was the capital of a big empire. Time is sure to bring many changes and in a few decades London may be a very different place.

You might let me have a list of the things supplied to you by Wallace as I want to check the account he has sent in. Order from him whatever you want—food, tobacco or cigarettes: it is much quicker and handier than sending them by parcel post. Don't hesitate to send for whatever you require. The books you requested last month are being sent today; your letter asking for them arrived after I had left for Rome. I hope that you will not have much time to read them in prison. God knows you must be heartsick of prison life, and with the prospect of a fourth consecutive Christmas in prison before you you cannot feel too cheerful. However, Nil Desperandum!

We expect Connie home to-morrow or Thursday; she didn't like her latest prison at all. We have a friend of hers staying with us now who was her cell-mate for a long time in the N.D.U. We had a letter from Conn yesterday, dated 3

Dec. and quite cheery. He seems to be in good form and is confidently awaiting his release before Xmas. He says he enjoyed your last letter.

I got a pretty bad cold on my return from sunny Italy* but I am now recovered. I can arrange, later on, to meet you in Holyhead on your return journey.

With fondest love and heartiest wishes for a Happy Birthday, Your affectionate

Pappa.

The earlier letter about the Treaty, in which Pappa had 'tried to put the best face on it', was written on December 8, 1921, and began:

May God save and prosper the Free State of Ireland! You have no doubt heard the good news that a settlement has been agreed to between the English and Irish nations. It is not quite all that we had hoped it would be, but it is very good indeed and very much better than anything which seemed within the bounds of possibility a few years ago. And we have to thank you and the comrades with whom you fought for the magnitude of the victory. We have not succeeded in establishing an Irish Republic for a united Ireland, it is true. But we have got the real substance and can afford to wait a bit for the name. The sovereign independent Free State of Ireland will be in actual existence within a month and you will be coming back to live in that Free State which your courage and sacrifices have helped to create. So rejoice and be exceedingly glad. Let no disappointment cloud your joy or diminish your legitimate pride in what has been accomplished. On your return I shall explain fully to you the real value—as distinct from the paper value—of what we have won. I believe that the convicts will be released as soon as the Treaty has been ratified by An Dail and the English Parliament and that will be, probably, within a week.

I have asked Mamma to send you on the biggest portmanteau in the house. Cord up all your books, make sure they are fastened securely and bring them all home safely.

*Pappa had been in Rome as Ambassador to the Vatican from the Government of the Irish Republic.

What had caused Pappa to change his attitude towards the Treaty so radically within exactly one week? 'Putting the best face on it' for a son in jail is not a sufficient explanation. Did the real 'substance' referred to on December 8 prove after all insubstantial? And was it in some way connected with the negotiations which Pappa had been conducting with the Vatican on behalf of the Provisional Government of the Irish Republic? I have been able to find no answer to this question in the vast accumulation of letters and papers now in my possession.

The convicts were not released before Christmas and on December 23 Pappa wrote to his 'beloved son':

> The Dail has not been able to make up its mind about the Treaty and last evening decided by 77 votes to 44 to adjourn its consideration of the matter to 3 Jan. So this means an end to all our hopes of having you home for Christmas. Poor Feargus! It is too bad, indeed; but never mind, my dear son, there is a good time coming and this is, I hope, the last big trial of the kind which the providence of God will permit to be inflicted on you. So keep up your heart and laugh English prisons to scorn. We were disgusted to hear that two extra days have been imposed on you for something which happened in Mountjoy before your transfer to Wormwood Scrubs. This is typical of English meanness, but let it pass. I was going to bring the matter to the attention of the IRA liason officer, but on second thoughts I decided not to!
>
> The handling of the position created by the Treaty did no credit to the Dail: they have spent too much time discussing the pros and cons of theoretical points instead of addressing themselves to practical affairs. However, no human institution is perfect and perhaps we expected too much of our representatives. Opinion is settling steadily in favour of ratification and, although nobody is madly in love with the Treaty, there seems to be nothing else to do in the present circumstances but to accept it.

Four days later Pappa was writing again:

> It will be fine to have you home for New Year's Day! You will see the first sun of 1922 shining on the slopes of

Kilmashogue and lighting up the top of the Three Rock and flecking with light and shadow the little trout stream out of which you so often fished a breakfast for yourself and Kathleen. And a good deep draught of our sweet Irish air will soon make the blood again run freely and warmly in your veins.

We are going down to Malahide this evening to see Cathal Brugha: he is greatly upset about the Treaty and thinks it ought not to be accepted on any account. Things are looking particularly ugly just at present. A double crooked game is being played against us and I should not be surprised if the Conference broke up this week. *The Irish Bulletin* got hold of a secret circular issued by the RIC Divisional Commander in Belfast organising a secret Orange army—and has published it! Of course the Cabinet will repudiate it but there it is and very significant, too. In addition the British Govt. is hastily pushing on the Partition Act arrangements to give Belfast full powers and in order to do so is committing all sorts of illegalities and riding rough-shod over its own precious Act. So we are by no means within sight of a settlement yet. 'Ulster' has now been paraded on stage and the marionettes wave their wooden arms and shout 'No surrender!' in the approved Orange style. Of course in this case the benevolent English Govt., anxious to do its best to effect a settlement, finds all its efforts thwarted by the irreconcilable quarrels between Irishmen themselves. What can you do with a hopeless people like this except keep a tight grip on them to prevent their killing each other? If Irishmen could only come to some agreement among themselves and tell the British exactly what they do want—there would be no trouble at all. Everything that a united Ireland asked for would be granted on the spot! And so the old game goes merrily on—just for the moment. But the curtain is about to be rung down on this tragi-comedy and to be rung up on a different style of drama presenting some very novel features.

[Alas! Pappa was wrong there: contemporary Northern Ireland proves *how* wrong. The equivalent of his next paragraph has appeared with monotonous frequency in Irish newspapers during the past decade.]

There has been great trouble in all the internment camps

26

since the truce. Conditions grow worse instead of better and the boys are having a rotten time. In Ballykinlar especially the British have gone out of their way to be nasty. They shot Alderman Tadgh Barry the other day just as he was waving good-bye to some released internees. A sentry pretended to think that Tadgh was trying to escape and shot him dead. There was great grief in Cork and great indignation everywhere. Friday and Saturday saw a very impressive funeral, the cortège coming from Ballykinlar by motor and being received by Volunteers and big crowds on the way down to Dublin.

We had a great day at the National University on Saturday when we installed President de Valera as Chancellor. It was a splendid turn-out with the Chancellor himself of course the most striking figure. He wore a robe of black velvet with rich gold trimmings and looked like both a ruler and a scholar; his tall figure and his thin ascetic face were fittingly set off by his magnificent robes. We gave him a great reception—and no mistaking its significance! What an extraordinary revolutionary change has the National seen! Who would have dreamed, a few short years ago, that an unknown and despised B.A. would on Saturday have been installed with great pomp and ceremony as Head of the entire university! Time! thou bringest mighty revenges! The IRA furnished a guard of honour and Kathleen, as Captain of the University Company of Cumann na mBan, mustered her sixty-five hefty cailin who made an impressive display. She also read an address in Irish to the Chancellor, who replied in Irish. Except for one speech, all the proceedings were conducted either in Latin or in Irish. The doctors' gowns with their various colours 'brightened up the scene' wonderfully. I was resplendent in a scarlet gown with maroon sleeves and a maroon hood lined with green silk. Next to the Chancellor's, it was the best robe in the show!

Everybody is looking forward to having you home, including Bob and Whiskers who are purring beside me at the thought. I hope you got the portmanteau and that you will find it big enough for all your books.

Fondest love from your own affectionate

Pappa.

Throughout his time in prison my father had received from Pappa as many letters as were allowable, some covering more than twenty foolscap pages and few less than ten. Each included a detailed account of the latest political developments and an assessment of how Dubliners of every shade of opinion were reacting to them. Pappa also occasionally reminded his son that 'the average Englishman is a decent enough fellow'—from which rather unexpected comment one may deduce that my father's letters (now lost) were betraying that obsessional anti-English bias which he was never to outgrow. Pappa was too kindly to condemn any race completely; therefore his hatred of British rule in Ireland led him to draw a not very convincing distinction between 'the average decent Englishman and the governing mind—for that is the only mind that finds expression in the country's corporate institutions—and it is a strange mixture of Saxon dullness and Norman cruelty'. So much for his faith in British democracy.

These letters give a wonderfully vivid picture of contemporary life in Dublin. Repeatedly 18 Garville Avenue was raided, sometimes when the house was empty, and once the British troops helped themselves to £5-10-0 which Pappa had imprudently left in a wallet in his bedroom. He got no satisfaction when he wrote to the C.O. complaining that the maid and the gardener could not be paid that week unless the money were restored. This was literally true—not a sob-story—and after the gardener had left in a huff there are some wry references to Mamma's unsuccessful attempts to replace his labours with Pappa's. Soon after, Maria, the maid, also left to get married and was replaced by 'Mrs Bruagh's maid, Agnes, who plays the melodeon beautifully and often entertains us in the drawing-room. She remembers you well: she says you are a nice young gentleman and not a bit proud as you spoke to her kindly one day when she was out with the Bruagh children.' So much for attitudes towards servants sixty years ago.

The burning of the Customs House and the various reactions of Dubliners to that event are graphically described; Pappa's own reactions were—as he admitted—very mixed. Then on June 1 he writes:

In Dublin now it is positively dangerous to walk the

streets. Not a day passes without four or five ambushes taking place. You are walking down say, Nassau St., when suddenly you hear a terrific explosion followed by a volley of rifle shots; you look round and see people rushing into shops, others lying flat on the ground, others running up the side streets! Trams tear along madly; horses gallop away from the cab-stands, women shriek, bullets whistle round your ears, bomb splinters are flying, wounded people lie about groaning—"oh! what a lovely war!"—and for a quarter of an hour you have a lively time of it. Scenes like this occur every day here in all quarters of the city. A girl was shot dead in Trinity College Park last week during a cricket match; and two men who were sitting on a wall at Clontarf were shot at and died a few hours afterwards. The why or the wherefore of these latter happenings never appears, but all sorts of rumours are flying round—many of them of the most contradictory kind. It is easy enough to see the *raison d'être* of the ambushes, but the other occurrences are terrifying and mysterious. Twice this week the tram on which I was travelling was held up by the English and all passengers (male) searched. On last Sat. at the corner of Harrington, Camden and Richmond Streets you could see four long lines of trams held up for searching purposes while groups of soldiers occupied the streets and stopped all vehicles—rifles at the ready and bayonets fixed, while officers nervously brandished revolvers and held them under the noses of all and sundry including women and children. The searching would make a cat laugh—I could have had half a dozen revolvers and a few bombs on me without the slightest risk of detection. And all that is achieved by this ferocious display is to delay and irritate everybody, to dislocate traffic and business and to call down curses—not loud but deep—on the stupid military. But the situation is not without its humorous side: it is delightful to listen to the former red-white-and-blue people—the bigoted Unionists—the erstwhile 'God Save the Kingers', expressing their views on the present régime. My word! haven't they changed! To hear them would do the heart of any Sinn Feiner good!

However, normal life continued too, as it does today in

Belfast, and most of Pappa's letters were devoted to descriptions of family outings, new plays, art exhibitions, bridge marathons, poker parties, long hikes in the Dublin and Wicklow mountains, cricket matches, croquet contests on long summer evenings, moonlight bathing parties at Greystones and gossip about friends and neighbours. The family news mainly concerned Conn, my father's ne'er-do-well younger brother, who when not in jail for political reasons was a constant source of anxiety lest he might end up there for non-political reasons. And there were many speculations about Kathleen's many admirers —which she should retain for further consideration and which she should discard without delay.

Some news items have a very modern ring: 'The strike of the Rathmines Council workmen is still on and we are without light and without "bin-men". As for the first we don't miss it for we have daylight till 11; but not being able to get rid of ashes and house rubbish is a bit of a nuisance. And the fun of the thing is that the dispute about hours is settled and the strike is being continued solely for the wages which were not paid during the time of the strike: workmen now want to be paid even for striking.'

Despite Pappa's horror of Partition, his references to the North all indicate that even in 1921 the average Dubliner felt it to be an alien place. On May 2 he wrote:

I was in Belfast on April 20 and 21 lecturing on 'Ancient Irish and Ancient Greek Education'. I had little opportunity to find out anything as I know practically nobody there, but I heard one important item of information from a 'big business' source—over 60% of those employed in the linen trade are out of work, the American trade has almost entirely ceased, there are big stocks on hand which can find no purchasers though they are being offered at prices slightly lower than the present cost of production. The boycott is telling very markedly. Otherwise the town seemed to me just as it was when I last visited it five or six years ago. It seems to have learned nothing and to have forgotten nothing. For instance I saw two lorry-loads of young fellows apparently returning from an excursion—probably factory hands— each lorry had a Union Jack floating over it; the Union

Jack floated too over that monstrosity in architecture known as the City Hall. King William on a white horse crossing the Boyne is still their beau ideal and to shout 'To Hell With the Pope' and to stone the 'bloody papishes' is still the chief duty of a 'loyal' Belfast citizen. They still live in the Ireland of 15 years ago and are unaware of the avalanche which is about to descend on them.

Belfast is an uninteresting place—it has only one fine street, the rest being either monotonous replicas of rows of workmen's cottages or dingy terraces of a would-be suburbia. The energy which I noticed on my last visit was replaced by a good deal of listlessness—owing to the ubiquity of the out-of-works, I suppose. Anyway I was very glad to get back to good old Dublin. I may have to go up again in a week or a fortnight—but I hope not.

Clearly Pappa enjoyed letter-writing. A midsummer day's solitary walking and trout-fishing in the familiar Wicklow mountains could spark off a thousand-word lyrical description of the landscape, the birds and the ever-changing Irish sky. And a sunny autumn afternoon spent strolling with Mamma around Lucan and the Leixlip demesne inspired at least another thousand words. Until reading these letters I had not fully appreciated how easy it was for Dubliners of that period to enjoy as much of country life as was desired. For a keen hiker, miles of untouched countryside were within walking distance of Rathgar—as was the sea, for a keen swimmer like Pappa.

In the autumn of 1922 my father left for Paris, to begin his studies at the Sorbonne, and he spent the next seven years in France. Money was so scarce that he only rarely returned home; most of his vacations were spent tutoring the two sons of a Russian émigré duke in the South of France. Unfortunately no correspondence has survived from those years—until 1928, when on July 9 Pappa wrote a long letter, liberally scattered with quotations from Julius Caesar and Shakespeare, in response to my father's decision to become a Benedictine monk. In the end he expresses no opinion but concludes, tantalisingly, 'I have a hundred things to say but it is just post-time so I shall wait till to-morrow.' Reading between the lines, however, one discerns disapproval. And there is an unwonted acidity in the last paragraph—'Fondest love from your mother. Send her a little note for herself—why have I to suggest this? Does your love for her not prompt it?'

If Pappa at once doubted the genuineness of his son's vocation he was quite right. The next letter to have survived was written only nine months later, on March 20, 1929, in response to my father's decision to marry a nineteen-year-old Swedish girl who was studying at the Sorbonne under the eagle eye of an aunt-chaperon. My father appears to have detested this aunt even more than he detested the English—and with good reason. She threatened to call in the police after her niece had spent a day at Versailles—without permission—in the company of a penniless Irishman.

This romance provoked Pappa to write a full-blown Victorian homily:

I must say that my first thoughts and feelings were made up of almost contradictory elements. In the first place there was a sort of disappointment: I had thought that your whole soul was so decidedly fixed on a monastic life that nothing could have diverted you from fulfilling a purpose which you had adopted, apparently, with such deliberation and determination. I had built up a scheme of thoughts for myself founded on *that* as on a first principle. And then you drop a bombshell—a living one, aetat 19—into my beautifully constructed building and blow the whole thing to smithereens in a second! But you did it in such an airy and unconcerned fashion that I haven't the heart to reproach you. Well, perhaps it is the best thing that ever happened. And perhaps it isn't: time alone can tell. I sincerely hope it is; I earnestly hope that it may bring you deep and lasting happiness. All the fond love of your parents' hearts goes out to you and we shall have nothing but the warmest welcome for the girl of your choice.

Your mother was not nearly so astonished at the news as I was; and I am sure that in her inmost soul she was delighted at the thought that you were saved from the ever-grasping arms of religious communities!

One thing I am really glad of; and that is that you made

the discovery of the possibility of falling in love before you had taken any decisive step towards ordination.

Believe me it is a great thing to be honestly and deeply in love; it lifts the whole soul to a higher level; and if the person loved is a good woman, then it is the noblest passion which can animate the soul of man. Love your sweetheart, then, with all the intensity of your soul—if she is a good girl and returns your love, you cannot love her too much. Pour out your affection without stint; and when she becomes your wife, wrap the whole warmth of your love so closely around her that she can never feel the cold breath of the world no matter how bitterly the winds of adversity may blow. But let your love be intelligent and unselfish. A good wife is the greatest blessing God can bestow on any man—a pearl beyond price; but that pearl must be cherished and safe-guarded at all costs. There are two sorts of love—a selfish and an unselfish one. The first seeks to make the beloved minister to one's own good: the second seeks the good of the beloved before all else.

And now to come down to earth. It is all very well to fall in love—but what about the future? You cannot ask anyone to marry you until you are able to provide a decent life for her—I don't mean affluence nor even an easy life, nor one devoid of struggle, or even, at times, of anxiety; but a reasonable prospect of the necessary things—a sufficiency of nourishing food, comfortable housing and warm, befitting clothing. I don't know whether you have come to any understanding with the girl, whether you are engaged or not. You have merely said you intended to marry her soon. To my mind, it is all too sudden and recent for any official engagement. It takes a certain amount of time for the growth and ripening of real love. But, if you are in earnest, you must set about making a living: you must have a definite realisable plan and you must follow it out steadily. What do you propose doing?

Love should purge you of a large element of that selfishness which clings to you. You are too apt to let absorption in your own intellectual concerns cause you to forget the position of those who love you dearly. For instance, you did not trouble to acknowledge the receipt of this month's

allowance. And that's only one incident. This is not a reproach, but a reminder.

Write soon—and more fully. Your affectionate

Pappa.

What happened next? Did the formidable aunt win? (I
cannot imagine my father—however much in love—with-
standing such a female for long.) Or, when the novelty had
worn off, did the nineteen-year-old bombshell lose interest in her
Irish suitor—so shy, impractical and inexperienced in the arts
of love? Or did my father take fright, upon reading Pappa's
homily, and decide that the responsibilities of marriage would
prove too taxing? Whatever happened, he was home for
Christmas that year—unmarried and unemployed—and he
never returned to France. In January 1930 he began a six-
month Library Diploma course at University College Dublin,
in April he met my mother again (they had last met three years
previously and had known each other as children), in July he
was appointed County Librarian for Waterford and in August
he and my mother announced their engagement.

At that time Ireland's Civil War was not long over and the
families of Dublin were still angrily arrayed on either side of an
ugly barrier. How ugly may be gauged by a remark made on
July 29, 1927, when my father's brother Conn wrote from
Ontario: 'Congratulations on getting your finals. I am quite
enjoying the experience of sailing on the Great Lakes. I saw in
the papers here that Kevin O'Higgins has been shot dead—
damn near time—the sooner they shoot a few more like him the
better. The Canadian papers described him as a martyr but
they had to admit he was the best hated man in Ireland.'
Kevin O'Higgins was one of the finest Irishmen of his generation
—but he was a Free Stater, and the Murphys were Republicans.

My parents' engagement therefore represented a considerable
mésalliance, between the son of a rabidly Republican family
and the daughter of a mildly Unionist family. But to give my
paternal grandparents their due, they saw the point of the
marriage within moments of being introduced to my mother.
By then she—being totally apolitical—had cheerfully adopted a
diluted form of Republicanism to meet the situation.

In general, however, the two families were never more than

distantly polite. To my father's family, my mother's relations were not only politically corrupt but barbarously unlearned, hard-drinking, irreligious, foppish and extravagant. To my mother's family, my father's relations were not only politically irresponsible but feckless, bigoted, prudish and riddled with intellectual pretensions that never came to anything. Happily these prejudices left me unaffected. I grew up fond of both families, unquestioningly accepting their covert mutual hostility as a fact of Irish life.

3

In November 1936 my father at last found a house to rent at a price we could afford. It was on the South Mall, Lismore's most respectable street, but the dwelling itself was so irreparably decrepit that no modern squatter would stay there overnight. Short of a leaking roof, it suffered from every defect buildings are heir to and, for the next twenty-one years, it decayed—usually quietly, but occasionally dramatically— about our ears. Dating from the 1820s, it was two-storeyed, semi-detached and covered in Virginia creeper. The fanlight and wooden porch were attractive, a pair of romantic stone urns graced the front garden and overgrown fuchsia-bushes billowed on either side of the hall door. The well-proportioned rooms had good marble mantelpieces and mock-Adam ceilings and the wide hall was tiled in cream and dull red—pleasant, old-fashioned, indestructible tiles. However, some past tenant with execrable taste had left the whole place superficially hideous. The hall was painted a dead laurel green, only relieved by irregular patches of yellow-grey mildew where the plaster had fallen off. (For years I was fascinated by those patches, seeing them as maps of undiscovered countries.) The staircase was covered with cracked red and blue linoleum which ill-matched the magnificent mahogany banisters. Upstairs were five rooms: three large bedrooms, a boxroom which became my playroom and another large room, complete with fireplace, which at some remote period had been converted into a bathroom. The bath stood on four gigantic iron lion's paws and resembled a modern child's swimming-pool. It was patriotically stained green and orange and had a shower-device, of considerable antiquarian interest, near the ceiling. This had become viciously perverted and it sprayed, with tremendous force, only onto the opposite wall. When my father had forgotten to warn three successive guests he put up a notice saying 'Please do not touch'. The lavatory also had its notice, to explain that the chain needed three morse-like pulls: long–short–long. The wash-basin could almost have been used as a bath and was without a plug: apparently none to fit it had been manufactured since the turn of the century. Had my father exerted himself he could, at the cost of a few pence, have remedied this and many other defects. But the idea of personally improvising a wash-basin plug—or anything else—would never have entered his mind and he judged our numerous discomforts too trivial to warrant expensive expert attention.

Throughout the house we found peeling beige woodwork and wallpaper that had faded to a uniform grey-brown. Everywhere the paper was coming unstuck and in the dining-room rats had eaten through it at several points, thus demonstrating the fragility of the basic structure. Dry-rot afflicted the floor boards and some other sort of rot caused the ground-floor ceilings to snow gently if anyone walked about too vigorously overhead. This perhaps explains why I have always moved rather lightly for one of my build.

At the end of the hall a semi-glazed door led to a narrow, dark, flagged passage with ominously bulging henna-distempered walls. Having passed a storeroom, a pantry and a larder one entered the kitchen. Here sly draughts sneaked up from damp non-foundations through gaps between ancient flags, and blatant draughts whined through the slits between rotting window frames and rattling panes. The roughly plastered walls were an evil shade of green and a temperamental coal-range stood in an alcove. A row of discoloured pewter bells hung high above the door; in our day these never responded to the relevant buttons being pushed but they emitted ghostly chimes when gales blew. A dozen iron hooks depended from the the rafters—"The better to hang yourself on, my dear," observed my mother as she toured her new home. In one corner a steep ladder-stairs led through a trap-door to an attic where the servants would have slept in the Bad Old Days. An adult could stand upright only in the middle of the attic floor and this retreat soon became one of my Private Paradises.

Behind the house were several collapsing stables and, beyond a wide cobbled yard, stood Lismore's recently opened cinema, the property of our landlord, who lived next door. It was enormous and no one could tell us what purpose it had originally served; it may have been a series of barns whose internal walls had been demolished. Mercifully our landlord did not prosper as a film-wallah and within a few years the local doctor had built a new 'Palladium'. Then the old cinema became another of my Private Paradises; in semi-darkness I leapt from row to row of moth-eaten red plush seats, being pursued by imaginary cannibals and collecting swarms of real fleas. These were not found tolerable by my mother, even when identified by me as rare tropical insects picked up while exploring in New Guinea.

Beyond the cinema were our garden and orchard, half an acre of wilderness which, despite consistent neglect, provided us for many years with an abundance of loganberries, gooseberries, apples and pears. At intervals my mother would remark on the advantages of growing one's own vegetables. Then my father would borrow some implements and might on the following Saturday be observed reclining beside a minute pile of cut brambles reading Plato's *Theaetetus* or the latest Dorothy Sayers. Like myself, he lacked the urge to cultivate. Our genes have perhaps resisted change since the Age of the Gatherers.

Although our new home was very nearly a ruin we tolerated it for the next twenty-one years. My mother must have abhorred these slum-like surroundings but she refrained, as always, from complaining about the inevitable. For a rent of ten shillings a week one couldn't, even in Lismore in the 1930s, expect very much.

The rent was so low not only because of the house's dilapidation but because of the previous tenant's suicide in the dining-room. This snag considerably influenced my destiny since it made it far harder to engage local maid-servants, or to persuade those who came from a distance to remain in residence. It was not that any ghost operated—at least to our knowledge —but the neighbourhood vociferously believed that a suicide without a consequent haunting was against nature.

As a child I always knew there was nothing to spare for

non-essentials. But I was never hungry or cold so it did not occur to me to interpret this condition as poverty. Nor did I ever long for the unobtainable, with one spectacular exception —a pony of my own. And since that desire so clearly belonged to the realm of fantasy it caused me no discontent. In Dublin I enjoyed the luxury toys of my cousins—rocking-horses, tricycles, pedal motor-cars and the like—yet I never asked or even wished for such things. They belonged to another sort of person who lived in another sort of world. And it was not a world I should have cared to inhabit permanently. It had no rivers, fields, woods, moors and mountains.

When we moved to the South Mall Nora was replaced by Old Brigid, a formidable character who for the next three years—scornful of ghosts—impassively controlled the whole peculiar Murphy establishment. It cannot have been easy to contend with a disintegrating house, an invalid mistress, a chronically vague master and a nasty child. Old Brigid, however, took the lot in her slow, purposeful stride. When the foul-looking sink came adrift from the wall she said nothing to my mother but fetched the plumber, a man who normally took weeks to answer any summons but who meekly accompanied Old Brigid to the scene of the disaster. When my mother needed some attention as lunch was being prepared the attention was promptly provided but the meal was never late or ill-cooked. When my father wandered off to the Library one morning wearing his dressing-gown and slippers Old Brigid pursued him, looking reproving but resigned, and handed him his jacket and shoes half-way down the Main Street. When I staged a tantrum because I could not have everything exactly as and when I wanted it Old Brigid said, "Now, Miss Dervla, I'll have no more of that nonsense—*if* you please!" And the tantrum stopped.

Despite her surface severity—or because of it?—I loved Old Brigid dearly. She always wore an ankle-length blue and white check cotton dress and a large starched white linen apron, without spot or stain. Every afternoon, while boiling the tea kettle, she also heated a ponderous iron on the hot coals, carefully placed it on its tin tray and ironed the next day's aprons. She was small and stout, with grey hair in a neat bun and shiny red cheeks and sharp bristles on her chin. In 1936 she was sixty-five and had been fifty-three years in the service of a Tipperary family whose last representative had left her an adequate annuity; but she found idleness uncongenial. Since we paid her two pounds a month she must have regarded the Murphys as a hobby.

Every morning Old Brigid bathed me at seven o'clock because the range idiosyncratically refused to provide hot water in the evening. Then she took me into the dark airing cupboard, which was considerably larger than the average modern bathroom, and told me fairy stories while drying me beside the gurgling, gleaming bulk of a gigantic copper boiler. I listened politely, concealing my bored disbelief. I had faith in only one fairy, Mr Dumbly-Doo, who was exactly my own height and wore silver boots and red leather breeches and a green silk shirt and a black velvet jacket and a gold brocade tricorne hat. A creation of my father—with acknowledgements to the leprechaun industry—Mr Dumbly-Doo occasionally left a mint-new penny under a certain stone beside a certain stile along a certain laneway. (I cherished these coins for their red-gold rather than for their purchasing power—though in those days that was considerable.) He did none of the exasperating things common to fairies in stories and since my father did not elaborate on his life style I was free to do so myself without feeling the victim of adult condescension.

This wary attitude towards fairy tales was part of my unremitting struggle against grown-up power. Despite the affectionate understanding provided by my parents, in their very different ways, I tensely suspected the adult world of some sinister conspiracy to make me conform. I could not have felt more fiercely about this had my parents been models of conservatism instead of the individualists they were.

Yet for all my rejection of the standard fairy tales I needed a fantasy escape hatch even more than most children do. So I created my own intricate world of magic animals and omnipotent teddy-bears. A family of the latter, comprising four generations, lived in the branches of my favourite tree— a superb elm, some 120 feet tall and reckoned to be more than 400 years old. Under that tree I spent countless hours, at all seasons, totally absorbed in the bears' doings and in their dramatic personality clashes. Each one had a clearly defined character and in time they came to seem quite independent of my controlling imagination. For a few years they—and their tree—meant more to me than any human friend.

That elm grew (and mercifully still grows) in the dense, dim wood which rises steeply from the Blackwater just west of Lismore Castle. The path leading down to it was an exciting tunnel through thick undergrowth. All around the other trees were old and tall, though dwarfed by its prodigious girth and height. Long before I had ever heard of pantheists, druids or sacred groves I used to stand at the foot of this elm, pressing with outstretched arms against its vastness, fingering its rough bark and looking up in reverence at the endless ramifications of its mighty branches. I was never to feel anything comparable under the influence of orthodox religious stimulants. But does it matter how we worship, if we worship?

All this of course took place only after I had been given licence to roam alone, at the age of seven. But long before that my chief amusement was telling myself interminable convoluted stories—if 'amusement' is the right word. The longing to be alone with the denizens of my imagination was so intense, and the amount of time I devoted to them so abnormal, that one of my father's sisters—a child psychologist—became seriously alarmed during a visit to Lismore.

No doubt there was something neurotic about my elated relief as I escaped to the garden or the attic, and about the anger I felt when interrupted by the necessity to eat, or go for a walk, or learn my lessons. I often looked forward to bedtime. Lying happily taut under the blankets, with my eyes shut and my imaginative throttles wide open, I was at last safe from adult interference. I well remember the physical symptoms of excitement during those sessions: my heart hammering, my fists clenching and unclenching, my face contorted as I rapidly muttered the latest instalment, *sotto voce*. No wonder my aunt, who had doubtless contrived to spy on a daytime session, felt concerned.

My mother, however, insisted that I was suffering from nothing more than a lively imagination. On principle she tended *not* to agree with her sister-in-law, who was very close to my father. And in this case she may have realised that my fantasy-world was a not unhealthy form of escapism. At some level I must have been aware of the domestic stresses and strains; and futile efforts to understand and adjust to them would have done me much more harm than my withdrawal into the company of golden calves, silver goats and arboreal teddy-bears.

As I seem always to have known the facts of life I assume they were simply absorbed from my mother during that phase of obsessional questioning when everything in nature arouses a child's curiosity. I therefore find it hard to understand the difficulties that even in this explicit age are said to surround basic sex instruction by parents. It is far easier to explain to a three-year-old how babies are made than to explain the processes whereby bread or sugar appear on the table.

By the age of six I was a proficient and dedicated masturbator and someone—probably Old Brigid—had infected me with an acute guilt complex about this hobby. So I consulted my mother, who said the activity in question was certainly not a matter to *worry* about. It was a babyish habit and quite soon I would grow out of it—just as I had grown out of wetting my bed. These remarks must have had the intended effect. Guilt evaporated and in time the 'babyish' habit was superseded by more cerebral sexual interests centred on scientific investigations of the male anatomy.

I was about seven when an outraged neighbour complained to my mother that I had been seen, on the public street, removing a little boy's shorts and examining him from every angle. All I can now remember is the colour and texture of this four-year-old's shorts. They had been knitted from coarse burgundy-coloured wool and as he wore no underpants I pitied him, reasoning that he must feel miserably scratchy.

The fact that this scene took place on the Main Street—"in broad daylight", as our neighbour several times emphasised, unconsciously implying that had it taken place in a dark corner it would have been less culpable—the fact that this could have happened shows how well my parents had thus far protected me from Irish puritanism. But there are limits. The time had come to risk unhealthy repression and my mother told me that never again must I do such a thing because little boys are very sensitive to the cold around that area, and could get a bad chill if stripped in the open air. I was not, of course, deceived. I had got the message that the relevant area merited special treatment and indeed was, for some utterly incomprehensible reason, Taboo. This new awareness gave the physiological differences between boys and girls an extra fascination; but my investigations, from now on, were more discreet.

Soon Providence favoured me; newcomers took the house opposite and within hours it became apparent that their eight-year-old son was a professional exhibitionist. He had perfected a variety of ingenious urinating techniques and his penis was public property. We were an ideally suited couple. He performed, I admired, and it occurred to neither of us that his penis could be put to other uses. Almost certainly he was ignorant of the mechanics of reproduction, as he was without curiosity about the female anatomy (he had five sisters). And it would no more have occurred to me to initiate an experiment than to smoke a cigarette. In my mind a clear line was drawn between the activities of grown-ups and children, and for all my defiance I was never tempted to cross this line prematurely. The world was organised in a certain way. There was a pattern and one felt no impulse to disarrange it.

The South Mall had been skilfully planned. Looking due north from our hall door one saw, scarcely six miles away, the 2,900-foot main peak of the Knockmealdowns, its smooth blue curve rising directly above one of Ireland's loveliest churches. A double line of stately lime trees led up to St Carthage's Cathedral and the broad, grassy sweep between them, known as The Mall, made a safe children's playground.

Four doors down from us, on the same side of the wide street, was a house rather like our own—but detached and in perfect condition—which had recently been bought by a family of outsiders who seemed no better than ourselves at integration with the natives. They were, however, devoted to children and during the spring of 1937 they regularly invited me into their garden to play with an exuberant young Airedale named Bran and a sentimental black cocker spaniel named Roddy. The garden covered two acres and almost every afternoon a few members of the Ryan family were to be found working enthusiastically beside the gardener. (Here I first discovered what fun it is to watch other people digging and pruning, mowing and raking.) For a month or so I could not be induced to enter the house, possibly because I was afraid of the hypochondriacal Mr Ryan, who never ventured out before midsummer but could occasionally be glimpsed peering unsmilingly through an upstairs window. Everyone, including his wife, called him 'The Boss' and regarded him with an unwholesome mixture of deference, resentment, concern and scorn.

Mr Ryan was a retired country schoolmaster, gruff, autocratic, keen-minded and at this time already in his seventies. Mrs Ryan—his second wife, much younger than himself— was gentle and placid with a subtle sense of humour. Beneath her placidity one could detect more positive qualities which if not repressed might, in the circumstances, have led to domestic disharmony. She, too, had been a school-teacher and the eight children of their union had been brought up mainly by her unmarried sister, who never seemed in the least like a frustrated maiden aunt but had a permanent twinkle in her eye. She smoked secretly—in the summer-house, to be well out of nose-shot of the Boss—and gave me all her cigarette cards.

Of the four Ryan sons two* were then curates, one was studying for the priesthood in Rome and the youngest was an army cadet whose buttons I loved to polish. Of the four daughters two were missionary nuns—educational pioneers in the remoter parts of Nigeria—and two lived at home. It was taken for granted that the Misses Ryan, though young, attractive and intelligent, would remain unmarried. Their ageing parents needed them and, having given five children to the Church, deserved them. They were never allowed enough freedom to be noticed by eligible men—though a father who had sired, in all, eleven children, and who could provide little financial security, might have been expected to consider both their emotional and economic needs. But in rural Ireland forty years ago Mr Ryan's despotism was not rare; and it was encouraged by Irish Catholicism, which has always given to involuntary celibacy the status of a virtue.

*One of those two was Mark, of whom there will be much more anon.

44

The Ryan family had produced several distinguished Gaelic poets and I much preferred their spontaneous 'Irishness' to the Murphys' turgid and embittered nationalism. Yet this comparison was unfair; for generations no Ryan had been directly involved in Irish politics and it is less easy to avoid bitterness when you have spent some of the best years of your life in jail, being treated as a common criminal. But perhaps what really appealed to me about the Ryans' tradition was its genuineness. They had a cultural integrity not often found, for historical reasons, in Dublin families. When my father and his brother were sent to Saint Enda's—the school founded by Patrick Pearse—and when the family went to the Donegal Gaeltacht for their summer holidays, to learn Irish, they were searching for something the Ryans had never lost.

In other ways, however, the Ryans' simplicity irritated me, even at the age of six. Everything was good and bad, right and wrong, black and white; and children who suggested the possible existence of grey areas were just being impertinent. I soon learned to hold my tongue, partly because it seemed right to conform to the standards of the household and partly because The Boss shared with my mother—for very different reasons—the unusual distinction of being able to frighten me. To an extent I probably found the Ryans' authoritarianism reassuring, but sometimes I was driven to secret tears when my rudimentary intellectual probings evoked an altogether unmerited sarcastic reprimand. To this day I remain puzzled by my emotional 'adoption' into this outwardly unyielding family. Clearly the Ryans liked having me about the place to soften the harshness of daily life; I was impulsively affectionate and as a family they conspicuously lacked demonstrativeness. But why did they not cultivate a child less liable to outrage their various susceptibilities and generally more tractable? Perhaps they furtively relished the stimulus of being outraged, or they may simply have enjoyed trying to raise my moral tone.

The Ryans and my parents never fraternised; whatever they might have in common, their differences far outweighed their similarities. So the relationship stuck at meteorological comment, though for years I spent as much time in the Ryans' house as in my own. Moving daily between two households whose attitudes, opinions and standards were often opposed might have led to some confusion had I been more pliable. But for me this tension was healthy, part of the process of learning to accept other people as they are.

During the '30s my parents' only local friends were a Catholic curate, a Fianna Fáil senator and the senator's elderly widowed sister, Mrs Mansfield.

Father Power was pompous, smug and plump; though a good deal more intelligent than Jane Austen's Mr Collins there were prominent affinities, including a weakness for titled nobility. Few people in the parish were prepared to talk interminably about his obsession—Early Christian Ireland— so he spent many evenings in our house, often bringing a half-bottle of claret and staying to supper. His brother was a wine merchant, but he seemed to imagine that a full bottle would give an air of debauchery to the proceedings.

I much preferred Senator Goulding because he completely ignored me. A bachelor, he was small, slight and energetic, with a calm, precise voice, a dry sense of humour and not a speck of self-importance. When in Lismore—he was often in Dublin on senatorial business—he attended Mass and received Communion every morning, and every evening he again went to church, and had there been an afternoon service he would certainly have attended that, too. He was, however, the best sort of devout Irish Catholic, not a craw-thumper but a man who tried to make politics honourable through the practical application of Christian teaching. Having served Ireland for more than half a century he died poorer than he was born.

Mrs Mansfield was childless and had been widowed young. One got the impression that she had unaccountably married beneath her and regarded Mr Mansfield's premature death as his one gentlemanly gesture. She lived in a rambling, three-storeyed corner house at the junction of Ferry Lane and the Main Street; and the fact that the ground floor was occupied by a pub—once the property of her late husband—was a circumstance so unfortunate that to have referred to it in her presence would have been like commenting on someone's club-foot—or wig. She and her brother affected to despise each other and had not exchanged a word, at least publicly, within living memory. They might be observed going to church by pointedly different routes: the senator trotting briskly up the South Mall while his sister sedately paced down the Main Street, tiny, slim and erect, the tapping of her silver-mounted cane being made to sound like heralds' trumpets through the sheer force of her personality.

When not going to church Mrs Mansfield was invariably accompanied by San Toy, an irascible Peke with chronic asthma. San Toy once attacked a bull-terrier, in a fit of sheer spleen, and the terrier was so astonished he simply ran away. Having witnessed this scene I always deprecated Mrs Mansfield's subsequent boastings about San Toy's gallantry when unjustly set upon.

Twice a week Mrs Mansfield called to drink tea with my mother and deplore the appalling inroads being made by democracy on good manners. She complained bitterly of being greeted with an 'Hello!'—she whispered the word as though it had four letters—by children whose parents she could remember walking in to Lismore on a fair-day with bare feet and scarcely a shirt to their backs. Those children of course knew no better; their elders had waxed too prosperous and brazen to teach them respect. But I, Dervla—she would swivel round to survey me through her lorgnette—*I* should know better than to *run* down the Main Street, endangering in my unseemly haste defenceless babies and feeble old-age pensioners. "A lady should never be seen to hurry, my dear."

"But she's not quite a lady yet," my mother would protest mildly—avoiding my vulgarly winking eye. Then Mrs Mansfield's expression would convey that if my mother did not act soon and drastically the necessary transmogrification was unlikely ever to take place.

Before I was old enough to wander alone I often attended Mrs Mansfield and San Toy on their afternoon walks. For one of her apparent fragility and gentility Mrs Mansfield was a stout marcher, not at all deterred—once out of sight of the neighbours—by rough going and the accompanying indignities of climbing over fallen tree trunks or crawling under wire fences. And San Toy availed himself of these occasions to prove that he was no mere effete aristocrat. It was Mrs Mansfield who introduced me to the pleasures of strolling

47

through old graveyards, striving to read weathered inscriptions and speculating about the fate of such as John Carney who, in 1811, at the age of fifteen, 'loved peace but died violently'. Of the consequences of this addiction there will be more anon.

4

One fine spring morning, when I was six and a half, my father escorted me to the local national school and my formal education began. I remember lying on the chalk-smelling floor boards of a huge, bright classroom, kicking in a tantrum and feeling tears running into my ears and noticing the chalk dust gyrating through a sunbeam. My father was standing over me looking helpless and worried and being assured by a little group of nuns that I would settle down the moment he left me.

I had not any objection, in theory, to starting school, but the moment I entered that classroom I panicked at the prospect of being confined within alien walls until some unknown nun gave me permission to leave. At home I chose to spend hours alone every day, yet if at any moment I suddenly wanted to be with my mother she was always accessible. Here, however, I was trapped in a situation where it would be impossible to reach her no matter how desperate my need. So I screamed and kicked frantically while the other children, who had all started school at the age of four, regarded me with amused scorn, and the nuns, raising their voices above my howls, repeated firmly that I would soon settle down and tried to edge my father tactfully towards the door.

Luckily I could not express my desolate sense of betrayal. Had my father realised that this was not just another bout of nastiness he might well have taken me home again, thereby setting a disastrous precedent. As it was I did settle down surprisingly soon after his reluctant departure, having discovered that I liked the nun who was to be my teacher. She explained that if ever I needed my mother *very* badly I could at once be sent home in the charge of an older girl. Whereupon

I discounted the possibility of ever again needing my mother very badly, either in or out of school hours, and by lunch-time being a scholar seemed a good idea.

Yet I did not mean to profit in the accepted manner by my educational opportunities. Indeed, having learned to read at home I felt that the essential part of my education had already been completed. The world was full of books and I intended to read as many as possible before I died. What I did not intend was to waste the best years of my life—the *only* years of my youth—studying inexpressibly boring things like French and arithmetic. I knew by then of my parents' plans: at ten I would be sent away to school, at eighteen I would be sent to the Sorbonne, at twenty-two or twenty-three I would return home with a degree in something or other and be welcomed as a complete, civilised human being. This programme might have fired many children with worthy ambitions, but I neither wished it to be carried out nor believed that it would be. We are born—I am convinced—with a certain basic fore-knowledge about the pattern of our lives and I always regarded those parental plans as pipe-dreams.

My teachers found me an awkward, lazy pupil and the educational methods of the day did nothing to help. Another discouragement, for a child without any linguistic ability, was the compulsory use of Irish as the language through which all subjects were taught in free primary schools—except, signi-ficantly, religious instruction. By the 1930s most Irish families had been English-speaking for generations and only a tiny minority were interested in reviving their own language. So this lunatic law was extremely unpopular. It produced millions of Irish citizens who were, as one wit sourly observed, 'illiterate in two languages'. The situation would be paralleled in Britain if Wales reconquered England and compelled all state-school pupils to study in Welsh.

Even as a character-forming influence, Lismore school did me very little good. My classmates, instead of forcing me into the sort of rough and tumble I needed to remove my corners, generally deferred to me and expected me to be their leader—an expectation which was disappointed, for it was not in my nature either to lead or be led. Also, most of the nuns were too lenient towards me and too openly appreciative of intellectual attainments which would not have seemed at all remarkable in another academic setting.

Fortunately there was one exception to this, whose class I joined when I was eight. Sister Andrew was a tall twenty-year-old with a pale long face, straight black brows and eyes that seemed to give off blue forked lightning during her rages. Verbally she flayed me and physically she battered me—often across the back, with a stout wooden pointer. If it is true that corporal punishment is inflicted only by the insecure, then Sister Andrew repeatedly betrayed her own uncertainty and inexperience. We were in fact using each other at this stage: she to prove that she could control even such a resolutely self-willed and obliquely insolent child as myself, and I to prove that I could and would withstand the adult world, however painful the consequences.

I remember sitting upright at my heavy wooden desk, with its cracked, brass-lidded inkwell and countless carved initials and the splinter under the left side of the seat on which I was wont unobtrusively to clean my finger-nails. Sister Andrew was bending over me, whitely angry, ordering me to write the letter 'h' in the approved manner. I knew quite well how to write a standard 'h' but I was determined not to do it according to the specifications; I had my own method, which I naturally preferred. And so, under Sister Andrew's flashing gaze, I deliberately rewrote 'h' as I thought fit. Meanwhile the rest of the class, who always relished our duels, watched with bated breath. Several emotions simultaneously possessed me in that instant: a spiteful sense of triumph, regret that our duel could not take place in dignified seclusion instead of in the middle of a classroom, fear of the physical pain that I knew was imminent and a sharp stab of shame because I could not but recognise the futility and stupidity of my own behaviour. This was one of the occasions when the pointer left bruises on my back. Since I was able to write a perfectly legible 'h' it might be argued that Sister Andrew should have ignored my method of achieving it; but then it might also be argued that I did not mean my defiant originality to be ignored.

For a year or so we were sporadically at war. Many were the afternoons when I hurried home, trembling with resentful fury, affronted, humiliated and longing for the balm of maternal sympathy. But these rages usually cooled on the way and I rarely mentioned Sister Andrew. The verbal flayings hurt me far more than the beatings, but I was shrewd enough to realise that if I repeated those criticisms verbatim my mother would simply add, "Hear! Hear!" Besides, complaints about the school authorities were discouraged at home and many years passed before I discovered how much worry my bruised back had caused on one particular occasion. From the '70s such violence looks primitive and uncouth. But in the '30s even doting parents, themselves too sensitive to hurt a fly, did not really object to having the hell beaten out of their wicked brats by somebody else. (N.B.—for the past thirty-five years Sister Andrew and I have been very good friends.)

An interesting aspect of childhood is the democracy of those who have not yet been trained to think or feel undemocratically. And one of the oddest functions of middle-class parents—which seems inconsistent with the civilising parental mission—is to destroy this democratic instinct for the sake of maintaining standards often of far less value to society than the attitude being sacrificed. At the age of seven or eight my classmates and I were not prepared to accept the operation of chance as a valid foundation for either superiority or inferiority complexes. The barriers built within the adult social world were unknown to us and differences in speech, manners, attitudes and interests neither embarrassed nor amused us; we simply ignored social frontier posts.

During this period my few school friends were wild and ragged. Tommy particularly attracted me because he hated wearing shoes and in all seasons removed his footwear outside the school gate before going home. To me running bare-footed symbolised the very quintessence of liberty and I soon became Tommy's only female intimate. With his gang I raided many orchards—including our own, which was stealthily approached from an adjacent field. I had been admitted to this all-male gang by virtue of my muscle-power. If necessary I could bear any two of these ill-nourished little boys on my shoulders to assist them over an orchard wall.

On Saturday afternoons I often went to Tommy's home for tea. He lived with his foster-parents in a tiny cottage and we were given hunks of hot, butter-sodden bastable-cake, its crisp crust delicately flavoured with the wood-ash beneath which it had been baked, and huge chipped enamel mugs of very sweet cocoa. This soon became my favourite meal of the week and I was desolated when my mother one day announced that in future Tommy and I must take it in turns to entertain each other. Cocoa made with milk instead of water, egg and cheese and tomatoes instead of bastable-cake.... I pleaded desperately, but in vain. "You *must* return Tommy's hospitality," said my mother in her that's-the-end-of-the-matter voice. "But you may have tea in the kitchen because Tommy might feel shy in the dining-room."

Gloom enveloped me at the thought of Old Brigid scrutinising our hands, vigilantly observing our table-manners and perhaps—I shuddered at the very possibility—perhaps even being brutal enough to tell Tommy not to lick his knife. As supervisor of a tea-party she seemed a poor substitute indeed for Tommy's foster-mother, who always reminded us to wipe our filthy hands on our backsides before we sat down and made gloriously comic slurping noises as she drank her tea from her saucer. Then I hit on a brilliant compromise: Tommy and I should have tea in the attic, where adults feared to tread because of dry-rot. My mother—always ready to view a situation from my angle—approved of this idea; and since Tommy would have nothing to do with my body-building menu we were given white bread and jam—for me a very special treat.

At my eighth birthday party Tommy looked miserable in shiny shoes and his First Holy Communion suit, now giving at the seams. The other guests were South Mall children—in whom I had very little interest, but they always asked me to their parties—and years afterwards I heard of the repercussions of Tommy's attendance. A few days later it was conveyed to my mother—through Mrs Mansfield—that if the Lynch boy were invited to my Christmas party the rest could be counted out. Of course my mother didn't realise it—how could she, poor thing, stuck in a wheel-chair all day?—but no one even knew who Tommy's parents were, and he ran barefooted like a tinker, and blew his nose in the gutter, and *stole* from people! Stole apples, and sold them on fair days to the poor mountainy farmers' wives!

My mother's reply was that she found Tommy a most attractive, spirited, intelligent little boy. Soon afterwards came Christmas and to my astonished joy I found that this year, for some mysterious reason, I was to be spared party-going and party-giving. But Tommy spent St Stephen's Day with us; he had long since lost his shyness and graduated to the dining-room where he delighted my father by showing a lively interest in astronomy.

The Lynches left Lismore a few months later, to my great though transient grief. And eventually Tommy, having won a series of scholarships—a more difficult feat then than now—went on to become a chemical engineer with a top job in ICI.

The neighbours quite often found Murphy standards unacceptable. I was seven when three small girls—sisters—were forbidden to play with me because I had assured them that every night a lion slunk across the rooftops of Lismore, hunting the crows which nested in the chimneys, roaring at the stars just to show he was very fierce and fighting with an orang-utan who lived in the cathedral belfry. Nightmares resulted and the parish priest received a formal complaint about my pernicious untruthfulness. When Father Power relayed this complaint to my parents they made no attempt to conceal their amusement. But my mother cautioned me against further terrorising of my contemporaries and advised me to write such stories down in future instead of telling them, as it were, in the market-place.

Thus began an enduring custom; every year I wrote long stories for my parents' birthday and Christmas presents. Only one of these survives, written when I was eight. In about three thousand misspelt words it describes the adventures of two boys in a jungle that, judging by the available fauna, extended from Peru to Siberia. Having throttled a sabre-toothed tiger with their bare hands, rescued a shepherd's baby from a condor and killed an anaconda with a poisoned dart my heroes returned to Ireland by an unspecified route and lived happily ever after.

In a letter to her father-in-law my mother reported that when I was four—not yet able to read—I picked up a Little Grey Rabbit book and pointing to the author's name on the title-page said, "When I'm grown up I'm going to write books and have my name there." My mother commented, "I think she means it. She is a very decided and determined child." This comment was probably regarded as the typical effusion of a doting mother, but it was correct. I did mean it. And I went on meaning it though none of my literary efforts, during childhood or adolescence, showed any trace of promise.

I preferred not to discuss my ambition with anyone—it was tacitly understood between my parents and myself—and from the age of about twelve I was well aware that I might follow in my father's and grandfather's footsteps and be a failed writer. But this did not deter me. I was not thinking in terms of success or failure, prosperity or poverty, fame or obscurity. To me writing was not a career but a necessity. And so it remains, though I am now, technically, a professional writer. The strength of this inborn desire to write has always baffled me. It is understandable that the really gifted should feel an over-whelming urge to use their gift; but a strong urge with only a slight gift seems almost a genetic mistake.

My parents naturally approved of these literary ambitions. Yet to have encouraged me too enthusiastically, in the absence of any discernible talent, would have been irresponsible. Fortunately my mother enjoyed nothing more than being a literary critic. Everything she read was dissected and an ill-written book, endured for the sake of the subject matter, made her look quite haggard. An aspiring writer could ask for no more suitable mother and after a tactful interval—never look a gift story in the syntax—my parents' Christmas and birthday presents would reappear to be torn phrase from phrase. During these sessions I sat beside my mother like the most docile of Victorian daughters, attentively absorbing her every suggestion. This was the one area in which I did not spurn adult advice.

In May 1938 we acquired a motor-car. I cannot imagine by what financial conjuring feat my mother managed that, but somehow a brand-new, dark green, four-door Ford Ten appeared—having been paid for before delivery, eccentric as that may seem to a generation reared on hire-purchase systems. Motor-cars were then a rarity in Lismore, yet ours was no extravagance; for my mother train-travel would have been intolerably troublesome and painful.

Almost every Saturday and Sunday, in all seasons, we

motored to the sea. ('Driving' seems to have replaced 'motoring' only after the second war.) My mother loved to sit in the car for hours with the windows wide open, parked if possible within reach of the flying spray; she was especially partial to mid-winter gales. Meanwhile my father would march briskly along beaches or cliff-tops while I did my own thing among rock-pools or sand-dunes. While Tommy was around he usually came with us.

On Saturdays we often paused in Dungarvan, a market-town on the coast, to shop at Miller's old-fashioned Select Family Grocers. Mr Miller, beaming and bowing, would hurry out to the car to discuss with my mother cheeses and rices and teas and coffees while an assistant, wearing a half-moon leather apron, hovered in the background ceremoniously bearing samples on a round brass tray. These my mother would closely examine before committing herself to the expenditure of ten or twelve shillings. I sometimes think of this scene as I push my sweaty way through a seething supermarket crowd, beneath the glare of strip-lighting, between cliffs of gaudy packages.

Occasionally Mrs Mansfield accompanied us to Dungarvan, but she never shopped at Miller's and I soon realised that she disapproved of our doing so. When I questioned my mother about this she looked embarrassed—an uncharacteristic re-action to any question of mine—and at once I knew that I had touched on one of the more sordid areas of adult misbehaviour. But she would, I was confident, tell me the truth. Then she said, "Mrs Mansfield doesn't believe in supporting Protestant shops."

Momentarily I suspected a red herring. "But that's daft!" I objected. "What does a shop's religion matter?"

"It doesn't matter at all," said my mother, "but many Irish people think it does."

Suddenly various pennies began to drop; now I understood obscure remarks that had been made in my presence by the Ryans, or by the nuns at school, or by Old Brigid or Tommy's foster-mother. I felt an overwhelming, angry disgust—perhaps my first step away from orthodox religion. There was no logical reason why I should have recoiled so violently, at the age of eight, from an attitude that had long been accepted as normal by the majority of my compatriots, both Catholic and

Protestant. Obviously I comprehended none of the practical or philosophical implications. I only knew that this was something contemptible, which should be opposed.

Next morning I reopened the subject at breakfast-time. I was sitting on a stool by the fire in my parents' bedroom, eating grapefruit, and my mother was still in bed, propped against a pile of pillows, her heavy, glossy, chestnut braids coiled on a pale green bed-jacket and the bible open on her bookrest. (She began each day with a chapter from the New Testament.) Overnight my agitation about religious bigotry in general had been aggravated by my particular grief about the Ryans and Mrs Mansfield and Old Brigid—people to whom I was deeply attached—being guilty of this evil. I felt threatened. What to make of a world in which some of my most respected adults had been suddenly revealed as wrong-doers? So I asked my mother, "Why can't somebody teach people not to be bigots?"

"It's difficult," she explained, "because bigotry is self-perpetuating." (She never believed in tempering her vocabulary to the unlearned lamb.) "Bigots are so sure they're right they don't even try to see any other point of view. But it's wrong to blame individuals for being bigoted—that's just another form of bigotry and sometimes it's worse because it's so self-righteous while pretending not to be. Usually people inherit bigotry—it's a sort of communal disease. So if you hear other children repeating nonsense about all Protestants going to hell, and so forth, don't lose your temper. Just try to make them realise that such beliefs are unchristian and stupid. Then at least—even if they don't believe you—they'll be aware there's another point of view."

I have never forgotten this conversation. My mother's response to my first serious querying of a widely accepted attitude had shown that in certain circumstances nonconformism was not merely allowable but desirable. At once my anxiety evaporated and I was full of happy self-importance, seeing my parents and myself as crusaders against the forces of evil.

I cannot recall many conversations or scenes from my first decade, but the few memories I have are very vivid, possibly because they mark emotional or mental advances.

One raw November noon, not long after my discovery of bigotry, I stood waiting for my grandfather outside Trinity College and as I watched the crowds hurrying across College Green I wondered, "How important are all those people? Soon they will all be dead. And I'll be dead. What *is* a person? Do we really matter? Or do we only think we do? Why are we alive?" As they formed in my mind I was aware of the enormity of these questions. And I remember a detached, fatalistic acceptance of the fact that even as an adult I was unlikely to find coherent answers. But I was also aware that merely by asking such questions I had acknowledged the mystery at the centre of things and so perhaps had already found as much of the truth as was necessary for me. Oddly, I made no attempt to try to relate these speculations to the formal religion which was so much a part of my life at that time. They belonged to a category labelled 'Private Important Thoughts'—Pits for short—and nothing would have induced me to discuss them with any grown-up. Does every child have, as I had, an image of what adults expect children to be? And do they all courteously preserve this image, outwardly, lest their adults might be discomfited, while inwardly they are becoming something quite different, full of Pits that have nothing to do with Dr Dolittle or stringing conkers? But perhaps there is something more than courtesy behind the dissembling reticence of childhood. A personality is forming, and loving adults are eager to help mould it—while the child is determined to remain in control of his own evolution. Also, nothing is ready to be exposed. Most artists dislike having their incomplete work considered and discussed and this analogy, I think, is valid. The child is incomplete, too, and is constantly experimenting as he seeks his own style of thought and feeling. And all this is going on long before puberty, at an age when many children are expected still to believe in Santa Claus.

Not long after my ninth birthday my grandfather and I had a brief, curiously moving encounter in the sitting-room at Charleston Avenue. My grandmother had died of cancer the year before, but the battleground of the bridge warriors still reeked nostalgically of cigarette smoke, coffee grounds and sherry fumes. It was cluttered with an assortment of very bad and very good furniture, severely ravaged by moth, woodworm and dust, and over the mantelpiece hung the arms of the Leinster Murphys—four Lions Rampant and three Sheaves of Corn. The blue, scarlet and gold had been dimmed by wood-smoke from the inefficient grate, but the motto was still legible: *Fortis et Hospitalis.* Pappa came upon me one day when I was standing on the hearth in the empty sitting-room gazing up at those lions. And he asked me, "Do you know what the motto means?"

"That we should be Strong and Hospitable," I replied.

"Yes—but physical strength and material generosity are easy. To have strength and generosity of the mind and the spirit is what matters. We must all have our faults—but never be weak or mean." Then suddenly Pappa looked comically startled; he was too humble and humorous to be able to lecture even a grandchild unselfconsciously. For a moment he stood staring through the window, twirling an end of his moustache and humming a snatch from *The Gondoliers.* Before I could think of anything to say he had left the room.

On our monthly week-end visits to Dublin we usually left for home after Sunday tea. In those days the journey took six hours—it now takes three—and being prone to car-sickness I preferred night travel which allowed me to cheat my disability by sleeping. Often I woke only next morning, to find myself in my own bed.

Once, however, I woke as we crossed the Vee—and experienced pure terror for the first time. Directly above the car a dancing wall of orange and scarlet flame was obviously about to engulf us. This gorse-fire had of course been deliberately started and was not even remotely dangerous. But as we chugged up the steep slope the flames spread swiftly, filling with their terrible beauty the blackness of the night. Fear paralysed me, until a turn in the road made it seem that we were about to plunge into the crackling, glowing, writhing heart of the inferno. Then I shrieked and clutched my father's shoulder—thus putting us in real danger. Even when my mother had calmed me a residue of fear remained and on future crossings of the Vee I both dreaded and longed for the superb fury of a burning mountain.

That same winter I inconsistently failed to panic even slightly

59

when there was ample excuse for hysteria. During a very frosty spell my father had put a rug under the car bonnet—and then, typically, forgotten to remove it. Half-way up the Vee I happened to notice, through a gap in the floor beside the foot-brake, an ominously flickering brightness. I stared at it for a moment, fully aware of the implications, and then said in a carefully calm voice, "I think we'd better stop. The engine seems to be on fire."

My parents, who were no doubt discussing some medieval heresy or other, took no immediate notice. Then, "What did you say?" asked my mother.

"I said the engine seems to be on fire." And I remember adding sourly, "So we'll all be blown up if you don't stop talking about religion and put it out."

An instant later my father was hurling the burning rug onto the roadside. For the next five hours he and my mother hardly exchanged a word on any subject, which I well knew presaged a monumental row as soon as I was out of earshot.

At about this time I was suddenly afflicted by an irrational terror of darkness. Electricity had not yet come to Lismore; at dusk the lamp-lighter went up and down the South Mall and Old Brigid lit the oil lamps and closed and barred the shutters and drew the curtains and, when I had been put to bed at seven o'clock, darkness was, officially, final. However, for reading illicitly I had a secret supply of candles and matches and my new terror was revealed to myself when I forgot, one evening, to smuggle these in from my playroom. The playroom door was a mere three steps away, across the landing, yet I felt sick with fear at the thought of venturing out into the total, silent blackness. Inevitably I then saw myself as a most despicable coward, a craven sissy, a lily-livered, weak-kneed, spineless rotter.

This terror quickly became a phobia that dominated all my waking hours. Sometimes I was tempted to confide in my mother, but pride inhibited me. As the days passed my dread of bedtime increased; this had become my regular test of courage and always I failed it. At breakfast-time I might have successfully persuaded myself that, that very evening, I would do what had to be done. Yet when the moment came, when Old Brigid and my father had said good-night and kissed me and gone, I simply lay listening to the mealtime noises in the dining-room below while little shivers of shame ran through my body. Night after night, I told myself that within minutes this torment could be ended—if I found the necessary courage. Then one very cold evening I did find it. I slipped out of bed, tip-toed to the door and began a deliberately slow tour of the whole of the first floor—including the airing cupboard and attic, which to many seemed quite spooky even by daylight. I moved silently through the dense blackness, my hands outstretched to guide me, and the thudding of my heart seemed to hurt my ribs. Something odd happened to my sense of time and the ordeal seemed to be taking place outside the normal framework of hours and minutes. But it was worth it. When I got back to my bedroom my self-respect was restored and all fear of darkness exorcised forever.

On most issues, at this period, I did confide in my mother. Yet already my attitude towards her was habitually guarded; while half of me needed comfort and guidance the other half was suspicious of interference. From my father I had inherited a certain shyness or gaucherie or tendency towards self-effacement—to this day I am not sure of the exact nature of the trait—and this was aggravated by observation of a woman who always seemed at ease in every sort of situation. Unwittingly, my mother gave me an inferiority complex I was never to outgrow. I recognised and took for granted the fact that in looks, intelligence and poise she set a standard I could never hope to reach and for years I heroine-worshipped her. Yet I may also have unconsciously envied her capacity to inspire such devotion—not only in myself but in many others. 'A magnetic personality' is the stock phrase. And as a child I expended a disproportionate amount of energy on testing myself against the power of that magnet.

5

One February morning in 1939 the possibility of Adventure appeared on our humdrum horizon. A letter from a German friend, who had shared university digs with my father in Paris, invited us to stay with him near Heidelberg for the month of August. And Pappa, who normally spent his summers with us, was invited too. A delirium of excitement seized me. Long train and sea journeys—I had never been on a train in my life —incomprehensible languages, foreign coins for spending not for collecting, strange foods, unfamiliar customs, weird clothes (Germany seemed to me as remote and exotic as Inner Mongolia)—in a word, Real Travel.

Then I saw that my parents, though themselves quite excited in their staid way, were hesitant about accepting Anton's invitation. For several years he had been campaigning relentlessly against Hitler and in my father's opinion 'things were getting much worse'. I had no idea what those things might be, or why their deterioration should effect our holiday plans, and I rejoiced to hear my mother observing that it would be very interesting to see it for oneself. I jigged up and down in my chair, unable to eat my boiled egg, and begged them to say 'yes we are going to Germany for our holidays'. As I had never known the parental word to be broken it seemed that if only they could be persuaded to make this simple statement no power on earth could prevent our going to Germany. But instead they said, "It's too soon to make plans. Let's say we'll go to Germany in August if by then it still seems a good idea."

As I went bounding off to school, my mother was already working out with pencil and paper how best to save our fare money during the next six months.

During this spring I was being prepared for my First Confession and First Holy Communion. These ceremonies represent an initiation rite of immense solemnity. According to Roman Catholic theology, a child attains the use of reason at the age of seven and from then on is capable of committing sins, both mortal and venial. Mortal sins, which 'kill' the soul by depriving it of sanctifying grace—a sort of spiritual oxygen—must be confessed to a priest before God will forgive them. The seven-year-old is also considered responsible enough to take Holy Communion, even though this sacrament is believed to involve actually absorbing into one's own body the flesh and blood of God himself. Confession and Communion go together —it is sacrilegious to receive Communion with a mortal sin on one's soul—and the preparations for the two ceremonies are designed to make an ineradicable impression on young minds.

The impression they made on mine seemed at the time comparatively slight though later events were to prove its force. I never doubted what I was being taught and I took the whole thing seriously enough to get ninety marks out of a hundred in the preparatory religious doctrine examination. Yet I just could not feel the emotions presented as appropriate when one is soon to receive Holy Communion. Perhaps my rationality was affronted by the doctrine of Transubstantiation —which provided my parents with one of their favourite theological bones—and as the weeks passed I became more and more aware of the inadequacies of my spirituality.

I was also troubled by a desire to ask inconvenient questions. The atmosphere at school naturally precluded these and I hesitated to ask my mother lest such irreverent wonderings might upset her. I therefore continued to speculate secretly, feeling increasingly guilty, until it seemed to me that my impulse to ask such questions could only lead to my being flung into Hell's hottest fires to writhe in torment throughout eternity.

Clearly the time had come to consult my mother, whatever her reactions, and on the eve of my First Confession I asked the most worrying question of all: what happened to the Sacred Host when one swallowed it? Did it continue to be God's body? If so, was it not grossly disrespectful to subject it to the routine processes of the human digestive system? And if it did not continue to be God's body, at what stage did it revert to being the piece of unleavened bread it was before the priest changed its nature at the Consecration of the Mass? (Not for nothing had I been exposed since birth to theological debate.) I was immensely relieved when my mother, instead of being upset by all this, looked positively pleased. But in reply to my question she only said that God, as the inventor of the human digestive system, could have no objection to being involved in its everyday workings. She added that many books, which I could study when I was older, had been written on this doctrine. Her reaction soothed my fears about hell-fire yet her actual answer did not satisfy me. I never doubted the Host's being God and I was made deeply uneasy by the essential irreverence involved in eating him. If I lacked the kind of superstitious awe my teachers were trying to inculcate, I did not lack reverence—described by Alexander Skutch as 'the chief of the religious emotions'. An instinctive reverence is, I believe, a part of every child's nature. But it needs to be carefully cultivated and this is why I have never regretted my Catholic upbringing; for all its peculiarities it encouraged my natural reverence to grow into something capable of surviving without the protective netting of formal religion.

Despite the build-up, my recollections of First Holy Communion Day are hazy. I chiefly remember acquiring an unprecedented amount of money, through sixpenny and shilling tips from the neighbours, and feeling very important and adult and conscious of having begun an entirely new phase in my life. The Roman Catholic Church is often accused of retarding the mental and moral development of its members—and so it does, in many cases. But the First Confession/First Holy Communion initiation rite, with its emphasis on the seven-year-old as a responsible person, probably hastens, at this stage, the maturing process. Or at least *can* hasten it, if those in charge of religious instruction are not themselves superstition-sodden autocrats.

Being mainly dependent on my parents for such instruction, I soon became familiar with the neat logic that underpins Catholic moral theology. To change the metaphor, this system of stylised thought can be enjoyed as a sort of intellectual ballet, full of harmony, grace, disciplined energy and calculated flexibility. But it never allows for the unplanned movement, the sudden burst of individual initiative, the leap of a solitary imagination. Just as ballet is only remotely related to how people move in everyday life, so this system is only remotely related to how they think and feel. It is an heroic attempt to strengthen the weak, reassure the fearful and give form to the formless. As such, it has been of inestimable value to Europeans for almost two thousand years. But now European man is growing up, as Bonhoeffer saw not long before my First Holy Communion Day.

Apart from its religious significance, the First Holy Communion rite in a small Irish town was, during my childhood, a provocation to rampant one-up-womanship amongst the mothers of little girls. Who would have the longest veil, the most striking wreath, the most becoming frock, the prettiest shoes and knee-socks, the smallest rosary-beads, the most lavishly illustrated prayer-book? Mothers who could never afford a square meal for their children spent absurd sums on outfits which were totally impractical since it was considered both irreverent and *déclassé* to wear them on social occasions. Once I heard my father muttering in his ascetic way that the clergy should condemn such inappropriate ostentation. But my mother defended it, arguing that by spending so apparently foolishly, people were expressing an awareness of the solemnity of sacramental rites—that for them extravagance was a part of worshipping. Many years later, when listening to criticisms of the lavish wedding-feasts of poor Hindus, I remembered her words. Had my father noticed the circumstance, he would certainly have deplored the fact that his daughter—attired in a Parisian outfit donated by her godfather—won this sartorial competition at a canter. But then my mother counteracted our status-improving victory by thriftily insisting on my wearing the frock 'for best' during that summer of 1939.

At the beginning of June my parents were more grieved than surprised to get a letter from Switzerland announcing Anton's 'disappearance'. (For several years he had been an outspoken opponent of Nazism.) As my father translated the news the sun was shining brilliantly across the breakfast-table, making the pot of marmalade glow amber. Then, precisely folding up the thin sheet of writing-paper, he replaced it in its envelope and said, "So, by August war will have come". He was not far out. But I cared nothing for the fate of a to me unknown German professor, or for the shadow of an unimaginable war; I mourned only the loss of Real Travel.

A few months later, I went one morning to fetch the news-paper and learned that war had been declared. Hurrying home, I relished the sense of crisis in the atmosphere and expectantly scanned a cloudless sky for the first bombers. But when I realised that Ireland was not going to be involved I lost interest in the whole distant drama. For me, its chief effect was to intensify the boredom of grown-up conversation; I regarded literature and theology as lesser evils than military tactics. Occasionally, however, I was diverted by Hitler's interminable monologues on the wireless. These I found irresistibly funny and I remember rolling under the dining-room table one day in an uncontrollable paroxysm of mirth. My parents, who both understood German, reacted otherwise.

Yet for my father the war was a source of considerable inner conflict; much as he detested Nazism he was psychologically incapable of desiring a British victory. (Very likely his secret wish was that Germany and Britain should do a Kilkenny cat act.) He temporarily resolved his conflict—to my mother's unvoiced, ironic amusement—by refusing to remember Anton and persuading himself that the evils of Nazism were a creation of British propaganda. This illusion he cherished until Anton, unrecognisable after six years in Dachau, reappeared among us to dispel it. Not indeed by his words, for he never mentioned his experiences, but by the brand-marks on his arms and torso and by certain personality changes which moved to pity and horror his closest friends.

Throughout the war I myself was straightforwardly pro-Germany in a light-hearted sort of way, as one might be pro-Scotland or pro-France at a rugger match. While reading such patriotic English stories as the Biggles books I automatically transposed names in my mind, to make the British the baddies and the Germans the goodies. And this was the extent of my emotional involvement. It is rather disquieting to remember how little the war meant to an Irish family without relatives or friends in Britain. While most of the world suffered, and millions of people died, we complacently pursued our almost-normal lives. At no time were we more than mildly affected by what was known to all but shoneens as 'the Emergency'. In most Irish minds of the period, our own mini-civil-war of the 1920s, in which some 700 died, remained The War. Eventually cigarettes were rationed, and as my father's conscience forbade him to use the black market his temper became uncertain towards the end of each month. I can see him now, carefully saving his cigarette ends in a flat, navy-blue Player's tin and rolling extra rations from them when threatened by nicotine starvation. It concerned me more that new books dwindled in number and became hard on the eyes when one was reading under the blankets by the light of a failing torch. Tea, sugar, butter and clothes were rationed; bread became virtually inedible and motor-cars disappeared—never to be replaced, in our case, since after the war we seemed to be even poorer than before. But most important of all, to me, was the fact that parcels could no longer come from Paris.

This restriction ended an era of acute misery. Before the war my generous French godfather had regularly sent me the current juvenile equivalent of Dior outfits and every Sunday morning I was forced into these detested garments and dragged off to Mass by my father to be exposed to the derision of the entire congregation. Those ordeals were as agonising as anything I have ever experienced. My Parisian ensembles would have been conspicuous anywhere; in Lismore I felt they made me look like a cross between a damn silly doll and a circus clown. On this one issue my mother refused to consider my point of view. Having longed for an elegant daughter to share in her own enjoyment of beautiful clothes, she had produced an uncouth little savage who only felt happy in shorts and shirts. So perhaps her insistence on making a fool of me once a week was a forgivable form of self-indulgence. Also, she may have hoped that one day I would begin to take an interest in the art of dressing, if exposed for long enough to pleasing fabrics and designs. But inevitably her determination to see me looking civilised once a week had the opposite effect. I came to hate even my normal quota of new clothes, until they had been so broken in that I was no longer aware of them—a phobia which persists to this day.

Looking back, it seems odd that my inherent unconventionality did not allow me to accept these Sunday ordeals as distasteful but unimportant. Thirty-five years ago, in an Irish provincial town, shorts were considered immoral on small girls—so in fact my everyday wear was as conspicuous as any of my Parisian excesses. Evidently, then, my aversion to the latter was based on something more than embarrassment at seeming different. Of course I loathed looking ridiculous as I slunk to our accustomed pew near the altar-rails, but I was made equally—if not more—uncomfortable by the element of artificiality introduced into my life by these pretty clothes. They and I did not belong together and though I could not then have articulated the sentiment, they made me feel vaguely dishonest. When we heard that my godfather had been killed while fighting with the Resistance forces I was quite incapable of the correct reaction.

That September I happily resumed my personal war with Sister Andrew. Beneath the tumultuous antagonisms which raged over the surface of our relationship, we were genuinely fond of each other. Yet we remained implacable enemies, outwardly, for another few years; and it was during this period that I invented my secret endurance tests.

These consisted of my regularly inflicting on myself increasing degrees of pain, until I was capable of such feats as walking three miles with a sharp thorn embedded in the sole of one foot. The imagination is unequal to what my psychologist aunt might have said had she discovered this little idiosyncrasy, but she would have been mistaken had she associated it with either sexuality or childish religiosity. My sexuality was at that stage quiescent and my religious sense never prompted me to go beyond the bounds of duty. I had simply discovered, while being beaten by Sister Andrew, that it was possible to repel certain kinds of pain. This inspired me to see if the same control could be exercised over self-inflicted pain. I struck the back of my hand, harder and harder, with a short, heavy stick; I tied thin twine around my fingers and pulled it tighter and tighter; I immersed my feet in hot water which I made hotter and hotter by adding to the basin from a boiling kettle— and to my astonishment the technique I had used at school always worked. But 'technique' is the wrong word and I am not sure what the right one is—perhaps 'instinct' would be a little closer to it. The process was as follows: I applied the painful pressure, hot water or whatever, felt the consequences acutely and then somehow contrived to send a message that numbed the pain even while the pressure was being increased. For instance, if I were experimenting with my left hand I could feel this message travelling down my left arm and checking the pain near my wrist.

I have mentioned this activity to only a few friends (one prefers to retain what small reputation one has for sanity) and though it seemed slightly peculiar to them it may well be a common juvenile hobby. At the time, it was to me merely a useful accomplishment, worth cultivating, and many hours that should have been devoted to the twelve-times-tables or the rivers of Europe were spent pain-repelling. I became so proficient that at the age of ten I could probably have earned a good wage as a circus performer. But as yet I had only tested myself through brief ordeals and when I embarked on more prolonged trials I found that my message-sending did not work in quite the same way. Instead, I had to develop an indifference to pain. This entailed practising mental detachment from bodily sensations, whereas I assume my pain-repelling to have had a physiological basis. I can still pain-repel at will; but not, significantly, if the pain is a nerve one such as lumbago or toothache.

An amount of common-sense was used in what sounds like a lunatic campaign. I rarely did anything downright dangerous —my hot-water experiments were the most perilous—nor did I ever attempt to endure any suffering that could objectively be considered excessive. Some twenty-five years later, while observing the reactions to pain of less pampered races, I wondered if my endurance tests had been prompted by some atavistic longing to reacquire a once universal power. They have certainly proved much more useful than the twelve-times-tables. Although the training course lasted scarcely three years I have ever since been almost wholly insensitive to what most Europeans regard as severe discomfort.

The strangest of all my childhood memories dates from this same period, which may not be entirely a coincidence. It concerns levitation; and I am comforted to know that some quite sane people—including Richard Church—have recorded similar memories.

What I recollect, or fancy I recollect, is standing at the head of the stairs, breathing very slowly and deeply for a few moments —and then, while holding my breath, proceeding to the foot of the stairs without touching steps, banisters or wall. Was this a recurring dream that for some reason became fixed in my mind as part of reality? My mother often read and discussed Saint Teresa of Ávila, so the concept of levitation was familiar to me and may have seemed so impressively peculiar that a realistic dream-cycle began. Another explanation, for a memory that is both wildly improbable and extremely vivid, is that one of my more extravagant fantasies became hopelessly entangled with reality. Yet neither of these explanations really satisfies me. The memory has about it a baffling matter-of-factness and coherence which seem to separate it from both dreams and daytime fantasies. I clearly recall making sure, before embarking on one of these trips, that only my mother was in the house, because I dreaded somebody witnessing what by any standards must have seemed outré behaviour. I also recall taking the practical precaution of keeping my right hand just above the banisters, and my left close to the wall, to save myself from falling should the system break down. And I retain a most vivid memory of the physical effort involved in this breath control—which, if it existed at all, can only have been some yogic talent that by a million to one chance I had hit on, possibly in the course of my pain-defying experiments. I have had an open mind on such subjects ever since my Tibetan friends convinced me that levitation—and other even odder phenomena—are not physically impossible. But if in fact I had acquired this curious skill, why did I so soon cease to practise it? Did I lose the knack as suddenly as I had found it? Or was I afraid? I remember being enthralled by my capacity to do something so extraordinary, but my 'trips' also provoked a profound uneasiness, amounting almost to guilt. It is slightly disconcerting to think that I shall never know the truth about this matter. Now, looking at small children, I often wonder what sort of private lives they lead.

*   *   *

As Wordsworth noted, the whole person is plain to be seen in the child, though unformed and unrefined. But in many cases the individual's true nature is radically modified by the pressures of his environment and the expectations of his family. It is sad to think that a generous, frank child may become a tight-fisted, shifty businessman if the pressures and expectations are so directed. But equally, as in my own case, a selfish, stubborn, sulky child may become quite an amiable adult.

Stubbornness and sulkiness were the weapons I used against my mother as she diligently laboured to eradicate—or at least suppress—my more anti-social vices. Even now it shames me to recollect certain scenes. Myself, aged nine or thereabouts, reading one damp July afternoon in the round, thatched, earwiggy summer-house; my mother asking me to post a letter, some fifty yards down the road; my snapped reply—"No! I'm reading—I won't go—I'm busy." Then the verbal battle and my mother's inevitable victory and my return from the post-office to sulk for the rest of the afternoon. Why did I so often start battles which I knew very well I was certain to lose? What devil prevented me from being normally helpful about everyday domestic chores?

In all circumstances my mother insisted on obedience, yet in spite of my surface sulks I never really resented her disciplining. She was almost always just—and capable of apologising if she had been unjust—so resentment would have been irrational.

My childhood relationship with my mother was relatively straightforward, but I still find it hard to understand my relationship, at any age, with my father. In a sense, nothing ever grew between us from the seed of child–parent love; it lived on through the years but remained underground; there was no blossoming to affirm its existence to the outside world—or even, for long periods, to ourselves. One of the conditions that hindered its growth was my father's inability to communicate with the young. He lacked any means of expressing his affection in an acceptable form and his rare attempts to get onto my level and be playful caused me acute embarrassment. Desperately well meant but blatantly phoney, these—I felt—were just making us both look foolish while widening the gulf between us. I much preferred his natural approach when he treated me as a pupil rather than a daughter. His own idea of

71

fun was a fact-packed lecture thinly disguised as a long walk. With the random questioning of small children he had no patience; this was an untidy, unscholarly way of going about learning—a bad habit, to be eradicated without delay. Significantly, I could never imagine him as anything but a tiresomely erudite grown-up, though I could easily picture my mother as a little girl.

For me, our regular Sunday afternoon walks were both physical and intellectual marathons. Week by week I would be tidily instructed about birds, or moral theology, or electricity, or Irish history, or geology, or English literature, or astronomy, or music, or agriculture, or the Renaissance. Often I wished that I were alone beneath my teddy-bear tree and then I would vindictively insulate myself against my father's voice; though to give him his due he presented all his information in carefully simple terms. Of course some of it fascinated me, despite myself, as several of his enthusiasms were by heredity my own—especially history and astronomy. On the whole, however, these didactic perambulations provided the wrong sort of fertiliser for the seed of love.

Just occasionally the barrier was lifted and we drew very close. My father had an unexpected flair for composing Learish nonsense rhymes and these charmed me utterly; when he was in one of his rare frivolous moods I would gladly have walked with him to the Giant's Causeway. Then I discovered that I had a similar flair—long since atrophied—and we enjoyed the harmony of collaboration or the stimulus of competition, each striving to outdo the other in dottiness and euphony. But the barrier always came down again at the end of these sessions, leaving us uneasily antagonistic for no discernible reason.

The reason could have been jealousy, an emotion one would expect to find in some rather virulent form in such an introverted family. Perhaps, being so worshipful of my mother, I resented my parents' mutual devotion. (Although according to pop psychology I should at that age have been so devoted to my father that I regarded my mother as a rival.) Yet I am pretty sure—as sure as one can be on such matters—that jealousy did not then influence any of our relationships. I was certainly given no cause for it. Together my parents lived their own separate child-excluding life, but I accepted this as natural and was never made to *feel* excluded in any unfair way. From an early age I took part in serious family conferences, and was admitted to the cupboard where the skeletons were kept, and generally was treated as a responsible, dependable individual. Years later I discovered that Pappa disapproved of my being consulted before family decisions were taken; he held that it is unkind to implicate children in adult affairs with which they are too inexperienced to cope.

Every summer Pappa spent July and August with us. I would guess that my father was his favourite child though apart from their common bibliomania the two were alike in no obvious way. Pappa was not merely 'good with children'; he truly enjoyed them and his annual arrival by train drew not only myself but a score of other children to the railway station. Yet he never gave pennies or sweets or treats to me or to any of his young friends. Instead he played with us endlessly—our own games in our own favourite haunts. And always he brought from Dublin a battered suitcase tied with rope and bulging with dog-eared children's books bought for twopence a dozen on the quays. No one—not even my mother—could read aloud as Pappa did. He involved us until we were transported beyond anything we knew of into other worlds that seemed to be suffused with a special Pappa magic, whatever the theme of the story or the author's style. Even the more restless of the smaller children—and those who were not accustomed to being read to and normally had no interest in books—even they would sit motionless for as long as Pappa chose to read.

Punctuality was the only subject on which I used to query Pappa's wisdom. He argued cheerfully that a capacity for ignoring time marks the truly free in spirit and that over-organised Western man has only himself to blame for the fact that our society would collapse if this freedom were widely enjoyed. His own indifference to time no doubt formed part of his attraction for children. But it made him another of Old Brigid's crosses. She, too, adored him, and considered it her duty and privilege to 'feed him up' during his holidays, and so if he had not appeared by 12.55 she felt obliged to go forth to quarter the back streets and lanes of the town in search of 'Dr Conn'. Luckily this did not happen too often since I shared my father's obsessional punctuality—which was perhaps a result of the havoc frequently wrought in his own life by parents who never knew or cared whether it was morning or evening.

There was a Franciscan quality about Pappa's affection for children and animals and the poor of all ages. It was without any element of paternalism or do-gooding; behind the gaiety which charmed us all lay a deep awareness of suffering and a love based on compassion and respect. For some reason he was always known locally as Dr Conn and he was a particular favourite of the old country folk whose dying traditions he collected for one of his unwritten—or half-written—books.

On a hot summer evening in 1939 an old woman from the mountain hamlet of Ballysaggart called to ask for Dr Conn's help and I answered the door. Explaining that Pappa was out, I offered to give him a message. The old woman hitched her black woollen shawl higher to protect her head from the midges around the fuchsia bushes. "When he comes back, could y'ever ask yer father to drive him out t'see me poor husband? He have a crool pain in his chest wit de past tree weeks. He can't even raise himself in de bed wit it. An' the docthur above on'y gev him on oul cough-bottle dat med him sick to his stummick."

I looked at the old woman in silence and felt wretchedly guilty, as though the family had been caught playing some nasty confidence trick on the entire district. Then I admitted miserably, "But Pappa isn't a real doctor. He's only a doctor of philosophy!"

The old woman shrugged. "Shure isn't that good enough? Isn't he a kind man wit brains? What more d'ye want?"

I tried to explain. "But you see it's not the right sort of brains—he wouldn't know what medicine you need. Philosophy has nothing to do with being ill. At least, I don't think it has," I added, suddenly wondering just what it did have to do with.

Next day I asked, "What is philosophy?" as Pappa and I were walking back from our morning bathe in the Blackwater. My father would undoubtedly have taken this question as the jumping-off point for an outline of the various schools of Western thought. But Pappa simply said, "It's the study of how to live contentedly and how to die peacefully!"

From my point of view our annual summer holiday in some

secluded seaside cottage was redeemed only by Pappa's presence. I enormously enjoyed our week-end trips to the sea, but I detested being away from home for an entire month. These cottages were never anywhere near a public library and, from 1940 on, petrol was rationed and I dreaded running short of books. There was little room for luggage in the Ford Ten with five passengers—including Old Brigid or her successor—and Parnell the all-black sheepdog, and Sibelius and Delius the cats, and my mother's bath chair on the roof. My personal baggage allowance was one large suitcase and to make the most of this I wore all my clothes, including two pairs of pyjamas, on the journey to the coast. But a single suitcase of books seemed meagre fare for a month, even if one chose only volumes that could stand rapid rereading.

However, it was the removal from my natural habitat that I minded most. Amidst the fields and woods and rivers and hills around Lismore I could enjoy myself as nowhere else. Already I wanted to travel to distant lands, so I might have been expected to welcome the substitute thrill of exploring remote stretches of the Irish coastline. But already, too, I had clear-cut ideas about *how* I wanted to travel. I wanted to wander alone, taking each day as it came, and even at the age of nine or ten it was impossible to pretend that a month in the domestic cosiness of a seaside cottage was any sort of substitute for such adventuring.

6

The autumn of 1940 was marred by a bizarre psychological affliction. Or perhaps it was a 'normal abnormality', given my keen interest in sexual equipment and the inhuman puritanism of the Irish Catholic Church. Because I had long been in the habit of closely observing mating animals I one day became convinced that my soul was permanently laden with mortal sins. This conviction rapidly spread, like a sort of mental septicaemia. Soon I felt that to wash above the knees or below the navel must also be a mortal sin. And so must chancing to see a male baby having his nappy changed, or noticing a cat feeding her kittens or a dog sprinkling a lamppost—or even hearing, at the other side of the partition that divided the school lavatory, the hiss of little boys urinating into the stinking gutter. At this stage my having long since given up masturbation was unfortunate. Something as tangible as that to worry about might have saved me from fancying myself corrupt right through because a dog peed in my presence.

What puzzles me now is the extent to which, during those months, school influences temporarily overcame home influences. On trivial issues small children will naturally follow school fashions, on important matters parental attitudes generally prevail. Moreover, at no other period of my life have I been prone to unhealthy—or even, some would say, healthy —guilt. Yet throughout this nightmare period I was half-crazed by shame and self-disgust.

The approach of puberty, combined with an incident which had occurred during the previous summer holidays, may have been partly responsible for this anxiety-state. Physically I was unusually mature and my mother had explained that my budding breasts must now be kept covered.

But I so relished the feel of the sun and the wind on my body that I often ignored her directive and wore only brief shorts when playing alone on the deserted beaches near our holiday cottage. Then one day three adolescent boys appeared abruptly from behind a rock, shouted obscene remarks and threw several well-aimed pebbles at my indecently exposed torso. And my eyes were opened, and I knew that I was naked . . .

A better balanced child would merely have been incensed by this tiny incident, or at worst slightly alarmed. But in an instant it made me see human sexuality not just as an example of nature's ingenuity but as something apart from the rest of life and capable of assuming ugly, obscurely threatening shapes. I told my mother about the incident by way of exorcising it, though the telling involved a confession of disobedience. Her reaction, as always, was steadying—"People can be unpleasant. But their unpleasantness needn't infect us if we don't want it to." Nevertheless, I now began to think about sex in a new, personal, speculative way (though I have no recollection of experiencing at the time any sexual sensations) and this made me much more vulnerable at school.

The reader may well wonder what methods were used by my teachers to unhinge me so disastrously. In fact sex was never mentioned: eight of the ten commandments were commented on in detail, but the other two were ignored. At the same time the impression was given that these were the most important of all, though the vices they forbade were too evil to be analysed as one could analyse the comparatively minor sins of murder, theft, slander and idolatry. It is remarkable, and quite sinister, that this message, stressing the incomparable heinousness of sexual sin, could be got across wordlessly. Somehow we were made hyper-aware of the horror and revulsion with which such sins must be regarded and in the process a horror of sex itself was deeply implanted in many a child's mind.

All this left no lasting mark on me though it profoundly affected the world in which I grew up. Behind the popular image of the gay, feckless, hard-drinking, charming, belligerent, eloquent Irishman lies an amount of muted yet intolerable suffering—which is shared by the victims' wives. The Irish incidence of mental disease and alcoholism is amongst the highest in the world, Irish people marry later than most others

77

—if at all—and the Irish male is noted for sexual immaturity. The Catholic Church has always been the obvious scapegoat here, yet it does not deserve all the blame. Our puritanism is peculiarly Irish rather than peculiarly Catholic; one finds it operating equally strongly among Northern Irish Protestants.

Members of celibate communities are often assumed to be unbalanced, tense, frustrated and generally unsuitable as educators. Yet many priests and nuns seem, to those who know them best, exceptionally balanced, relaxed and fulfilled. However, when celibates do go dotty they go very dotty indeed, frequently in rather nasty ways, and one of my teachers—not Sister Andrew—should never have had anything to do with children. She regularly interrupted our history, geography or arithmetic lessons to gratify herself by terrorising us. Obviously she believed in her own fevered descriptions of Hell and the Devil and the conviction with which she spoke made her harangues all the more blood-curdling.

I was unsettled not only by this poor creature's words but by the evident sick satisfaction she obtained from frightening us. I recall one of her sessions with particular vividness because I was sitting in the front row just below her desk. She had a high-pitched voice which became little better than a squeak when she was enraged or excited and on this occasion, as she spoke, fine beads of sweat broke out on her hairy upper lip. She was telling the 'true' story of a ten-year-old Co Waterford girl who one day committed a filthy mortal sin (the adjective told us that it was sexual) and next day fell into a stream and was drowned. Because she had not been to confession, or made an act of perfect contrition, the Devil promptly dragged her soul down to Hell where she was doomed to an eternity of tortures which Sister X assured us were indescribable though this did not deter her from attempting to describe them in considerable detail. None of us thought to ask our mentor the source of her information on this case. It was a cruel coincidence that I came under the influence of such an unstable woman during the unhappiest phase of my childhood.

At noon every Saturday I went to confession with my classmates, as was the custom. We sat in restless rows near the three confessionals, examining our consciences and memorising our sins while awaiting our turn to enter the stuffy, anonymous darkness of the box. During my guilt period I used to envy my companions whose rapid reappearances, following the muffled drone of the absolution, indicate their freedom from moral problems. It made me feel doubly depraved to think of the innocent content of their confessions, which I knew would go something like this: "Bless me, father, for I have sinned. It's one week since my last confession. I forgot to say my morning prayers three times. I was distracted at Mass on Sunday. I stole five sweets from my brother. I told three lies to the nun. I was disobedient nine times. I hit the girl next door. That's all, father." Then they would be given three Hail Marys for penance and would cheerfully emerge to commit the same crimes— more or less—during the week ahead.

I always chose to confess to Father Power. The other curate too plainly conveyed the extremity of boredom to which juvenile misdeeds drove him and the parish priest was eighty-five, stone deaf and apt to confuse 'impure thoughts' with adultery. While in the confessional most Catholics regard their confessor not as the neighbour who calls for a chat but as an impersonal representative of God. Therefore it was easy for me to put Father Power in the picture. But his calm reassurances and careful explanations achieved nothing. Like any mentally deranged person, I was isolated in a private world of my own, beyond reach of common sense. Father Power repeatedly urged me to confide in my mother, but this was no help as my inability to do so was an integral part of my disease. I was so far gone that I feared losing her love if she discovered my vileness. When I explained this to Father Power he again tried unsuccessfully to make me see the absurdity of my terrors; had he not been bound by the seal of the confessional he himself would certainly have warned my mother of her daughter's pathetic state. More acceptable was his advice to confess only four times a year instead of once a week and to stop keeping a tally of my sins in the copybook I had specially set aside for the purpose. But unfortunately even this counsel did not reach to the root of my obsession—though it came near enough to it. However, it stimulated an enjoyable argument with Sister X who furiously asked if I wanted to 'lose my soul' when I told her that in future I would not be joining my class at confession time. I declined to explain that I was acting on Father

Power's advice; why should I divulge to her what went on in the confessional? Besides, I was delighted to have a chance to deflate her single-handed. I did not then clearly recognise her contribution to my problem, but I disliked her more than anyone else I had ever known. (And indeed, now I come to think of it, I have never since met anybody I disliked as much.)

Sister X had a very long nose, with a ludicrously thin tip, and her angry flushes always began at this tip and radiated outwards like a spreading wine stain on a yellowing table-cloth. "I'll be looking for you tomorrow!" she squeaked threateningly as I watched her nasal indicator turning crimson. "Mind you're here at a quarter to twelve sharp with the rest! You should be ashamed of yourself, even thinking of rejecting God's grace! It's the Devil is putting such wickedness in your mind— he wants your soul for himself—and at this rate he won't be long getting it!"

Such a challenge to do theological battle made me briefly forget that this was my own current belief. I replied that no Catholic was bound to confess more than once a year and that if I were forced to confess by anyone else the sacrament would be invalid. This final point took Sister X right out of her depth, as it was meant to do, and she sounded like a fork on a plate when she exclaimed—most unconvincingly—"I'll report you to the Canon for this!" (The Canon was our parish priest, a saintly old gentleman who was known to abhor the very mention of Sister X's name.) As she swept from the schoolroom giggles erupted among my classmates and in an instant she was back to give us all an hour's detention. But I knew that she knew that she had been beaten. And vengefully I rejoiced. She brought out the very worst in her pupils—apart from turning them into nervous wrecks.

Years later my mother told me that by the end of November she had begun to worry about my being so obviously off form. She mentioned her concern to Father Power, who at once suggested a mother–daughter conference on the relevant commandments.

The day before my ninth birthday I woke early and tried to read but could not concentrate. At that age birthdays have an epochal significance and I felt that if my tenth year began as inauspiciously as my ninth was ending this misery must continue for every day of the next twelve months. As I lay in bed, staring unhappily at the grey-brown damp stains on the ceiling, I heard my father coming upstairs—but instead of going straight into the bathroom to shave he came to my door and said that my mother wanted to see me. As she did not usually encourage me to enter her life before breakfast-time—rather the reverse—I went downstairs reluctantly, expecting a lecture on some newly discovered misdemeanour. But no; she was in a very gentle mood and invited me into her bed for a snuggle. And then she asked directly, "What's making you so unhappy?"

For weeks I had known, deep down, that a conference with my mother was the key to freedom if only I could bring myself to take the risk of using it. Now that key had been put in my hand—and I did use it.

I shall never forget my mother's laughter as I lay there with my arms around her neck and my face buried in her hair. She had a deep, rich laugh and soon I, too, was laughing— dazedly, scarcely able to believe that within moments my tragedy had been transmuted into comedy. When I returned to my room to dress I felt just as one does on wakening from a complicated nightmare: elated by the simplicity of reality.

My mother's amusement had been perfectly genuine, but beneath it she was gravely disturbed by my account of Sister X's mental torturings. Already she was weary of another aspect of school life; every afternoon, before I could safely be admitted to the house, she had to supervise the fine-combing of my hair over a basin of Lysol outside the back door. So now it was decided that a combination of head lice and faulty theology sufficiently justified my removal from Lismore school.

While debating what to do next, my mother taught me—an arrangement which I favoured. She used teaching methods not then fashionable in Irish national schools. Instead of presenting knowledge neatly cut up into small bits she showed me how to go about collecting my own information and so made learning seem fun. Yet even she could not reconcile me to the German language. Nor could I cope with Irish or French, which my father had been inflicting on me since I was born. Latin was the only language for me. That I enjoyed, and was good at, knowing I would never be expected to make a fool of myself by speaking it.

Many nine-year-olds would have missed the social side of school life, but this loss never worried me. Apart from Tommy, and a girl with the unlikely name of Charity, all my primary school relationships were superficial. For a time I felt that I should have several friends, because children in books usually had, but I soon found that promising to meet for play at a certain time unduly restricted my private life of reading and roaming. Had the choice been wider I might have felt otherwise; I was overjoyed when Charity joined our class and revealed that she, too, was enslaved to Hugh Lofting, Arthur Ransome and Richmal Crompton. Soon I had got her a special pass to visit the library whenever she liked and for the next six months we were Best Friends. But then her army father was posted elsewhere and thus ended my first close friendship, as distinct from the sort of tribal comradeship I had enjoyed with Tommy.

A few days after Christmas my mother broke it to me that in January I was to go as a boarder to an Irish-speaking coeducational school. Naturally I was devastated. It had always been understood that I would go away to school at the age of ten and I could scarcely credit my parents' treachery. But in an odd way this sense of having been betrayed kept me calm. Parents who loved me so little must not be allowed to see how much I cared—a melodramatic reaction which carried me through my initial grief and disillusionment. Then suddenly going away to school began to seem an interesting idea; to my own surprise part of me was one morning quite looking forward to it, though I had never yet been separated from both my parents for more than a few days. But soon I was again shattered by the discovery that books in English were forbidden at the College. Despair overcame me; this was equivalent to depriving an alcoholic of his bottle or a chain-smoker of his packet. Yet I never made any attempt to alter my parents' decision. On details I argued interminably with them; on major issues I meekly deferred to their adult wisdom even if their reasoning seemed obscure. Or if, as in the present case, my antennae told me that they were not themselves in perfect agreement.

This was one of the few occasions when my father made a

decision, for personal reasons of his own, to which my mother only grudgingly assented. Where the use of English was totally forbidden it seemed possible that within a year even I would have acquired a working knowledge of my native tongue. For nationalistic reasons my father wished me to be as fluent an Irish speaker as himself. Besides, if I were ever to pass an examination some action had to be taken to remove whatever blockage prevented me from learning languages. Or so my parents thought; for years they would not accept the simple fact that I had not inherited their linguistic gifts. They mistook stupidity for laziness and my mother—who held no strong views about the Gaelic Revival—probably agreed to this experiment as a general disciplinary measure.

At the beginning of 1941 the 'Emergency' had not yet banished all motor-cars from Irish roads and we drove to the College on a cold, dark, wet January afternoon. The hedges were hardly visible through swirling curtains of rain and we were all, for our various reasons, apprehensively silent. Real, live boarding-school authorities were an unknown quantity to me, but I felt that they might prove much more dangerous in life than in literature so I had been afraid to pack even one illicit book. And now I was sick with anguish at the thought of parting from my parents. When the grey school buildings loomed sombrely out of the rain and fog, on their bleak and windswept cliff above the sea, I remarked that there would be no need for any lingering once my luggage had been unloaded. And my mother agreed that this was so.

When we had said our brisk good-byes my father decisively banged the car door and I turned into a long, empty corridor. Most pupils travelled by train and had not yet arrived. A young master appeared, said something curt in Irish and disappeared, carrying my suitcases. I hurried after him, down the ill-lit corridor and up a steep staircase. The whole place reeked of Jeyes Fluid and boiled onions. Then I was put in the care (not quite the *mot juste*) of a freckled twelve-year-old with sandy plaits and a shrill, bossy voice. I can still see her frayed pale green hair-ribbons and her look of contempt when she realised that I understood not a word she was saying.

In the icy, barn-like, whitewashed dormitory there were no cubicles but only rows of beds with vociferously broken springs and lumpy, unclean mattresses. My bed stood almost in the centre of this desolation and as I paused forlornly beside it, wondering where to hang my clothes, I realised that such a complete lack of privacy would add an unforeseen dimension to my hell. I shivered and needed to go quickly to the lavatory. Half-a-dozen older girls were gathered in a far corner, wearing overcoats and stuffing themselves with sticky buns. When I asked for the lavatory in English one of them threw a boot at me and shouted angrily in Irish. My bladder was about to fail me and I broke into a cold sweat—literally, for I remember pushing the hair out of my eyes and noting the chilly moisture on my forehead and thinking that this must be what authors meant by 'cold sweat'. I had assumed that *in extremis* we could talk English; now it was plain that to do so, under any circumstances, would bring some instant punishment from my uncouth and intimidating seniors. Mercifully a lavatory chain was pulled nearby at that moment and I rushed gratefully towards the sound.

Back in the dormitory I found my suitcases open and their contents scattered on the bed. The girls were examining everything critically and the discovery of my school-books provoked much mirth; I was so tall for my age that from these they deduced extraordinary stupidity. They expressed the opinion that I must be mentally retarded by using graphic traditional gestures, while shrieking with laughter. Then they came on a packet of sanitary towels—proud emblem of my recently acquired womanhood—and used other gestures, not then understood by me; no doubt their comments were to match for they lowered their voices and muffled their sniggers. As I could see no friendly—or even neutral—face anywhere I suppressed my rage and stood by helplessly until the enemy lost interest. They left the dormitory linking arms, scuffling, giggling and shouting each other down. I thought of Mrs Mansfield, who would almost have fainted to witness such behaviour, and the image of her trim little figure, with San Toy trotting regally to heel, sent me hurrying back to the lavatory to weep. Already I had resolved that my enemies would never see me weeping.

At six o'clock a jangling bell summoned us to the refectory for high tea. Most of the other pupils had now arrived, but I seemed to be the only new girl though there were several new boys—all of whom, discouragingly, spoke effortless Irish. As I took my place at one of the long, scrubbed wooden tables, each with mounds of thick bread and scrape placed at intervals down the centre, I vowed that this educational experiment must be made to fail as expeditiously as possible. Since English was forbidden, I would not speak. And when the futility of having a dumb child about the place impinged on the authorities, they would expel me. Nothing could be simpler. As I am naturally taciturn the prospect of maintaining silence for an indefinite period did not dismay me. And to compensate for the lack of books I would secretly write one myself.

Of course things did not work out quite like this. I was far too demoralised by homesickness to concentrate on writing anything more than letters and my misery, instead of diminishing as the days passed, became more acute. There was not even one remotely congenial character among either staff or pupils and I had immediately become a favourite bullying target for the more sadistic seniors. These also regularly robbed me of my weekly food parcel—an Emergency innovation—and they did use English to threaten to retaliate if I reported them. It is easy to see how I brought out the worst in these schoolmates. To them I must have seemed intolerably priggish, precocious, precious, pedantic and pusillanimous. There was no point of contact; in every sense we spoke different languages. Inevitably my memories of this ordeal are biased and the reality may have been a trifle less barbarous than what I recollect. Yet the essence of the atmosphere remained unparalleled in my experience until I worked as a waitress, almost twenty years later, in the canteen of a home for down-and-outs in East London.

Therefore this episode, despite its brevity, was one of the most valuable in my limited educational career. At Lismore school I was subtly accorded privileges by many of the teachers because I seemed 'different'. At Ring I was given hell for the same reason and thus I learned that standards other than my own were not only acceptable to, but preferred by, large sections of the population.

My parents wrote long letters three times a week but refrained from squandering their petrol ration on me. In my

Sunday letters home I never asked for a visit but regularly reported that I was learning *no* Irish and cunningly emphasised the physical hardships of school life. In fact I took these in my stride—apart from the atrocious food they seemed no worse than the rigours of home life—but I felt that my mother would be more disturbed by health hazards than by complaints about bullying. So I graphically described how—after an inadequate lunch—we were driven out every afternoon, whatever the weather, to play camogie (the feminine of hurling) on pitches hock-deep in mud—and how we then had to sit in an unheated prep. hall for two hours wearing damp socks.

These letters were not greatly exaggerated and as a result of over-exposure and underfeeding I developed severe bronchitis in the middle of February. After forty-eight hours I was almost too ill to walk, yet the matron merely dosed me with some ineffectual syrup. Everyone had snuffles and coughs and she did not pause to distinguish between penny plain and tuppence coloured. So I wrote an extra letter to my parents, one Wednesday morning.

On the following afternoon they arrived unannounced, and despite a keen east wind discerned in the distance their wheezing ewe-lamb, feebly wielding a camogie stick. Moments later I was in the car, drenching my mother's shoulder with all the tears not shed since our parting. And in the headmaster's office my father was being told that I had made little progress with my Irish and seemed 'unable to fit in with the rest'. "I should think not!" muttered my mother, as we drove off. While I was changing and packing she had had an opportunity to observe a cross-section of 'the rest'.

7

During my absence from home Old Brigid had at last retired to her cottage near Cappoquin and been replaced by one Maggie—unenthusiastically described as 'adequate', fading to 'better than nothing', in my mother's letters. As we drove towards Lismore I found it hard to imagine life without Old Brigid, but I would have been a good deal more upset in any other circumstances. Having just regained Paradise not even her loss could dilute my joy and on being assured that I might visit her weekly I philosophically accepted the idea of Maggie.

I did not, however, accept the reality of Maggie. She was sharp-boned and purple-hued and her voice rasped and she always looked discontented—with some reason, as a servant chez Murphy. We disliked each other on sight; to me she was an unloving tyrant, to her I was a saucy little puppy. And the chances of our ever coming to terms were much reduced by my having to take to my bed at once and stay there for three weeks, during which time Maggie found herself toiling up and down stairs every few hours with trays of such delicacies as were then available. (I particularly remember dark-brown beef-tea, jars of Calves'-foot jelly and a weird, chewy ginger-based concoction which was alleged to do wonderful things for the bronchial chords.)

Even in our Spartan household bronchitic patients were permitted a fire in their bedroom and it was typical of my mother's feeling for servants that she always asked my father to take on the consequent chores—which he most willingly did. Old Brigid had greatly appreciated his help, but it quickly became obvious that in Maggie's estimation such face-losing behaviour on the master's part drastically lowered our status. For a few weeks after my recovery she and I sparred daily; I

87

was missing Old Brigid dreadfully, resenting Maggie in proportion and making my feelings plain. Then one morning she left without notice to become housekeeper to an elderly, childless couple who lived in a comfortable new house where no one had committed suicide.

Having been born with 'a weak chest' I was accustomed to enjoying a few weeks of invalidism each winter and I revelled in being free to read, almost without interruption, for fourteen hours a day seven days a week. Whatever the theologians might say about Heaven being a state of union with God, I knew it consisted of an infinite library; and eternity, about which my parents were wont to argue with amusing vehemence, was simply what enabled one to read uninterruptedly forever.

The only interruptions I welcomed during these withdrawals from the world were Dr White's visits. He treated me with the sort of rough affection one bestows on a large dog and gave me delicious syrup from a bottle excavated with difficulty from the depths of his greatcoat pocket and told heart-stopping stories about his soldiering days in India and South Africa. Sometimes he advised me to rest my eyes, but this advice went unheeded as I took no interest whatever in any of the standard children's games or pastimes. (A serious handicap nowadays, when I have a more versatile child of my own.)

I remember the perfection of my happiness—a perfection not often attained in this life, as I realised even then—when I woke on a dark winter's morning and switched on the light to see a tower of unread library books by my bed. From them I would look caressingly towards my own books on their shelves around the wall and reflect that now I had time to reread; I could never decide which was the greater pleasure, rereading old favourites or discovering new ones. For a moment I would lie still, ecstatically anticipating the day's bliss. And sometimes it would cross my mind that only Pappa could fully understand how I felt.

There is a difference between the interest taken in books by normal readers (people like my parents) and the lunatic concern of bibliomaniacs (people like Pappa and myself). Everything to do with books mattered to me and I fretted much more over their wartime deterioration—that squalid gravy-coloured paper!—than I did over butter rationing or inedible bread. (Clothes rationing I of course considered a blessing in disguise.) After a quick glance at any open page I could by the age of nine have told you the publisher of most children's books—and often the printer and illustrator, too. One of my hobbies was rewriting blurbs which seemed inadequate and I collected publishers' lists as other children collect stamps. During June and July I often prayed for rain; on fine days I was supposed to be out in the fresh air, but on wet days I could go to the county library headquarters and help unpack the new books that came by the hundred, in tea-chests, at that season. The sight, smell and feel of these books so intoxicated me that I often refused to go home at lunch time. I had an agreement with my parents that when the children's books came I could always help unpack, regardless of climatic conditions. I would then—to my father's sensibly silent disgust—seize on the least worthy volumes (Biggles and so forth) and beg to be allowed to borrow them even before they had been initiated into public circulation. But my father did not believe in Privilege so I had to bide my time—very sulkily. It must have exasperated my parents that for so long I preferred exciting stories to good writing. At every stage of childhood I completely rejected all the classical fairy stories, and Lewis Carroll, Captain Marryat, Louisa Alcott, Kipling, E. Nesbit and any volume that I suspected might be intended to improve my mind. But neither, to be fair to myself, would I read Enid Blyton when she began to pollute the literary atmosphere. I was uncompromisingly middlebrow; and so, with minor modifications, I have remained to this day.

As the librarian's daughter I did have one priceless perk. When public library books become too battered and disgusting for rebinding or recirculation they are 'Withdrawn From Circulation', stamped to that effect and despatched either to fever hospitals or to the pulpers. And among those glorious, revolting heaps of 'Withdrawn' books—their pages interlarded with evidence of the diet of the rural reader—I was free to wander and take my pick and carry the noisome volumes home by the armful to be mine forever. (Many of them are still mine; no one ever steals them.)

I went through one appalling crisis in relation to 'Withdrawn' books. At the age of eight or so I had a compulsive secret vice—

crossing out the author's name on the title page of old books and substituting my own. This could be done without fear of detection in unfrequented corners of the library; but then, in bed one ghastly evening, I suddenly realised that some of the books I had been abusing might go, not to the pulpers but to a fever hospital. If this happened both my iniquitous vandalism and my vain ambitions would be exposed to a shocked and derisive public. This hideous possibility so tormented me that I could not sleep. As my parents were listening to the late news I crept downstairs and confessed all to my mother—who remained astonishingly unperturbed. She assured me that the defacement of such books was forgivable and that no fever hospital patient was likely to report on my little weakness to the world press—which would in any case be disinclined to take the matter up. I always enjoyed the irony with which she put things in perspective; curiously enough, it never made me feel foolish.

By the spring of 1941 most Irish working girls had emigrated to earn good money in English factories and our next five years were dominated by the comings and goings of maid-servants. The best were those too young to emigrate, who usually responded well to my mother's training; but no sooner had she imparted the rudiments of domesticity than they were clutching a ticket for Paddington and saying often tearful farewells. This relay system offered no reward for weeks of hard work. Gone were the days when my mother spent her mornings reading, or listening to concerts on the wireless, or teaching me. Now she was lifted into her bath chair after breakfast and wheeled into the kitchen to supervise the cooking and other household tasks. As a bride she had been unable to cook an egg, but in everything she was a perfectionist and her zealous study of the art of cooking had such sensational results that despite Emergency limitations I have never anywhere eaten better than I did then in my own home.

Several of our non-treasures had to be dismissed within days for intolerable personal filthiness (there was the celebrated case of the louse on the table-napkin . . .) or irredeemable incompetence, or both. Some were petty thieves, others were incorrigible 'borrowers'. One sixteen-year-old was detected by my father returning through the kitchen window from a military hop at four o'clock on a summer morning, clad only in one of my mother's nightgowns. My father imagined her to have been sleep-walking and apologised profusely for having chanced to observe her in dishabille. My mother assessed the situation more realistically and next day patiently lectured the girl on the hazards of associating, in the small hours of the morning, with the licentious soldiery.

As Lismore was a garrison town throughout the war our younger maids' morals were a source of constant anxiety. Those who arrived knowing nothing of the facts of life had to be given sex instruction even before they were taught how to make coffee. And for a few this instruction came too late. These usually stayed longest; when they discovered their condition their bewildered fear was pathetic and whatever their professional defects my mother never had the heart to dismiss them.

One eighteen-year-old precipitately gave birth under the kitchen table with me in fascinated attendance. When the drama was all over bar the afterbirth I rushed into the sitting-room exclaiming that it was just the way cows did it. Perennially unflappable, my mother said "How interesting"—and now would I please take some blankets to the kitchen and wrap the baby up well before going to the Post Office to telephone for an ambulance.

It had always been clear that Josie was weak in the head and as her parents now rejected her—an unusual reaction, amongst Irish country folk, to 'little accidents'—my mother felt obliged to act *in loco parentis*. The authorities did everything possible, and more than was ethically allowable, to force her to give up her baby; but under the influence of maternal love, she showed unexpected strength of character. When we visited her in the County Home in Dungarvan my parents were so moved by her determination to keep her child that they entered the argument with a few well-chosen remarks about the legal rights of parents. They also guaranteed to look after both mother and son until Dr White could arrange for their admission to some suitable hostel. I never forgot this example of how the uninformed and inarticulate citizens of a democracy may be bullied and confused by bureaucrats—both clerical and lay.

Eventually Josie and son departed to a nun-run hostel and we got occasional postcards, laboriously inscribed in capital letters, telling us of George's progress. (To my father's disgust the child had been named in honour of the King of England.) A few years later Josie called one afternoon to introduce her husband and month-old second son—who had been born, she happily informed us, during the honeymoon. George was now a fine lad and seemed on excellent terms with his amiable step-father. Obviously all concerned were going to live happily ever after.

The Josie drama had provoked much comment throughout the neighbourhood, yet not even she could compete with Cattie. Cattie arrived the day after my father had been immobilised by sciatica. She looked middle-aged but claimed to be twenty-two. She was tall and gaunt and grey-haired and never removed her Wellington boots; when my mother hinted that she might find another form of footwear more comfortable indoors, she snapped enigmatically, "I has me notions!" A few days later she acquired another notion and took to carrying everywhere, under her arm, a sweeping-brush. Even while bearing laden trays into my parents' bedroom she stuck to her brush; and when my mother—speaking timidly, at this stage—suggested that she might find it more convenient occasionally to lay it aside, she snapped, "It's a need!"

That night sounds as of tap-dancing came from Cattie's room and large quantities of plaster fell from the dining-room ceiling. Next morning, before dawn, weird rhythmic wails, as of an oriental widow keening, became increasingly audible from the direction of the kitchen. I was thrilled. Indisputably we had a fully fledged lunatic on the premises. But when we held a council of war after breakfast it disconcerted me slightly to realise that my parents took Cattie's overnight deterioration quite seriously. The district nurse was due at ten o'clock to minister to the two invalids—my father was temporarily almost as incapacitated as my mother—and we decided to ask her to telephone Dr White.

At that very moment a shrieking Cattie came storming up the hall and burst into my parents' room brandishing the sweeping-brush. Her face was distorted and she was yelling—"I'll fork ye! I'll fork ye!" By any standards she was an alarming sight. It soon transpired that she believed my parents to be two fried eggs and the brush a fork. Afterwards I saw the joke, but not then. I rushed to my mother and clung to her and she whispered—"Fetch the guards!" But such crises prove the strength of the herd instinct. My mother's order made sense, yet I could not leave that room while Cattie was darting about with contorted face poking her fork towards the two defenceless fried eggs. If murder were about to be done, let us all die together. Only when Cattie's expression relaxed, and she began again to tap-dance and to chant quite cheerfully, did I flee onto the street and beg a passer-by to fetch the garda sergeant. Then the nurse arrived and said, "I told you so!" because for days she had been warning us of our peril. Within an hour the unfortunate Cattie had been removed, under sedation, to the nearest lunatic asylum—from which she had been discharged, we then discovered, only two months previously.

After this débâcle my mother observed dryly that our neighbours probably regarded it as a 'judgement' on the Murphys. My parents' attitude towards unmarried mothers was condemned by many as a scandalous condoning of immorality. Like middle-class communities everywhere, our neighbours abhorred and feared illegitimacy. And being Irish Christians, their abhorrence was compounded by the uniquely nasty odour they could detect emanating from sexual licence. A few managed to pay lip-service to Christian charity, but not one would have encouraged an unmarried mother to keep her baby. To rear one's bastard was considered far worse than merely having it furtively and quickly giving it away for adoption; allowing the maternal instinct to take over branded one as a brazen hussy. Therefore middle-class girls never did keep their babies. I often heard my parents denouncing this vicious hypocrisy—one could feel the viciousness vibrating through the anti-Josie vituperations of some of our neighbours. Their moral code was of the primitive sort that seeks confirmation and reinforcement in the merciless punishing of delinquents. A century earlier they would have formed part of the grimly gleeful crowd around the scaffold at a public hanging.

Josie was the cause of my historic argument with Mr Ryan— 'the Boss'. I say historic because it was unheard of for anyone— never mind a child—to defy this formidable patriarch.

The scene was the Ryans' living-room. The Boss was sitting

in his symbolically uncomfortable wooden armchair by the fire; I was lying on the hearth-rug at his feet reading a book about (appropriately) volcanoes; Mrs Ryan was rolling a skein of knitting wool into a ball and Mark—the eldest son, home for the week-end because he was then Diocesan Inspector of Schools—was changing the batteries in the wireless.

Suddenly the Boss began to criticise people who encouraged shameless young girls to display their wickedness in public. Immediately I got the reference though by Ryan standards no child should have known what was being discussed. Thus I was provoked to defiance both by loyalty to my parents and by compassion for Fallen Women in general and Josie in particular. Sitting upright on the hearth-rug, I accused the Boss of hypocrisy. This word was a recent addition to my vocabulary and it pleased me to use it, despite what I knew must be the cataclysmic result.

There was a shattering silence. The Boss and I stared at each other fixedly like belligerent tom-cats. Those ice-blue eyes seemed unnervingly expressionless: years later it struck me that at that moment the Boss may well have been trying not to laugh. But of course he had to fight his autocratic corner and as the argument developed I became very angry indeed. No doubt my opponent was deliberately egging me on—that would have been characteristic—and though the words exchanged have been forgotten I perfectly remember the unfamiliar adult quality of the anger that consumed me. It was unlike anything I had ever felt during my tantrums; now I was being angry on someone else's behalf. But unfortunately I was also being outrageously and uncharacteristically impertinent—which indicates that this incident released much long-repressed hostility to certain aspects of the Ryan ethos.

The Boss always kept by his side a heavy walking-stick which somehow had the appearance of a weapon, though it may never have been so used, and suddenly he picked this up, shook it at me and said—"Get out!" Seizing my book I fled, meaning to go straight home. Neither Mrs Ryan nor Mark had taken any part in the argument, but now Mark quietly hurried after me. He laid a hand on my arm and said that he needed help in the orchard. We understood each other so well that the most important things could always be left unsaid. Without even

94

glancing at him I knew that he had approved of my stand against the Boss—at least in principle, though he would have wished me to use more self-restraint in what I actually said.

It was a golden October afternoon, following the first of the season's gales. Autumn's cosy/melancholy tang was spicing the air and the leaves were turning on the neat beech hedge, with an arch at either end, which divided garden from orchard. Under the trees the long grass was still wet, though all day the sun had shone while a romping wind chased white clouds. We collected windfalls in oval wicker clothes-baskets; when full these were carried down to the back gate and from there the 'eaters' would be given away to the children of the town and the 'cookers' to a certain clique known unambiguously as 'the poor women'.

We scarcely spoke as we moved about under the trees, watchful least we tread on our harvest, bent double, parting the long grass with our hands, then straightening up to remove from an apple its cargo of snails or slugs or earwigs or beetles and to decide whether or not it was still worth saving. We often spent almost silent hours together in the garden, Mark working steadily, I helping enthusiastically if the job appealed and desultorily if it didn't.

Towards teatime Mark suddenly said, "I think you must apologise to the Boss before you go home."

Holding a hard, dark green Bramley I looked up at my companion with a mixture of resentment and resignation. It was one of my more disagreeable traits that I usually resisted having to admit a mistake or make an apology. But Mark had a power over me unequalled by—and never to be equalled by—anyone else's. Furiously I dug my finger-nails into the apple: they were sore for days afterwards. Then silently I followed Mark down the path and meekly I trotted into the living-room to offer my apologies to the Boss—who received them with a non-committal growl.

As I passed through the kitchen, on my way home, Mark handed me a chunk of home-made fudge—in 1942 a rare treat.

For my tenth birthday my parents gave me a second-hand bicycle and Pappa sent me a second-hand atlas. Already I was an enthusiastic cyclist, though I had never before owned a

95

bicycle, and soon after my birthday I resolved to cycle to India one day. I have never forgotten the exact spot, on a steep hill near Lismore, where this decision was made. Half-way up I rather proudly looked at my legs, slowly pushing the pedals round, and the thought came—'If I went on doing this for long enough I could get to India.' The simplicity of the idea enchanted me. I had been poring over my new atlas every evening travelling in fancy. Now I saw how I could travel in reality—alone, independent and needing very little money.

This was a significant moment in my life, and not only because of the consequences in the far future. A ten-year-old's decision to cycle to India might have seemed to many adults an amusing childish whim. But by giving me material for dreaming about something that I knew could be attained, it offered a healthier outlet for my imaginings than my usual escapist fantasies. It also gave me a purpose that was, or seemed to be, quite separate from my obsessional desire to write—which diversification of ambitions was an excellent thing. Naturally I never discussed my plan with anyone; I well knew how it would be regarded by my elders. Nor did I feel any particular urge to talk about it; it had enough substance not to need the reinforcement of conversation. Oddly, it never developed into an obsession: as I grew older months could pass without my consciously thinking of it. Cycling to India simply became part of the pattern of my future. In the same matter-of-fact way many youngsters think of the remote but inevitable day when they will graduate from university or join their father's firm or inherit the farm.

Clearly ten-year-olds are not interested in Hindu sculpture or Brahminical philosophy or Sanskrit literature; at that age even the *Jungle Books* bored me. My only personal links with India were Dr White's nostalgic bedside tales of the North-west Frontier Province and a weirdly impressive painting by a Hindu of the mythical source of the Ganges. This extraordinary picture—a wedding present to my parents from a friend of the artist—had fascinated me (so my mother said) since I began to focus in my cradle. Yet one doubts if it had any influence on my cycling plans. I merely wished to travel far beyond Europe for travelling's sake, and taking all geographical and political factors into consideration New Delhi seemed the most interesting Asian capital that could conveniently be approached by bicycle.

Apart from future plans, owning a bicycle gave me freedom to roam much more widely than I had ever done before. And within a week of my birthday I had very nearly roamed into the Elysian fields.

One sunny, frosty December morning I set out to cycle to the foot of the Knockmealdown Mountains, some eight miles north of Lismore. I took a picnic, and ate it by a lively brown stream, and then thought it would be fun to climb to the top of Knockmealdown—an easy little mountain of just under 3,000 feet.

I had been up several times before, with my father and Pappa and sundry guests, and was familiar with the easiest route. But somehow the climb took longer than expected and as I approached the top the weather began to change. The air lost its crispness and the Galtees to the north-west disappeared as clouds came rolling south over the plain of Tipperary. Before I was half-way down both the clouds and the dusk had overtaken me. But I was too inexperienced to be immediately afraid. For ten or fifteen minutes it all seemed a glorious adventure and I never doubted that I would soon hear the stream and feel the road beneath my feet. Not until darkness came, and the mist turned to rain, and a wind began to moan, did panic threaten. Then I stumbled into an old turf-cutting that should not have been on my route and burst into tears.

Pulling myself out of the icy water—I was soaked through— I recognised the extent of my stupidity. Plainly I was lost for the night and, though I never doubted that I would get home eventually, my parents could not be expected to think so. It is far from clear to me now *why* I assumed that I would survive a mid-winter night on an exposed mountain without food or shelter. It is precisely this irrational faith in one's own durability which can earn an undeserved reputation for courage.

Having accepted that I was lost, and that no rescue party would dramatically save me because no one knew in which direction I had cycled, I kept moving for what felt like hours, still desperately hoping to find the road. I tried not to think of what my parents must be suffering. Even at ten, mental or emotional suffering had the power to move me as physical

97

suffering could never do. I was now feeling for them a great deal more than if they had, for instance, been seriously injured in a motor-smash.

Already I felt weak with hunger, my leg muscles were throbbing and my sodden clothes seemed heavy as lead. At this point my secret endurance tests were justified. I had never inflicted on myself anything comparable to my present trial, yet I believe that by using the techniques I had so often light-heartedly practised I kept moving for longer than would otherwise have been possible.

I was close to collapse when I came on a low stone wall. Knowing my mountain, I realised that I must now be on its east or north side; had I still been on the south side I would have had to cross a road to reach such a wall. From its existence I deduced a cottage at no great distance and felt a resurgence of hope and energy. I groped on eagerly through the darkness, following the wall, and then came not on a cottage but on an unoccupied animal shelter, built of stone and roofed with turf. Inside were great mounds of cut bracken. I stripped naked and buried myself in a mound and not even the thought of my parents' distress could keep me awake.

When I opened my eyes the sun was rising and the wind was tidying the clouds away. As I struggled to put on my sodden clothes I felt not only stiff and weak but very ill. Stumbling out of the shelter, I saw a cottage some hundred yards away: but it was deserted. A boreen led down to a narrow road and there I realised I was above Newcastle. Now, in daylight, with my safety assured, I ceased to worry about my parents and felt only a considerable fear of their reaction to my escapade. I sat by the roadside to await rescue and in my debilitated condition the imminence of my mother's just wrath was too much for me. I was weeping dismally when an astonished farmer came along on his donkey-cart and picked me up.

The rest is a blur. For some reason I was taken to a priest's house—perhaps there was no local gardai barracks—and fed and put to bed by the housekeeper. When I came to I was in my own bed, running a high temperature and feeling too terrible even to want to read. And I had to stay in bed for the next fortnight while there were mutterings in the background about pleurisy.

My parents never once reproached me for having put them through eighteen hours of hell; possibly they considered the experience itself sufficient punishment. It must also have been obvious that I had learned my lesson and would never again embark on such a reckless adventure. I willingly promised to tell my mother, in future, exactly where I was going when I left home for a day's cycling; and this satisfied her, though both Mrs Mansfield and Father Power urged her to put me on a much tighter rein. Curiously, I felt during those years that she molly-coddled me to humiliation by closely watching my diet, making me change my clothes if they got damp and sending me to bed at seven-thirty. Yet short of throwing me into the middle of the Irish Sea in January, and telling me to swim for the shore, she could scarcely have been less fussy about my physical safety.

Years later my mother admitted that despite being frantically worried throughout that long night she had known I was safe. My father, on the other hand, had decided by six-thirty that I had been killed. But apart from notifying the gardai and checking nearby roadsides there was nothing immediate to be done and my mother had discouraged the formation of what could only have been an ineffectual search-party. Father Power and Mrs Mansfield had both spent the night at our house, providing moral support, and by breakfast-time even Mrs Mansfield was not entirely sober. (On Christmas Day, and during periods of extreme nervous tension, she coyly accepted the addition of a little whiskey to her tea. Two teaspoonfuls made her quite merry and three induced a degree of hilarity she would normally have considered most reprehensible.)

When the good news was brought from Newcastle, Father Power drove my father to collect me; our own car had been put on blocks by this date. Surprisingly few of the neighbours ever heard of my misadventure and I was grateful to my parents for not publicising it; to have become the laughing stock of the whole town would have been intolerable. Now I feel that in such ways they were over-protective and that it was wrong to spare me this part of my punishment. It would have done my bumptious ten-year-old pride no harm at all to be wounded in such a fashion. I did of course voluntarily confide in Mark, from whom I hid nothing. With him I felt no need, either then or later, to project an image of myself that was an improvement on reality.

By 1942 I had come to detest those educational Sunday walks so much enjoyed by my father; and one day I decided to use cycling as an excuse to break with tradition.

My mother looked stricken when I defiantly announced that I would not be going for any more long walks with Daddy because Sundays must henceforth be left free to practise long-distance cycling. This transparent excuse did not for a moment deceive her and after a tiny, tense silence she said quietly. "But that's absurd. You have plenty of time for cycling during the week."

Then the truth came out—or what at that time I imagined to be the truth. "Daddy's so *boring*!" I exclaimed miserably. "I can't stand it and I'm *not* going with him again and anyway I'm *ten* so why should I be forced to go for walks like a little girl?"

Staring at my mother, I was appalled to realise that she, like myself, was close to tears. Then I knew that she saw my point. But her first loyalty was to a man whose vulnerability was not any the less extreme for being so far below the surface. Recovering herself, she reasoned with me gently, tacitly admitting that I had a case but stressing how unkind it would be to rebuff a loving father who so enjoyed our weekly walks. As I listened I knew that she was right, but I didn't care. Or rather, I was determined to act as though I didn't care. Deep down I cared so much that the guilt bred by this calculated cruelty remained with me for twenty years.

Why did I feel such an overwhelming compulsion to detach from my father, even though I fully recognised that my doing so would hurt him as perhaps nothing else could? Had our inability to communicate driven me to an extremity of frustration that could only be relieved by meting out the punishment of rejection? For he was the grown-up, the powerful one and it must all be his fault . . . We might have been basically indifferent to one another, as parents and children quite often are, and then we could have casually sustained an amiable, meaningless relationship. But our bonds were very strong; we understood each other intuitively in a way which to me, on the threshold of adolescence, may have seemed a violation of my spiritual privacy.

I do not know how my mother explained away my decision to my father, or if she even tried to soften the blow. But I never again went for a walk with him and he accepted my defection without a comment, a query or a protest of any sort.

A few months later, while we were all in Dublin, an incident occurred which I now regard, perhaps exaggeratedly, as one of the saddest wasted opportunities of a lifetime. My father had arranged to meet me at an aunt's house for lunch, but he was late; half-an-hour passed, and an hour, and still he did not come. Then it was lunch-time and we all sat down to our grilled cutlets and creamed carrots. There were meringues for pudding, but by that stage I was in a daze of terror and grief. My father must have been killed in a car-crash—he was a notoriously absent-minded driver and had borrowed my aunt's Morris. I felt certain that I would never see him again and remorse about my cruel aloofness devastated me. But I must not make a fool of myself by fussing and fidgeting in front of all those grown-up cousins who were accepting Uncle Fergus's non-appearance with what seemed to me heartless placidity.

My father had in fact telephoned at twelve-thirty to explain that he had been delayed, but no one had bothered to inform me. When at last he arrived I nonchalantly said "Hello" before slipping away to the lavatory to be sick. (Even today the mere sight of a meringue makes me feel queasy.) Then I went out to the garden to talk to the dog.

Later, as my father drove me back to Charleston Avenue, I desperately wanted to tell him about all that I had suffered at lunch-time because I thought he was dead. But I could not. Many years passed before I realised that even a slight reference to my ordeal might have significantly altered our relationship at a crucial stage. After that summer, we grew further and further apart on the surface while retaining our indestructible and uncomfortable mutual flair for reading each other's thoughts.

As my leg muscles grew stronger my cycling ambitions grew bolder and soon I was longing to cycle the twenty-five miles to Helvick Head. But fifty miles in one day sounded a long way. Frighteningly long, for one who had never yet attempted more than thirty. The project began to worry me. I passionately wanted to achieve those fifty miles yet I dreaded failure. It would be so un-live-downable for ever if I could not make the last few miles and had to signal for help. Eventually I mentioned the idea to my mother, very casually, as though it were a matter of no great consequence.

"Probably I could easily do it," I said; and years later she told me that as I spoke I looked at her with an expression of the most pathetic doubt and anxiety.

But she kept the conversation on the casual note I imagined I had sounded. "Of course you can do it," she said cheerfully, "if you want to do it enough."

Thus encouraged, I left for Helvick at six o'clock on a radiant June morning—a morning all blue and gold and green. The air smelt damp, warm, rich and full of promises. From every tree, bush and hedge came the harmonious confusion of birdsong, seeming to celebrate my own joyous excitement. As I turned towards the coast, and settled to the rhythm of pedalling, I experienced an exaltation I have never forgotten. The vigour of my body seemed to merge with the eager abundance all around me and in an almost sacramental way I became totally aware of myself as a part of nature. Unconsciously, I had taken another step away from the faith of my fathers.

On the previous evening the wireless had guaranteed good weather, but my mother pretended not to have heard. Before I went to bed she gave me the first pound note I had ever been in charge of (to be returned if not needed) and remarked that should the weather deteriorate, or my bicycle break down, or some other disaster occur, I could spend the night in a Dungarvan hotel.

In fact there was no hitch of any kind. By six-thirty I was home, nauseated with exhaustion and bursting with pride. The last twelve miles had been torture, but I would not tarnish the glory of my achievement by admitting this. And even during that terrible final stage part of me had relished the sense of power derived from driving my body beyond what had seemed, at a certain point, to be its limit.

Yet without my mother's moral support I would never have had the courage to attempt that trip at that age. It was fortunate for me that she was not as possessive as she was dominating.

Her influence over me was so strong throughout childhood that had she wished to destroy or stunt me she could certainly have done so. Instead, I was aware of being regarded—and respected—as a separate personality rather than as an incidental appendage to the adults in the household. At the time I took this for granted: now I know what an uncommon attitude it was in the Ireland of my youth.

Some people imagined that my unusual upbringing was a result of being the only child of an invalid. But my mother's mothering would have been no less odd, I feel certain, had she been in rude health with a family of ten. As a perfectionist, and a woman who saw motherhood as an important career, she approached child-rearing in what I can only call an artistic spirit. Given as raw material a newly conceived child, she saw it as her duty and privilege to form an adult who would be as physically, mentally and morally healthy as intelligent rearing could make it. Physically she was completely successful. The other aspects of a child's health are, alas, less amenable to maternal regulation.

My childhood diet was generally considered freakish. Up to the age of sixteen I drank four pints of milk daily and was allowed no tea, coffee or fizzy drinks. Sweets, chocolate, ice-cream, cakes, sweet biscuits, white bread and white sugar were also forbidden. My 'treats' were muscatel raisins and fat, glossy dates in gay boxes. Included in my staple diet were raw beef, raw liver, raw vegetables, wholemeal bread, pinhead porridge and as much fresh fruit and cheese as I could be induced to eat. Naturally I flourished. And one can understand what it must have meant to my mother to look at me as an adolescent and to know that I was capable of enjoying, to the fullest extent, what she had lost.

8

Fanciful though this may sound, the Blackwater River was among the chief and best-loved companions of my youth. To me, it has always seemed Lismore's most tangible link with the saints and sinners and scholars of the past. Many centuries ago it was most appropriately known as *Nem*, an Irish word meaning 'Heaven'. Much later, Spenser mentioned it in *The Faery Queen*—'Swifte Awnaduff which of the English man is Cal'de Blackewater'. Later still, some enthusiastic Victorian tourist (Thackeray, I think) decided to rename it the Irish Rhine and this inanity—as absurd as calling Swat the Switzerland of the East—has earned him the undying gratitude of the Irish Tourist Board.

The Blackwater—one of Europe's great salmon rivers—rises near Killarney and flows for seventy miles through the counties of Kerry, Cork and Waterford. In the twelfth century both Dromana House and Lismore Castle were granted charters entitling their owners to extensive fishing rights and even now these charters of King John of England remain good in law, much to the annoyance of certain local rod fishers.

A river shows different aspects to the fisherman, the naturalist, the trader, the artist, the soldier, the boatman and the swimmer. I formed my relationship with the Blackwater as a swimmer. Before I can remember, my father regularly immersed me in the cool, dark silkiness of its depths and I swam almost as soon as I could walk. It is a good thing to have had a river among one's mentors; its strength develops the body, its beauty develops the soul, its agelessness develops the imagination. Also, its moods teach respect for the mindless power of nature. The Blackwater is very moody: it has deep holes, sudden floods, hidden rocks, tricky currents and sly weeds. It claims at least three lives a year and I was not allowed to bathe alone until I was twelve. Although I could easily have broken this rule without being detected, it never occurred to me to do so.

Our shared devotion to the Blackwater had always been important to my father and myself. It was not simply that we were both keen swimmers; our bathing was as much a rite as a pastime and during the summer, whether the weather was summery or not, we met outside the Library at five-thirty every afternoon and went together to the river. But at the beginning of this summer of 1942, only a few months after I had spurned those Sunday afternoon mobile lectures, what was to become of our traditional bathing-rite? I could not decently imply that I was now prepared to endure my father's company as a convenience. Yet if the custom were allowed to lapse my swimming season, which normally opened in mid-May, would have to be postponed until Pappa arrived at the beginning of July. My father might have been forgiven had he chosen to leave me excruciatingly impaled on the horns of this dilemma. Instead, he remarked at breakfast-time one fair May morning, as he had been remarking on such mornings for as long as I could remember, "I think we'll need our togs today". This was much more than I deserved, and I appreciated it.

A new phase of our relationship had begun. I was consciously in control and my father no longer tried to be educational without direct encouragement. Astronomy was then one of my main interests and it pleased me to be lectured on it day after day. Probably an observer would have detected no strain as my father and I considered the solar system. Yet a great sadness underlay our relationship, an awareness that somehow we had failed each other and that what now existed between us was merely a civilised façade to conceal failure.

Another of my hobbies at that time was the Black Death and related subjects. For a few years past I had been fascinated by diseases, epidemics, surgery, new medical discoveries and the like. Had I not been so committed to the writing life I would have wished to be a surgeon. My interest in corpses and skeletons was profound. I had never actually seen a human corpse, but I longed to observe closely the phenomenon of putrefaction. For this purpose I installed a dead rabbit in my bedroom. My observations, however, were unsympathetically terminated

when the rabbit reached an interesting and therefore percep-
tible state. In the same cause, I cultivated the society of an
aged British Army pensioner and begged him to describe in
detail all the corpses with which he had become acquainted
during the First World War. But he was tiresomely evasive,
plainly considering me mad and morbid. So I had to make do
with disintegrated skeletons, which could not even be brought
home for study. At the beginning of my osseous phase I had
pranced into the dining-room one lunch-time brandishing a
skull and expecting my parents to greet it rapturously. But my
father had declared the appropriation of human bones to be
unseemly, irreverent and possibly unhygienic and I was made
to return my trophy to its source without delay. Fortunately—
because I was hungry at the time—its source was nearby. In
those days the ancient graveyard surrounding St Carthage's
Cathedral was a wilderness, full of briars and romantic melan-
choly, and by visiting it shortly before a burial one might find,
beside the newly dug grave, a femur, a few ribs, a length of
spine or even, on very good days, a skull. My ambition was
eventually to assemble a whole skeleton by hiding my bits of
bones in the furthest corner of the graveyard and adding to
them from other ancient graveyards in the area, when the
local paper informed me a burial was about to take place. But
it was all too difficult and in the end my Identikit skeleton came
to nothing. Or rather, it came to an embarrassingly large heap
of bones which, belatedly inspired by some flicker of respect for
the mortal remains of various people, I surreptitiously transferred to an open grave on a wet December afternoon when
no one was likely to be about.

Scientific interest was not of course the only motive for my
graveyard prowlings. Children are enthralled by mortality and
unlike many who have felt the touch of Time, are able to con-
template it detachedly. As a child with no personal experience
of bereavement I was thrilled by the dramatic finality of death
and fascinated by the mystery of what follows after. Many an
hour did I spend sitting on old tombstones cheerfully reviewing
eschatological possibilities.

I had long since rejected the harps, angels, massed choirs and
other such tedious impedimenta which furnish the Heaven of
Christian folklore. My parents had carefully explained that this

picture of Heaven must not be despised since it represented the honest endeavour of simple people mentally to conceive the inconceivable. The real bliss of Heaven, they went on—and they obviously believed this—was in spiritual union with God. And the real pain of purgatory was in spiritual separation from God. But when I considered the matter, as I relaxed on a tombstone or peered hopefully into an open grave, it seemed to me a good deal easier, and no less consoling, to believe in union with Nature rather than with God. One could see it happening—'dust to dust'—on the physical plane. And when one thought, for instance, of wireless waves, it appeared there were enough odd things going on in the natural world for it to accommodate also the immortality of the soul. This immortality always made sense to me, but at no age did I find it necessary, despite my basic arrogance, to think of my own soul maintaining its existence for ever as a separate unit indelibly marked 'Dervla Murphy'. Physical extinction was an unpleasant thought and one saw the need for a comforting belief in an after-life. Yet death was made no more acceptable, to me, by the traditional Christian strivings to bring within our comprehension what is simultaneously admitted to be incomprehensible. When I eventually came upon it, that school of Buddhist philosophy which suggests that after death the individual soul can dissolve, to continue its existence by forming parts of other souls, suited me much better. And not many years ago, in *The Golden Core of Religion* by Alexander Skutch, I found perfectly expressed what I was beginning to grope towards as a ten-year-old: 'If immortality is, or will become, attainable by the human soul, it must be within the possibilities of that great, all-embracing, infinitely varied, and still imperfectly explored system of orderly, interrelated events which we know as nature. Only by regarding spiritual survival as natural, in the same sense that our birth, our thought, our aspiration, and our body's final dissolution are natural, can we who have been nurtured on science and philosophy hold faith in it. If the spirit survives its body in the course of nature, as in the course of of nature the light from a beacon on a hilltop goes coursing through outer space long after the fire has died, then it is reasonable to believe that its survival depends upon such intrinsic qualities as the intensity of its love, the unity of its aspirations, its coherence and the absence of passions that tear it asunder.'

As for Hell—which Irish Catholics are so regularly reminded of as a possible destination—having put behind me the terrors induced by Sister X, I ceased to take it seriously. I agreed with my parents that one cannot accept the paradox inherent in the concept of a God who is infinitely merciful and just and yet condemns countless unfortunates to an eternity of suffering.

A few weeks before my eleventh birthday I was cured of grave-robbing by a somewhat macabre experience. It was one of those still, moist, dull November afternoons when the country-side can be felt drifting into winter sleep. Cycling by the edge of a thick wood, I suddenly got a strong scent of badger. For years I had been longing to find a set, so I climbed a low stone wall and, sniffing like a terrier, forced my way through the dense tangle of rhododendrons, holly and briars that flourished beneath the trees. But soon I lost the scent and as my clothes had already been much damaged I decided to return to the road by a less destructive though longer route.

Zig-zagging between the trees, looking out for squirrels, I moved slowly uphill towards the track that I knew bisected this wood. Then I came unexpectedly on an odd little building, standing in a small clearing but half-hidden by briars and laurels. It had a vaguely ecclesiastical appearance and I felt both puzzled and uneasy; there was something faintly sinister about this inexplicable edifice lurking in the depths of a dense, deserted wood. Approaching closer, I noticed that the door had been forced open—quite recently, for the wood around the lock bore fresh scars. Advancing to the threshold, I peered into the gloom. As my eyes adjusted I saw big shelves and big, long boxes. Coffins, in fact. They had been hacked open, stripped of their lead and left in disarray. Then I saw the corpse, lying almost at my feet. It was dark-skinned and shrunken but very plainly a woman. Here at last was my yearned-for chance to make a close study of decomposition. I turned and fled.

Terror seemed to suffocate me as I tripped over brambles and slipped on the dank leaf-mould. The whole wood became an Arthur Rackham thicket and I was afraid to raise my eyes lest I might see discoloured corpses enmeshed in its thorny shadows.

Only when I reached the road did I realise that my face as well as my clothes had been ripped by briars. Blood was trickling onto the collar of my gaberdine and I wondered frantically how I could explain away those scratches. I decided to fabricate a fall off my bicycle to cover both the scratches and my shaken condition.

Why did this desecrated family vault so unnerve someone who hitherto had revelled in the gruesome? Was I so shocked and terrified simply because I had been taken unawares? Would I have reacted differently had I entered the wood not to track a badger but to seek out the vault? Or was I undone by the considerable difference between a skeleton and a corpse? There is always a temptation to try to unravel one's own inconsistencies and I still find this incident baffling.

It took me months to regain my nerve fully. I slept soundly that night—no doubt exhausted by emotion—but as I opened my eyes next morning the memory came back and I groped for my light switch in panic.

Nightmares started that evening; these were, according to my mother, the first from which I had ever suffered. When I awoke screaming my parents were listening to the gramophone and no one heard me. Realising where I was, I switched on the light and felt glad that my silly yells had not been noticed. But then I was afraid to switch off the light or to sleep again. I tried to read but was too tired and tense. Soon afterwards my father came upstairs, saw my light and looked in to demand sternly what I meant by reading at half-past ten? He switched off my light without waiting for a reply and left me sweating and shaking in the dark. When I turned on my illicit torch it didn't really help. I needed the full glare of the ceiling light which left no corner shadowy. My nightmare had been of shadows, and vilely coloured objects—brownish-grey, yellowish-green, yellowish-brown, greyish-green, yellowish-grey—a kaleidoscope of unearthly, corrupt tinges and indistinct forms moving slightly. And yet surely *not* moving, because they were dead . . . (Ever since, most of my few nightmares have been in this ghastly Technicolor.)

When I knew that my parents would be in bed I switched on the light again but, being used to a dark room, was unable to sleep for what felt like hours. Then I dreamt that my mother was dead and that I was searching for her body in a cave where at the far end corpses were dancing in a circle. I knew they would not let me pass though my mother was waiting for me beyond them and, if I reached her soon enough, could be brought back to life. I awoke, calling her hysterically, to find that it was past my usual getting-up time. As I dressed I was already dreading that night. Half of me longed to confide in my mother, but the other half forbade me to ask for help.

However, unlike my earlier fear of darkness, these horrors were altogether outside my control. Only by forcing myself to stay awake could I escape them. My symptoms of strain and exhaustion soon prompted my mother to investigate and when all had been revealed we decided that until my nerve had mended there was no alternative but for my father and me to exchange beds. Part of me rejoiced then to be free of those lonely terrors, while another part resented this admission of dependence and the consequent loss of privacy. My own room was important to me beyond calculation. The rest of the house—indeed, the rest of the world—seemed in a sense alien territory where adult writ ran; only in my own room could I freely expand. (Of course when I began to cherish decomposing rabbits under the bed my expansion had to be curtailed; but such crises were rare.) Thus, sleeping in my parents' room felt like the worst sort of indignity, with overtones of serfdom. I remember resolving one night, as I lay discontentedly curled up in my father's bed, that even should I happen to acquire a husband, by some unlikely chance, I would never share a room with him. Naturally we would share a bed for procreative purposes, but clearly there must be a clause in the marriage contract stipulating separate rooms. It did not then occur to me that post-procreation I might feel disinclined to trek to an Inner Sanctum.

At the age of eleven my bedtime was still seven-thirty, bizarre as this may sound to modern children, and usually I had been asleep for a few hours when my father wheeled my mother's bath chair across the hall. (My parents' bedroom would normally have been the sitting-room and the dining-room had to serve as our general living-room.) With the maid's help my mother was lifted onto her bed; she had lately become so heavy that no one could lift her unaided. Then, after the maid's departure, my father gently undressed his wife, gave her the bed-pan and made her comfortable—as they say in hospitals—for the night. Once she had been placed in a lying position she could move only her head so it was essential that she should be left completely relaxed. To achieve this, with the aid of strategically placed cushions under her locked knee-joints and ankles, involved much patient effort on my father's part—and much fortitude on my mother's, since at this stage of her disease every movement was painful. To me, of course, the whole thing was routine; if I chanced to waken I remarked neither my father's patience nor my mother's fortitude.

One night, not long before Christmas, loud sobs came from my mother instead of the usual subdued chit-chat about Thomas Aquinas or Balzac or whoever. Confusedly I diagnosed another nightmare; then I woke fully and accepted that this was reality. After a moment my mother began to talk fast, in an unfamiliar, blurred voice, and very cautiously I peeped out from beneath the blankets. She was virtually unrecognisable: flushed, incoherent and—this was the dreadful thing, unimaginable yet true—not in control of herself.

It was as though the mountains had toppled into the valley or the sun fallen out of the sky. I must somewhere have seen somebody drunk; at all events, I knew what was wrong. But this did not help. How could my own mother, the very epitome of composure, have been reduced to such ignominy within the few hours since I had kissed her good-night?

My first positive reaction, after those worse-than-nightmare moments of fear, bewilderment and grief, was a determination that my mother must never know that I had witnessed what seemed to me her degradation. I could see no meaning in such hideous chaos. But I was convinced that for her to know that I knew would compound the degradation. And though I abhorred this travesty of what I honoured, I did most keenly feel compassion.

At first my compassion was perhaps no more than a reflection of what I had seen on my father's face as he bent over his wife that night. But it soon became a great deal more. My mother drunk was a goddess with feet of clay, and viewing her as a demoted deity ultimately strengthened both my love and my respect. Inflexibly stiff upper lips can stunt sympathy within a family. Had I never glimpsed my mother with her defences down I might never have been able to measure the demands made hourly on her courage.

Next morning all seemed as usual though my unfortunate mother must have been feeling very unusual. My father knew that I had been awake and no doubt considered discussing the psychology of what had so disturbed me. He could easily have made me understand that what I had seen was not in the circumstances abnormal, however regrettable. Yet more than our personal barrier prevented any such discussion. We would both have felt disloyal and thus, for me, one tension would have replaced another. Probably my father appreciated this; and the avoidance of a subject which distressed us both came to form between us one more subtly strong bond of unacknowledged intimacy.

I never again—during childhood—saw my mother drunk; but throughout the following weeks I waited uneasily, night after night, for the horror to recur. Even after my return to my own bedroom in February I remained on the alert and every few months, over the next year or so, I knew the horror was happening. By the end of that time it had become a grief rather than a horror because pity had replaced incomprehension and disillusion. Then gradually I realised that a battle had been won and that I need not be anxious any more.

What was the battle? What combination of stresses forced my mother to seek a release incompatible with her character if not with her heredity? The greater part of her life was of course one unending battle and of its phases and inner agonies I know almost nothing; I never had that insight into her nature which I had into my father's. Only her husband knew and this was as it should have been. But now, looking back and guessing as one might guess about some figure in history, I would say that at this time my mother was feeling especially acutely her inability to have another child.

Also, what had by then become the problem of my education was beginning to cause a rift—if that is not too strong a word— between my parents. I was to have gone away to school in September 1942; for as long as I could remember that date had been fixed in my mind. Yet in December 1943 I was still at home—aged twelve—because the servant crisis had become chronic. This grievously worried my father. My mother also was concerned, as she was soon to prove, but by temperament she was not a worrier. Moreover, she attached less importance than my father did to the academic education of girls; and she had already assessed my potential accurately enough to know that I would never shine very brightly in the intellectual firmament, whatever opportunities were given me. Thus my parents were no longer in perfect agreement, as parents, and this, added to the strains of our everyday life at the time, must have affected their whole relationship.

By Christmas 1943 my own feelings about the situation were mixed. I dreaded another bout of homesickness yet had come to regard boarding-school not only as a glamorous adventure but as an escape from my domestic duties. For almost two years I had been acting as general servant, under my mother's direction, during the—lengthening—intervals between maids; and it had been conclusively proved that I was devoid of whatever virtues and talents go to make a good housewife. My duties were of course limited: I shopped, cooked, washed up and lit the fires. Nobody cleaned, except at week-ends, when my father abstractedly pushed an Electrolux over the more obvious floor surfaces. Luckily he enjoyed cooking and was good at it, even under Emergency conditions, so we had edible meals at week-ends. But from everyone's point of view these maidless interludes were trying.

As fuel and power were strictly limited all our cooking had to be done on two tiny electric rings in a damp kitchen that throughout the winter felt colder than out-of-doors. If both rings were used simultaneously livid blue flames leaped from the wall and the whole house was fused. As electric elements could not be replaced, my father improvised repairs of which he was very proud. Inordinately proud, my mother thought, since his ingenuity had rendered our rings potentially lethal. We then had to emulate Cattie by always wearing Wellington boots while cooking.

Why do certain utterly insignificant moments stick in the memory? For some reason I distinctly remember standing in the kitchen wearing Wellingtons and a heavy brown tweed overcoat and stirring a pot of chicken soup while reading

Clouds of Witness. Household chores were not allowed to encroach unduly on the real business of life. By then I had long since perfected the art of peeling apples, scraping carrots or tailing sprouts without ever lifting my eyes from the page. But during very cold spells my mother insisted on my doing all 'portable' jobs, such as preparing vegetables, beside the feeble fire of damp turf that smouldered in the dining-room. This meant having improving books read to me while I scraped, peeled or chopped. I still associate the smell of celery with the storm that broke over Missolonghi—as described by André Maurois—a few moments before Byron's death.

I was now at an age when most juvenile bookworms have voluntarily turned towards Dickens and the Brontës, but my literary tastes remained woefully undeveloped: William and Biggles were being betrayed only for the sake of Lord Peter or Sherlock Holmes. Nor was this, as might be expected, a reaction against parental expectations. No pressure was ever directly put on me to read the 'right' books; even my rather idealising father had to recognise that mentally I was slower than average and that pressure could only be counter-productive. But meanwhile my mother continued to tutor me in her own unorthodox way. By the time I was ten she had aroused my interest in many of the great writers, musicians and painters—*as people.* She had a gift for discussing their characters as though she were gossiping about the neighbours and years before I approached their work I had strong views about them as individuals. To some extent this must have subsequently influenced my literary judgements. It may be no coincidence that I have never greatly cared for the works of Richardson, Balzac or Dickens—none of whom I could warm to, as men— while I became passionately addicted to Fielding, Shelley, George Eliot and Wilde, all of whom I had admired and loved from early childhood. On the other hand, though I found Sterne, Meredith and Ruskin personally unsympathetic, *Tristram Shandy* and *The Egoist* remain to this day among my favourite novels and for years I had an irrational reverence for every word written by Ruskin on any subject; there can be few of my generation who had read the entire Collected Works from cover to cover by the age of twenty. (I cannot even remember now *why* I became so addicted to him.) As for Dr

Johnson—Boswell's *Life* was my mother's other bible, and the doctor with his Mrs Thrale and his Hodge, and all his oddities and kindnesses and pomposities and aggressions and profundities, seemed almost to belong to our own household.

My mother's immersion in the lives of the great was obviously a form of escapism from the narrowness and dullness of Lismore's social circle. Unlike my father and myself—both essentially of recluse material—she enjoyed the art of conversation and must have felt acutely her lack of congenial company. Her other great consolation was music, but that did not provide the stimulus of such psychological puzzles as 'Why did Ruskin marry?' or 'Was Tolstoy technically a sadist?' or 'Is T. S. Eliot jealous of Hardy or just too limited to appreciate him?' Yet it is probably true that music was her greatest, as it proved to be her most enduring, consolation.

My own awakening to music was an experience only comparable to first falling in love. From the age of a few hours, as the reader may remember, I had been exposed to music. Yet for eleven years it remained to me no more than a noise—neither pleasant nor unpleasant but so important to my parents that it must *never* be interrupted unless the house itself was demonstrably on fire. (I had once spoken during a wireless concert, to announce that a chimney was on fire, and had curtly been told not to mention such trivia until the interval.)

Then came that unforgettable moment. It was on a stormy January evening and from my bedroom window I was gazing at a flaring sunset of crimson and gold and purple and orange. As I watched my mother began to sing in the room below—something she was apt to do at any moment for no apparent reason. But on this evening an unfamiliar excitement possessed me. My heart began to race and I felt as though I had moved into another world—a world where the human spirit enjoyed a freedom I had never before been able to imagine, a world of infinite mystery and yet of infinite clarity and simplicity. That my musical awakening should have come through my mother's voice rather than through the gramophone or the wireless was scarcely a coincidence.

My first appearance in print came a few months later. Mark had drawn my attention to a children's essay competition in a weekly provincial paper. Prizes of seven-and-sixpence, five shillings and half-a-crown were being offered for the three best essays submitted weekly. Competitors must be under sixteen and were free to choose their own subject. I had at once protested that I could not possibly win. "Rubbish!" said Mark. "Go home and try." So I wrote five hundred words on 'Picking Blackberries', in prose as purple as blackberry juice.

The *Cork Weekly Examiner* came out on Fridays and I counted the days and then at last was standing in the newsagent's shop unfolding the paper with trembling hands. Looking down the pages I felt the nausea of suspense and could scarcely focus. Then I found the competition corner. My heart leaped like a salmon at a weir. The unbelievable had to be believed; Dervla Murphy had won first prize (aged twelve). And to crown her glory the other winners were aged fourteen and fifteen.

I moved out of the shop and stood on the Main Street, dazed with triumph, reading *myself* in print. Then, sickeningly, disappointment came. Three words and the structure of a sentence should have been changed before I posted my entry. It might have won first prize, but it was feeble—very feeble. Even had those changes been made, it would have been only mediocre. I resolved to forget 'Picking Blackberries' and do something better. I had yet to learn that one never writes anything of which one does not feel ashamed on seeing it in print.

But of course 'Picking Blackberries' could not be forgotten just like that. However mediocre, it *was* in print and had earned me seven shillings and sixpence, the largest amount of money I had ever acquired in one day—even more than the price of a new Arthur Ransome, because my father could get books at trade rates. Eager to share my victory with my parents, I pedalled quickly up the morbidly named Gallows' Hill to the County Library.

Not until I sat down to write this chapter did I see the significance of that action. The newsagent's shop was equidistant from our house and the Library, and I might have been expected to hurry home to tell my mother first—she with whom I habitually discussed my literary endeavours. Given the seriousness of my approach to writing, this tiny achievement was to me of enormous importance. And my impulsively choosing to share it first with my father must, I think, be interpreted as a salute to our special closeness—if not actually as an indirect gesture of atonement.

My parents were suitably impressed by my breaking out in print, but when I went on to win this competition five weeks running they became uneasy. Finally my father decreed that I must compete no more. I saw the point and reluctantly agreed to retire—but not before using the situation as a lever to raise my pocket-money from three to four (old) pence a week.

As a precaution against what Mark called 'swollen-headery' my mother reminded me that despite having taken the *Cork Weekly Examiner* literary world by storm my apprenticeship was going to be a long one. She need not have worried. I was well able to assess for myself the quality of my rivals' work.

9

The year 1944 was marked by some strange experiences. These I have already described elsewhere,* but their significance was such that they cannot be omitted from any account of my childhood.

One harsh, dark March afternoon a squealing hinge made me look through the kitchen window. A young man was entering the cobbled yard from the abandoned cinema, which meant that he had climbed our eight-foot garden wall. Yet I felt not at all alarmed, possibly because I was never prone to be made uneasy by the unconventional. Or it may simply have been because the young man looked so amiable and vulnerable. As he stood at the back door I noticed that he seemed rather apprehensive and very tired. He was tall, broad-shouldered and handsome, and I marked a Kerry brogue when he gave his name as Pat Carney and asked, diffidently, if he might see one or both of my parents.

In the living-room my mother's bath chair was close to the sulky wartime fire of wet turf. She seemed oddly unsurprised by our visitor's original approach route and my curiosity was further sharpened when she asked me to leave her alone with Pat. Ten minutes later Pat was back in the kitchen. He said that he had been invited to stay for a few days and that my mother would like to speak to me. Then, pausing inside the living-room door, I did begin to feel alarmed. Never before had I seen my mother looking so distraught. Mrs Mansfield and San Toy were coming to tea so there was no time to waste on euphemisms. In a couple of sentences I had been told that Pat was on the run, wanted for the murder of a Dublin detective-sergeant. He had come to us as a protégé of my father's

*A Place Apart (John Murray 1978).

118

elder sister who, never having recognised the validity of the post-Treaty Irish government, was an active member of the illegal IRA. On no account must any caller be allowed to see our guest or any trace of his presence. As I continued to stand by the door, paralysed with astonishment, my mother made a gallant preliminary bid to sort out the ethics of the situation. "This young man is a criminal though he regards himself as a patriot. No doubt his elders are chiefly to blame. They are using his muddled, foolish idealism. But we can talk about it later. Now please show him his room and give him a meal."

I walked down the hall in a joyous daze. This was the stuff of which fantasies are made, yet now it had become part of the reality of my own life. I was to prepare a meal for a man on the run who would be hanged if caught. My mother might have saved her breath. Of course Pat was not a criminal, or muddled or foolish. He was a most glorious patriot, heroically dedicated to the reunification of Ireland. No one had ever suggested that my grandfather and father were criminals because they belonged to the Old IRA. One had to be logical. I was badly jolted when I discovered how strongly my father disapproved of Pat. But then I reflected that he (my father) was very old (forty-three). And I made allowances for the fact that at that age some people just can't have the right reactions any more.

Listening to my parents, I gathered that for some days they had been half-expecting Pat without knowing exactly why he was on the run. Now they were disagreeing vigorously about how they should deal with him and it gave me a certain sardonic satisfaction to observe them both being inconsistent; at twelve, one likes the feet of clay to appear occasionally. My father should have been the one to welcome—or at least tolerate—Pat, while my mother (given her ancestry) should have been the one to reject him. Instead, my father coldly argued that it would be sinful to shelter someone who had deliberately killed an innocent man in the course of a seditious campaign against a lawfully established government. And my mother warmly argued that it was unthinkable, sinful or no, to betray someone whose coming to our home was an act of faith in our humanity. She insisted that allowances must be made for Pat's sick idealism. To which my father, sprung from generations of rebels, replied austerely that it would prove impossible to govern the state if hectic emotionalism were to be accepted as an excuse for murder. My mother then suggested that he should go at once to the gardai barracks and report on Pat's whereabouts. But he didn't.

My parents seem never to have debated the ethics of capital punishment; presumably they accepted it, in theory, as the appropriate penalty for murder. Yet had it not been employed in Ireland during the Forties, as part of the government's anti-IRA campaign, they might well have refused to succour Pat. When such a decision can lead directly to a death sentence it requires more moral courage, or moral arrogance, than either of my parents possessed.

From their point of view an awkward situation was being compounded by the need to impress on me that giving refuge to Pat did not mean condoning his crime. In the end they gave up pretending to unravel this tangled skein for my benefit, which was sensible of them since I well knew that they were incapable of unravelling it for their own. I had in any case already come to my own conclusions and was only listening to their dutiful dissertations out of politeness. Yet I vaguely sympathised with their discomfiture; though they repudiated Pat as a violent man their consciences compelled them to allow for the fact that he saw himself as a soldier fighting a just war—a dilemma that in present-day Northern Ireland has again become familiar to many.

Pat stayed with us for a fortnight, but he and I never referred directly to his peculiar status and he made no attempt to influence me politically. We played round after round of rummy and he gave me lessons in map-reading and taught me how to whistle through my fingers so piercingly that I can be heard two miles away. To me this marvellous companion seemed a magic sort of person, an intelligent grown-up who had retained all the wondering enthusiasms of childhood. And my intuition was right. It was Pat's tragedy that he had never outgrown either the innocence or the ruthlessness of youth.

My parents also became very fond of Pat and deeply concerned about him. Night after night they argued patiently in futile attempts to make him see the error of his ways. Soon he seemed a member of the family—quite an achievement, in view of the strains imposed on all the adults concerned by his presence in the house. Had he been detected under our roof, my father would not have perjured himself by denying any knowledge of his identity and so would certainly have been imprisoned—as his sister was soon to be, on Pat's account.

Our guest was careful never to go too near a window and any knock at the door sent him rushing upstairs. Remembering how I relished all this melodrama, I wonder now if I fully understood that we were truly dicing with death. But my light-hearted approach may well have helped by easing the tension generated between the three adults. Pat knew that I took the game seriously enough to keep all the rules, and I was made deliriously proud by his entrusting to me the addressing and posting of his letters. One morning I went into his room to leave fresh linen on the bed and saw an automatic by the pillow. For years this was to rank as the most thrilling moment in my life. I tingled all over at the romance of that weapon—symbol of Adventure!—gleaming black and lethal on the white sheet. It never occurred to me that in certain circumstances it could be used to kill the local gardai, the fathers of my play-mates. But then it was impossible to associate the gentle, considerate Pat with any form of violence or cruelty.

One evening Pat said good-bye instead of good-night and when we got up next morning he was gone. We heard nothing of him for several months, but his luck did not hold. He was eventually captured in my aunt's house, while asleep, and tried in Dublin before the Military Tribunal. Then he was hanged by the neck until he died, at eight o'clock in the morning on December 1, 1944. His real name was Charles Kerins.

In Waterford city, where I was by then at school, December 1, 1944, was a morning of violent wind and slashing rain. Just before eight o'clock I was queuing for my breakfast. I knew of Pat's attitude towards his sentence and at the moment of his hanging, when the gong in the hall was signalling us to enter the refectory, I experienced an almost hysterical elation. Then, curiously enough, I ate my usual hearty meal. It was against the nationalist tradition in my blood to mourn such deaths, for that would have been to imply that the sacrifice was not worth while.

Our mail was distributed during the mid-morning break and two worlds met when I stood amongst my classmates and—

while they chattered of hockey and drank their milk—read a letter from a friend who had been hanged three hours earlier. With his letter Pat had enclosed a silver ring made on the prison ship in Belfast by a comrade of his, 'Rocky' Burns, who was later shot dead in Belfast by the RUC—or perhaps the B specials. I wore the ring constantly from that moment until my fingers and my ideals outgrew it—developments which conveniently occurred at about the same time. But I have it still and I would not part with it.

A few days later I had a letter from the aunt in whose house Pat had been arrested. She wrote:

My dearest Dervla,

There is no need to tell you that Charlie Kerins met his death with the greatest possible courage and bravery. I was allowed to visit him on Wednesday and Thursday last and he gave me courage, too. I am more than sorry that you could not have seen him—he was so proud and happy to die for Ireland that one could not feel depressed—sad indeed—heartbroken—but not depressed.

I spoke to the priest who heard his confession and he told me that it was a privilege to meet him and that he had no doubt whatever he had gone straight to Heaven. He offered his life with Our Lord for all the people of Ireland. He had no bitterness against his enemies. For the week before his execution he heard Mass and received Holy Communion every morning. On the very morning he was hanged he sang two songs for the wardens, 'Kevin Barry' and 'Kelly the Boy from Killane'. As one of the warders said, 'he was the only happy man in the prison' during the terrible week before he was hanged. The following is a copy of his last letter written to me.

Mountjoy Jail
December 1st 1944
6.30 a.m.

'Dear Dr.,

'In case I haven't left a souvenir to some person I should have, please explain that the number at my disposal were limited.

'I haven't time to say much but I'm sure there's no necessity. All I ask is that the ideals and principles for which I'm about to die will be kept alive until the Irish Republic is finally enthroned. This I feel sure will be accomplished before very long despite all the labours of traitors and hypocrits as right will prevail.

'Thank everyone who has done anything on my behalf, good-bye and good luck in the future.

Charlie.'

Ireland has another martyr and we must all feel proud to have known him and to have been his friends. I'm sure he doesn't need our prayers but I will ask you to pray for your sorrowful

Aunt Kathleen.

At this stage I realised that Pappa, too, had been closely involved with Charlie and held more extreme political views than I had ever suspected. By 1944 he no longer agreed with my father that the twenty-six county government of the Irish Free State (since 1937 known as Eire) was legitimate and should be whole-heartedly supported. To him, then, de Valera was a traitor who had thrown in the sponge before the thirty-two counties had been freed from British rule, and he considered it his duty as a patriot and an honourable man to oppose the Dublin government. But he had never preached sedition to me, no doubt because to have done so would have been to risk confusing my young mind and dividing my loyalties between father and grandfather.

A few weeks later I had a letter from a fourteen-year-old cousin, the daughter of my father's younger sister, which indicated that extreme Republicanism was successfully being passed on to my own generation.*

10, Charleston Ave.,
1 January 1945

Dear Dervla,

I hope you are well and had a very happy Christmas. Thanks for the letter, I was delighted to get it. I'm glad you are now more used to school. Do you know what G. K.

---

*In fact the writer soon out-grew her extremism, being by temperament tolerant and objective.

Chesterton says about education? He says that it is being taught by somebody you don't know about things you don't want to know. I don't altogether agree.

Wasn't it awful about Charlie? I'll never forget the day of his death. The night before the people went to say the Rosary outside the prison for him but the police would not let them near it. (By 'they' I mean Republicans—in fact some were not but just pitied him.) Then they decided to say the Rosary aloud in procession while walking back to town but in O'Connell St. the police baton-charged them and injured two girls!! And this in a Catholic country ruled by an Irish Government!!!! However when the Nuncio heard of it he must have said something because for the first time in *four* years the government allowed a notice in the newspapers announcing that a Mass would be said for his soul and we all went to it. It was very sad but as he died such a brave death and is nearly sure to be in Heaven it is not so bad. He was laughing and happy up to the very last and the night before he said *he would not change his place for any man in the world.* He even forgave the CID who always pushed him around and maltreated him. He was so brave that the warders wept and the CID in the Castle said he was the bravest man they ever executed!! And that's saying something! I was glad to hear he left you a ring. He sent me a signed picture and left me a crucifix. I'd better stop now because if I don't I'll go on and on and on. I always do on the subject of Charlie. When you next come to Dublin I'll tell you all about Charlie, Aunt Kathleen and the raid on our own house. Give my love to Aunt Kitty and Uncle Feargus. I hope you have a very happy new year.

Lots of love and kisses,

Constance.

Had I lived in Dublin I might either have been much more deeply influenced by Murphy Republicanism or reacted earlier and more strongly against it. As it was, I followed exactly in my father's political footsteps, during this period, and despite the emotionalism aroused by Charlie's tragic career I reserved for de Valera (Charlie's 'murderer', according to Aunt Kathleen) the sort of devotion expended on less orthodox heroes by my Dublin cousins. To me 'Dev' was one of the greatest Irishmen who had ever lived—indeed, one of the greatest MEN—yet like my mother I was apolitical by nature and I cannot recall ever arguing about this with the more extreme of my relatives. Dev was not, in my eyes, a politician. He was an heroic, almost god-like leader of the nation who had never belonged to the dreary world of party politics but ruled us from an immeasurably higher plane. This of course was fantasy on my part, an adolescent's glorification of a sincere, romantic and very powerful personality. But behind the fantasy there was some truth. Now many of Dev's ideals seem to me either absurd or distasteful. Yet he did have genuine ideals, he was no mere politician out for personal power, and looking around today one realises that neither in Britain nor in Ireland is there any individual with the leadership qualities of Churchill and de Valera.

Unlike Pappa, Aunt Kathleen had no inhibitions about dividing my loyalties; she was such a fanatical Republican that she would not have scrupled to subvert anyone by almost any means. In July 1944, when she was in prison following the arrest of Charlie in her home, she wrote me the following letter —carefully designed to steer me towards the mainstream of contemporary Republicanism.

Mountjoy Prison
2.7.44

My dearest Dervla,
    It just struck me that you might like to have a letter from me and to know what life is like here. Well, considering everything, it's not so bad. The first and most important thing is that everyone here treats me with great kindness and consideration. The ordinary diet is not very appetizing—in fact I couldn't tackle it, but I have been put on hospital diet which means that I get two pints of milk and two eggs a day and beef tea for dinner. Also I can be sent in food from outside. However, I find I'm not at all hungry and I had to ask Isolde not to send me in food because it was a waste of money.
    This is the routine—the cell door is opened at 7 am and you may get up if you wish to. I stay in bed until breakfast is served and I usually take that in bed. As a rule the cup of

tea is all that interests me. The cell is locked then for about an hour while the wardens have their breakfast. At about 10 I have a bath, which I enjoy immensely. After that I potter around—tidy my cell, wash my cup and saucer, etc. I then go out for exercise—I can walk around or sit down and read or just think—and I have plenty to think about! I can also read the paper which is sent in each day. Dinner is at 12.45—beeftea and bread and milk. The cell is locked until about 2 after which I may go out into the grounds again. The high light of the day is my visit (usually at 4.0). I can see two people at a time but in the presence of a warder and a detective. The visit usually lasts from 15–30 minutes. The children come to see me in turn. I have not seen Pappa yet as he has been away in Limerick. Sunday is the dullest day here as there can be no bath and no visit. Mass of course is a great consolation. The ten days I was in the Bridewell included two Sundays and there is no possibility of getting Mass there.

After the visit I have tea, bread and butter and a boiled egg. Then I go out to sit in the grounds and before coming back to my cell at about 8.30 I spend a little time praying in the chapel. Although in the usual way there is no meal between 4.30 pm and 7.0 am I have my own tea and a tea-pot and I make some tea every evening. My door is locked at 9.30. However, I have the privilege of having the light on for a few hours so I read in bed until the small hours. Although the bed is very comfortable it's not so easy to sleep —all sorts of things come into your head and keep you awake. This morning I woke at 5 and was thinking of the morning last summer when you and I and Anne went out before sunrise to pick mushrooms. We didn't get any but I think it was well worth while to see the dawn over the mountains and the stars, that were so bright when we started, fading away one by one.

Daddy told me that you have all decided that it is best for you to go away to school next September to the Ursulines in Waterford. I'm sure you'll like them—they are the only nuns I ever really liked. Isolde and Niamh went to the Ursuline Convent at Forest Gate when we lived in London and they *loved* it. I know, of course, that they were day-pupils and how lonely you will be at first—but I know too that you have plenty of grit and backbone and that you'll do your best to be happy when you know that the only reason you are being sent away from home is that your wonderful mother is an invalid and that she and Daddy are prepared to give up the joy of having you always with them for the sake of your education.

Do you remember when I saw you last, and we were looking at Daddy's Active Service medal, you asked me if I had ever been in jail? When I said no you remarked that I was the only one of my family who hadn't been—well now I'm no longer a blot on the family escutcheon—in fact I'm more like a skeleton in the cupboard! I can hardly believe that you are only twelve years old when I remember how tall and strong you are—why, you'd make two of me!

Your affectionate Aunt Kathleen

When the present round of the Troubles began in Northern Ireland, Aunt Kathleen was soon to be seen in the Republican ghettos of Belfast. Perhaps she merely went north as an 'observer', but that seems unlikely. It would not surprise me to discover that although well over seventy, and in poor health,* she was gun-running. Where there are godfathers there can also be godmothers. And to this day the name of 'Dr Kathleen' brings an affectionate gleam—and occasionally even a tear—to the eye of many a Provo.

*She died in 1973.

10

Molly arrived in May 1944. She was fat and forty and placidly uncritical of our house and its inmates. She baked delicious soda bread, of which she ate immoderate quantities, and could cook two dishes well. (Irish stew and bacon and cabbage.) Her reactions were prodigiously slow; half-an-hour after something had amused her she would disconcert those who did not know her by bursting into apparently unprovoked laughter. Yet she was such an enormous improvement on her immediate fore-runners that in June I was measured for my school uniform. Two battered trunks, still bearing French luggage labels of the 1890s, were lowered through the attic trap-door into the kitchen and going away to school became a reality.

I began mildly to dislike the idea as August dwindled. With Molly in the kitchen and my freedom restored the environs of Lismore seemed to have a lot more to offer than the environs of any convent school. Yet the novelty of the adventure still appealed and I was not seriously fretting.

Miss Knowles, the Jubilee district nurse, had by this time become a valued family friend and I was overjoyed when she offered to escort me to school, *in loco parentis*. We were to travel to Waterford by train and this, oddly enough, was the first train journey of my life.

The carriages and corridors were gay with the scarlet and dove-grey of the school uniform and long before we got to Waterford I had begun, unexpectedly, to enjoy the sensation of belonging to a distinctive community. This says a good deal for my schoolmates. Of course they ignored me; as a new girl I was officially beneath contempt. Yet there was no antagonism in the atmosphere; clearly I was not unwelcome.

The school stood isolated on a height beyond the city,

behind smooth high walls. Its grey stone buildings, solid and dignified, spread themselves in spacious, well-kept grounds that were brilliantly patterned and richly scented by September's flowering of roses. A not unpleasing air of monastic austerity and formality prevailed. One was aware of entering a world of orderliness and precision, certainty and calm, where the unpredictable could not happen, unless by some act of God. And even an act of God, one felt, would soon be made to conform to the relevant rule or regulation.

Yet there was no aura of dour oppression. In the wide, bright hallway we joined a dejected group of obviously new girls who were waiting with their parents to be received by the headmistress. All around us the golden parquet floor shone like a lake at sunset and the walls had been freshly painted cream, with pale green woodwork, and opposite the handsome oak hall-door was an alcove holding a gaudy life-size plaster statue of the Blessed Virgin Mary. The broad staircase swept upward to the left of the door as one entered and when my eye followed its stately curve I saw, whizzing down the banisters, a wiry girl with frizzy ginger hair and a demoniacal grin. As she slowed slightly to negotiate a bend she glanced down the corridor that ran at right angles to the hall, saw a nun approaching, promptly swung outwards off the banisters, hung for a moment by her hands, dropped six feet into the hall and lurked behind a pillar looking blasé.

I held my breath. What grisly punishment would be meted out to her? The nun could not have failed to notice . . . But it had all happened in such a way that the nun could pretend not to have noticed, without any loss of face, and as she passed the pillar she simply paused to say a suave "Welcome back!" to the ginger acrobat. This little scene neatly epitomised the whole spirit of a school where the pupils had enough respect for the staff not to defy them openly and the staff had enough respect for the pupils not to repress them.

By then it was my turn to be presented to the headmistress—traditionally known as The Hat. She was small and thin and red, like a carrot. As we shook hands I wondered if her toes were as red as her fingers. Perhaps she was a secret drinker, I thought, noting the ruby nose and remembering Jeff. All in all, she looked one of Nature's less agreeable blunders. And I felt she was coming to an identical conclusion about me. However, our instant mutual antipathy worried me not at all. A liking for The Hat might indeed have inhibited my rule-breaking; that we had at once recognised each other as Natural Enemies was much more satisfactory.

In the second-floor junior dormitory Miss Knowles helped me to unpack and another new girl, having read my luggage labels, introduced herself as Sally Dowling. Our fathers had done time together in Wormwood Scrubs (the Irish equivalent of having been in the same house at Eton) and she, too, was the only child of comparatively poor parents—and her mother was a semi-invalid. With her raven-black hair, aquiline nose, deep-set grey-green eyes and almost copper-coloured skin she looked not unlike a Red Indian. She was eighteen months younger than I, but we were to be in the same form for she was very clever. She also had a lot of quiet self-assurance and when Miss Knowles had said good-bye she appointed herself—gently, not bossily—as my guide and mentor. It was hard to believe that she, too, was a new girl. That very evening she and I established the foundations of a comfortable, easy-going, dependable friendship. Our devotion to each other was deep, but undemanding, undemonstrative, unsentimental, almost masculine; and throughout the next two years we never once even came near to quarrelling.

However, my new friend was of no help when I woke for the first time in my cubicle. I had slept well, but as I opened my eyes homesickness engulfed me. It was almost a physical sensation, like being knocked down and rolled over and over by a wave. And it was all the more devastating for being unexpected. When saying good-bye to my parents I had felt just a little wistful, yet now my loneliness seemed to be even more acute than three years earlier. Then homesickness had been mitigated by the sheer horror of the place and its denizens, much as lumbago takes one's mind off tonsilitis. But here my personal anguish was unadulterated and I lived through the next week in a stupor of misery. Even to think about those seven days, thirty-five years later, is painful.

Then one morning I woke and something had slipped into place and I felt happy all through. There had been no gradual recovery; on the seventh day I had felt no less miserable than on the second or fourth. So it was with a sense of incredulous relief that I lay in bed on that eighth—Wednesday—morning, looking at the early sunlight streaming onto my pale gold cubicle curtains and realising that I was happy.

This happiness lasted for the rest of my schooldays. Undoubtedly it was in part a result of freedom from those incongruous domestic responsibilities which I had had to shoulder, for much of the time, during the past few years. At school I was leading a life appropriate to my age and I enjoyed every moment of it. I also enjoyed not being the only pebble on the beach. My parents tried to avoid spoiling me, but any only child—particularly with a strong-willed, perfectionist mother—inevitably receives an unwholesome amount of attention. At home everything to do with me was of prime importance and in itself this constant exposure to parental concern was an infringement of privacy, though never so intended. At school I missed my own room and my long, solitary hours out-of-doors, yet in a sense I had greater liberty to be myself. I was no more or less important than some hundred and twenty other girls and this anonymity pleased me. My parents were agreeably surprised by my enthusiastic letters home. They had expected me to resent the lack of physical freedom, at least during my first term. But I was a more adaptable animal than they knew. And they had been clever in their choice of school.

A grimly authoritarian régime would either have broken my spirit or provoked me to run away—probably the latter. But Waterford's Ursuline Convent allowed enough scope for me to lead my own kind of life without inviting disaster. (The Hat threatened to expel me three times; but this, I now feel, was because of my private feud with her rather than because I had unforgivably challenged The System.) The atmosphere was relaxed without being permissive—to this extent, a replica of home—and I liked most of my schoolmates and all my teachers. Also, I greatly enjoyed disliking The Hat.

I soon developed a passion for a senior girl and became weak at the knees if she smiled graciously at me when we chanced to pass in the corridors. This was known as 'having an affec' for so-and-so, the so-and-so in question being described as one's 'affec'. My affec was an amiable sixteen-year-old to whom I wrote countless sonnets in praise of her beauty—an attribute which existed chiefly in my beholding eye. Most of these sonnets were seething with subliminal sexuality, as I was fascinated to discover when I came upon them recently in a rusty tin box. Frances also caused me to expend much mental energy on devising schemes which would lead to our meeting more frequently in the corridors. Not that one ever actually talked to one's affec; that would have been a major breach of both school regulations (the age groups were rigidly segregated) and school tradition. It is interesting that we schoolgirls voluntarily reinforced this particular school rule with our own code, almost as though we were unconsciously aware of the need for protection from our burgeoning sexuality. By immemorial custom, everyday communication was restricted to the humbly adoring look and the regal smile of acknowledgement. However, school dances were held twice a year, on the feasts of St Angela and St Ursula, and then each affec asked her admirer, or admirers, for one dance (no more), during which verbal exchanges were permitted. But these occasions seldom or never generated immortal repartee.

I was a keen but undistinguished player of netball, hockey and tennis, and I founded a clandestine rugger club for those whose athletic tastes were more robust. We played in an out-of-bounds ploughed field and had two seven-a-side teams called Clongowes and Castleknock. Most of our fathers had been to one or other of those colleges and during the Leinster Senior Cup competition the whole school became hysterically involved. As we had no wireless at our disposal illicit telephone calls were made to Dublin to find out who had won each round. When I boasted of an uncle who in prehistoric times had once, during an influenza epidemic, been selected as a substitute for the Irish team my stock soared and even the seniors looked at me with respect.

I was such an unsatisfactory scholar that a school dedicated to self-glorification through examination results would have had little use for me. It must have been plain that even at the end of six years I would pass no examination since I applied my mind to only two subjects, English and history. And even during English classes I was selective, regarding grammatical sessions as needless because one knew most of it anyway by instinct. To this day I cannot tell the difference between parsing and analysis. By the end of the first month I had dropped domestic science, art and music, all subjects for which I had no aptitude whatever. Secretly I longed to be a really good pianist like my mother, who had all sorts of impressive awards from the Royal Academy rolled up at the back of a drawer, but my music mistress believed that I suffered from some sort of musical dyslexia and would never be able to master any instrument. So I had at my disposal, almost every day, two and a half hours more freedom than my classmates. And naturally my division mistress wanted to know how I proposed to spend all this spare time.

"Writing books," I replied succinctly.

"I see," said Mother Ambrose. "Well, in that case I think you'd better work in one of the empty music rooms. Anywhere else you'll be constantly interrupted. And I imagine you need peace and quiet for writing books?"

"Oh yes!" said I. "Silence is essential. And no interruptions."

"I thought as much," said Mother Ambrose. "Though of course"—she added reflectively—"Jane Austen managed to write quite a few rather good books in between receiving visitors and doing the household chores. But I expect she was different. May I read your book when it's finished?"

"I'm afraid not," I said apologetically. "It won't be good enough for anyone to read. It's not that sort of book. It's only practice."

Each term I produced at least one full-length, lurid adventure story set in nameless Foreign Parts where the political crises were even more ambiguous than in Ireland and led to a profusion of warm sticky blood, choking emotions and gallant last-minute rescues. No doubt this 'practice' was a development of my teddy-bear-tree fantasies and I often became so involved that I had to continue writing during prep-time and on Saturday afternoons when I should have been mending my clothes. Mother Ambrose can hardly have remained unaware of these irregularities, but she made no serious attempt to check them. Just occasionally—pandering to my passion for long words—she would comment on the 'unarrested disintegration' of my underwear.

For other reasons, however, I was constantly in trouble. Such rules as were specifically designed to transform us into young ladies aroused my most profound contempt and I rarely bothered to conceal the fact that I had broken them. Yet I soon developed a fierce loyalty to the school and however I might defy its traditions within the precincts I took care to behave impeccably on the rare occasions when I emerged into the big world wearing school uniform. Both my defiance and my loyalty were uncalculated, which may explain the nuns' tolerance; perhaps they saw that although I was never going to fit into their particular mould I had a certain objective regard for it.

Thirty-five years ago not even the most senior girls at an Irish convent boarding-school were allowed out during term time, with or without supervision, to pursue either entertainment or instruction. Entering the school grounds on the first day of term, one knew that unless something extraordinary happened one would not leave them for the next two or three months. Nor did we have visitors, because of wartime travelling restrictions, and our half-term merely meant no lessons on a Friday and lots of sticky cakes for tea three days running. Being averse to such confections this was no treat for me. Raising my plate I would say "Whizz?" and whoever first replied "Echo!" won the prize. This corrupt Latin greatly offended me and I aroused much derision by allowing the pedantic paternal genes to take over and attempting to restore "Quis?" and "Ego!" As Sally pointed out, with her usual brusque logic, this was a damn silly attitude considering so many respectable English words are corrupt Latin or corrupt something else.

Our lives were as enclosed and almost as sheltered as the nuns'. Yet within its own boundaries, both physical and mental, this school world was full and rich—if somewhat unreal to outsiders. It was made separate, distinct, self-sufficient and unassailable by the underlying strength and esotericism of its own traditions. And though it is argued that modern educational methods provide a better preparation for adult life, I still feel that there was an instinctive wisdom behind the fuddy-duddyism of the old system. A variety of 'ologists insist that the physiological and psychological changes of adolescence impose severe strains on the whole personality. Yet, as a society, we react most strangely to our new awareness of adolescent 'problems'. Are we trying to dodge them by forcing the maturing pace? My happy, limited school provided youngsters with as tranquil an environment as possible in which to come to terms with adulthood at the pace nature intended. The reassuring atmosphere of security and stability may well have helped us more than sophisticated insights into current affairs, cultural trips to the continent, 'projects' here, there and everywhere, and illustrated lectures on every conceivable subject including contraception.

I was now for the first time in a situation where relative poverty might have been felt as a disadvantage. During the holidays most of my classmates did all sorts of exciting things like hunting and sailing and competing in swimming galas and tennis tournaments and gymkhanas. Had I longed to enter this alien world I might soon have become miserable. But I continued to accept the fact that other people led other sorts of lives and no change in my own way of life seemed either possible or desirable. Perhaps it did not seem desirable simply because I knew it to be impossible; while one half of me throve on fantasy, the other was cheerfully pragmatic. So it rarely occurred to me that my apparently humdrum background was in any way defective. Books, after all, were my only real concern—the reading, collecting and possible writing of them—and other interests, however keenly pursued, were essentially peripheral. Anyway the idea of sailing did not greatly appeal to me; by all accounts it involved sharing a small space with far too many people for much too long and I preferred to enjoy it only vicariously in Arthur Ransome's world. Riding of course was another matter. One of my first memories is of being run away with by an allegedly angelic pony belonging to a horsy godmother in Co Kildare. A glorious mixture of terror and elation surged through me as I clung to the creature's mane. (I was to feel nothing comparable for the next quarter of a century, until I found myself galloping by mistake up a valley in the Western Himalaya on an Afghan stallion.) To everyone's astonishment I remained *in situ* while the pony took me twice round the paddock. But then he decided to show off at the jumps . . .

I fell with five-year-old animal expertness and my mother, who had witnessed all this from her bath chair, was too shocked to utter. My godmother, on the other hand, was so delighted by the whole performance that she promptly offered to give me a pony for my next birthday. But this generous gesture was decisively checked. To my parents, at the best of times, there was little if any difference between the Bengal tiger and the common cob. For years I believed that we could not possibly afford to keep a pony; now I suspect that this was one of the few areas in which my mother allowed herself to be over-protective. And so when listening to horsy classmates discussing their ponies I occasionally felt a wistful envy.

In one respect, however, I did for a time suffer acutely at school as a result of being 'different'. Children take even the most bizarre situations for granted, if these have always been a part of daily life, and easily form the habit of not thinking about certain matters that might be distressing to dwell upon. At intervals throughout my childhood I had registered receiving the neighbours' sympathy because my mother was an invalid—and this had puzzled me. My own unthinking acceptance of her invalidism was so complete that I could not understand why anyone should make emotional comments. This acceptance was encouraged by her own determination to lead as normal a life as possible. To be a good housewife and mother from a bath chair is not easy, but in so far as it could be done she did it. In my eyes she had no aura of 'differentness' and her high spirits and capacity for enjoying simple things made her exceptionally congenial to a small child.

Yet she was not as other mothers were. And this realisation, when at last it came, had a disproportionately upsetting effect on me. It was as though a dam had burst, freeing my long-restrained awareness of her difference which then inundated my stability. Suddenly, I couldn't take it. My frantic craving to be, in this respect, like everyone else compelled me to lie. Impulsively I would say, "When my mother and I were coming home from a long walk . . ." or, "My mother is such a fast walker it's hard to keep up." Being naturally truthful, like Alice, these aberrations troubled me. My mother and I did indeed go for long walks together—but I was pushing her in her bath chair. Also, she *had been* a fast walker, and I tried to convince myself that to change a tense was to tell no more than a half-lie. But I was too well grounded in moral theology for this to work, even temporarily. My intention was totally to mislead and therefore my lies were full-blooded and shameful.

Here were the makings of another 'scruples crisis', in a different key, but mercifully it did not develop. As the shock of my objective appreciation of my mother's invalidism wore off, I lost the compulsion to mislead. But it left me with an embarrassing residue of false information imparted, which throughout the rest of my schooldays occasionally rose up to confound me.

After my thirteenth birthday I began joyously to tick off, on the calendar in my cubicle, the days of December, and my heart seemed to swell with sheer happiness at the thought of being home again. Yet when I stepped off the train at Lismore, not having seen my parents for three months and ten days, a feeling of anticlimax and an oddly demoralising shyness overcame me. Although my parents meant no less to me than they had done in September they did mean something different. My attitudes to them had changed and I confusedly imagined it necessary to conceal this natural process as though it were some hurtful form of disloyalty. I had unconsciously transferred part of my allegiance to a world I valued all the more because parents were excluded from it. Most children who are happy at boarding-school revel in the secret-society aspect of school life. The cryptic slang, the apparently illogical customs, the usually logical rules and regulations laid down not by Authority but by generations of pupils—for me all this added up to a thoroughly satisfying existence in which grown-ups seemed insignificant and children taught each other as much as—or more than— they learned from their elders.

Inevitably this existence weakened the bonds between my mother and myself. I no longer confided everything to her or idealised her as the perfect companion. Instead, I became absurdly secretive about the most trivial details and went out of my way to try to break the links created by our mutual interests. As for my father, I now comprehended in a more adult way the strains and stresses of his life and felt correspondingly more guilty about our atrophied relationship. But this made it seem even less possible than before to take any remedial action.

Only one relationship remained unchanged. With Mark I could still discuss anything, to him I could reveal any idiocy or inconsistency, in his company I never felt it necessary to pretend to be other than myself as I was at that moment. Then, and for many years afterwards, I took my good fortune for granted, not realising how rare it is to be always totally at ease with another human being.

At the start of those Christmas holidays my father greeted me at the railway station with the news that Molly had just left, but had promised to send her youngest sister as a replacement in the new year. She had pronounced that in winter our kitchen would 'perish a brass monkey' so it seemed to us that this promise betrayed a certain lack of sisterly concern. The Emergency fuel shortage was by then acute and no doubt sub-zero temperatures had accelerated her departure. But when I viewed the situation with that new detachment gained at school it occurred to me, for the first time, that our servant problem was perhaps being aggravated by my mother's archaic expectations. She had her standards and was incapable of compromising if those she employed could not or would not accept them. Unlike my father and myself, she understood whatever weird impulse makes the Englishman dress for dinner in the jungle. "We may be poor, but we needn't live like cavemen" was her battle-cry. A table had to be laid with the correct multiplicity of instruments placed in their correct positions, though the plates came from Woolworths and the forks and spoons were of aluminium. The maid's uniform had to be immaculate and she had to know, or quickly learn, how to wait at table. (Her lessons were frequently a rich mine of comedy.) The kitchen might be falling around our ears, but every corner of every cupboard had to be kept spotless, and the outsides of saucepans scoured no less thoroughly than the insides, and the tea-towels boiled daily. Naturally enough, simple girls off the side of a mountain, who had never before seen a vegetable dish, never mind a napkin-ring, were confused if not positively intimidated by all this nonsense. Nor could I approve of it and in my more rebellious moments I mentally and unjustly labelled it 'side'. ('He has no side to him' means, in Ireland, 'he is a simple man, without affectation or pretension'.) To me this formality seemed both incongruous and irritating against the background of our ramshackle and poverty-stricken home; to my mother it symbolised something profoundly important. Now I can understand that she needed to uphold order and dignity as props to her own morale. But for many years no such explanation occurred to me and our divergence on this point was to become a running sore within the family.

My earliest Christmas memories are associated with Old Brigid, who ritually opened the season on November 1 by making the plum-puddings while grumbling obliquely about not being allowed to make a cake. Pappa sent a Christmas cake from Bewleys every year, but Old Brigid, who had never in her life been to Dublin, despised 'them shop things'. Each year she declined cake with an offended air, explaining darkly—"I wouldn't trust meself to it."

Annually another layer of plaster fell off the kitchen walls because of over-exposure to plum-pudding steam. Yet my memory, practising romantic selectivity, presents that kitchen as a cosy place during (pre-war) mid-winter. Pools of golden lamplight were fringed by friendly shadows, in December a ham hung from the rafters and while the oven was being 'got up' the huge shiny black range roared and glowed, all amiable and animated.

While Old Brigid went through her plum-pudding routine— unhurried yet superbly efficient—I knelt on a chair at one end of the massive, scrubbed-white kitchen table and slightly opened the deep drawer. Then, every time the range needed stoking, I swiftly hid a fistful of fruit. And at the end of the day, while Old Brigid was intent on settling the pudding basins into their giant oval iron pot, I transferred my loot to the nearby guichet and rushed into the dining-room to conceal it in the sideboard. This operation was inspired not by greed but by my predilection for outwitting authority. Most of the loot went to Tommy, whose parents couldn't afford plum-pudding. (Childhood was less complicated before the consumer society had begun its evil hypnosis of the young. It would never have occurred to me to pity Tommy because his family was even poorer than my own and it would never have occurred to Tommy to envy me.)

The two unique features of Christmas Eve were the repeated appearances of unfamiliar postmen at unpredictable hours— up to 11.00 pm—and the plucking, gutting and desinewing of the turkey. In those pre-supermarket days one bought one's turkey in a state of nature and to remove the sinews, without taking most of the leg-meat with them, was an art not everyone possessed. Old Brigid knew the theory of it but found my father a singularly inept collaborator. And for me the joy of watching those two struggling with the bird—one on either side of the pantry door—far outweighed the pleasure I got next day from eating it. This was the one occasion during the year when my father might be heard using bad language. If the struggle had gone on for half-an-hour or more, and then a pound of meat came away with a sinew, he was capable of saying 'Damn!' under his breath. Whereupon Old Brigid would cough loudly in an attempt to save my ears from pollution.

I had a circle of well-trained relatives and friends and from the age of six onwards the shape of my Christmas presents never varied—only the size. For me the glory of Christmas morning was the sight and smell and feel of new books. I don't remember book-tokens—perhaps they hadn't been invented—and occasionally there were duplicate volumes. But that was an advantage rather than a problem; in my privileged position I could exchange unwanted volumes for something long coveted, on our next visit to the Dublin bookshops.

Our Christmas ritual never varied. On Christmas Eve we listened to the carol service from King's College Chapel and afterwards we broached the Christmas cake and I was allowed to drink lemon cordial instead of milk. At midnight my parents listened to Mass from the Vatican and I—from the age of nine—went to the parish church. At ten o'clock on Christmas morning—after present opening—we sat down purposefully to a gargantuan mixed grill. Normally my parents were very light breakfasters and my mother in any case strongly disapproved of fries; but this meal was designed to keep us going until four o'clock when—true to Dublin tradition—we dined by candle-light as dusk became darkness.

To me, who habitually went to bed at seven thirty, Midnight Mass was among the most exciting events of the year. That walk through the dark, expectant night, its silence broken only by other hurrying footsteps and cheerful greetings; the packed church clumsily decorated with holly; the quivering, golden blaze of votive candles around the crib; the familiar carols being sung so badly they frequently seemed unfamiliar; the platitudinous Christmas sermon that allowed one to play at keeping a sentence in advance of the preacher without often dropping a point. Then the walk home through a night that seems always to have been frosty and tingling and starry and glittering—though I dare say this is an illusion—and so to bed, after mince-pies and a hot lemon-drink, in a stupor of happy exhaustion.

We never went away for Christmas or had anyone to stay and there were no treats like going to the pantomime. At noon on Christmas Day Mrs Mansfield and her brother came by different routes for a drink and sat at opposite ends of the room affecting to be unaware of each other's presence. Mrs Mansfield always proudly presented us with one of her own plum-puddings and my mother always evinced suspiciously eloquent gratitude. This gift was discreetly passed on to the Wren Boys who called in their droves on St Stephen's Day. Although those were delicious puddings—I often ate their litter-brothers when visiting Mrs Mansfield—it was common knowledge that San Toy actively participated in his mistress's washing-up and, as her scullery was ill-lit, my mother thought it hideously probable that many of the dishes attended to by San Toy never found their way into the sink. I failed to see why that mattered, after eight hours' boiling, but my mother's approach to hygiene was more emotional than scientific.

Our Christmasses, then, had always been times of contentment rather than excitement. And when that contentment evaporated for me, after my first term at school, nothing remained to distinguish Christmas beyond a lot of extra hard work in the kitchen. I tried to conceal my new anti-Christmas sentiments and never hinted that I would have preferred to celebrate by going off for a day's solitary cycling. Just as I had earlier felt obliged to pretend to believe in Santa Claus, lest adult feelings might be hurt, so now I felt obliged to pretend to be enjoying our modest festivities. I knew, however, that my mother sensed and was saddened by my new indifference to the old traditions. And I also knew that her own enjoyment was marred by my having to act as general maid instead of being a schoolgirl on holidays. Yet she tried to conceal this regret, perhaps prompted by some irrational guilt, or feeling that since nothing could be done to improve my lot it would be psychologically unwise to offer sympathy. Now I can see that those three weeks contained the seeds of much that later went wrong between us.

Rather to our surprise, Molly's 'youngest sister' did arrive in the new year carrying all her possessions on her back in a sack smelling strongly of poultry droppings. She never made any secret of the fact that she was Molly's illegitimate daughter and she looked like a slim edition of her mother. Her name was Brid, which is pronounced 'Breed'. My mother said "I hope she doesn't", but in due course she did. After what my parents delicately assumed to have been a spontaneous abortion she developed 'an affec' for my mother. This, in mild forms, was not uncommon amongst our adolescent skivvies, but Brid's devotion was so excessive that she had to be forcibly restrained from spending all her wages (£1 a month) on such votive offerings as bull's-eyes and liquorice allsorts. But these developments were all in the future when I repacked my suitcase on January 12 and said good-bye to my mother in the kitchen where she was explaining the function of a casserole to an incredulous-looking Brid.

I was glad of Brid's presence during that brief farewell. My new antagonism towards my mother had in no way diminished my love for her—only my ability to express it. The sadness of this parting was quite unlike my straightforward loneliness of the previous September. Now I was eager to get back to school and I grieved not because the holidays had ended but because they had fallen so far short of expectations. Instead of enjoying a happy reunion I had lived—without then realising it—through the prelude to an eighteen-year conflict.

Even more distressing, at a deeper level, was my new, mute sympathy for my father's situation. Throughout the holidays I had seen him working hard, in the evenings and at week-ends, on the translation of some French theological tome. And I was shattered by the significance of this not unsuccessful attempt to fatten the family purse. For as long as I could remember my father had been writing novels, and paying precious money to have them typed, and sending them to publishers, and bearing up when they were rejected. In recent years I had sometimes thought vaguely that his apprenticeship was being rather long.

Yet I had never doubted that one day a typescript would be accepted, putting me in the gratifying position of having as father An Author. (Why I should have assumed his ultimate success, when I felt no such confidence about my own literary future, is not now clear to me.) Therefore his becoming a mere translator was to me a grievous personal disappointment, quite apart from the sorrow I felt on his behalf. And my understanding that he had awakened from a dream was illogically made even more painful by the fact that those hours previously spent on enjoyable if unprofitable novel writing were now being spent on hack-work to pay my school-fees. I felt sorry for my mother, too. All her married life she had been encouraging and guiding my father's endeavours with endless patience and tact: and presumably with a certain amount of hope.

Nor would such hope have been unjustified. After my parents' deaths I found all those typescripts in a tea-chest, under a neat file of kindly rejection slips. I looked through them— feeling ridiculously uncomfortable, as though I were eaves-dropping on a soliloquy—and was amazed equally by the interest of their irrelevant philosophical asides and by their complete lack of basic narrative skill. Had my father not been so single-minded about writing novels he might have made quite a good essayist—though possibly not a publishable one, in an age when essays are (one hopes temporarily) out of fashion.

As my father and I stood waiting on the station platform, awkwardly exchanging banalities, I felt his inner defeat as keenly as though it had been my own. And I longed to be able to convey, however indirectly, my understanding and sympathy. But we were too aware of each other's moods and reactions to be of any mutual comfort. We knew that we were uniquely vulnerable to each other's perceptions and both of us were too proud and too reserved ever to let the barriers go down.

The train was full of children returning to Waterford schools in self-segregated groups. I joined the Ursuline coach and remained by the door to wave dutifully to my father. When he was out of sight I felt oddly *released*; yet I did not immediately merge with the rest, much as I had been looking forward to rejoining my friends. Suddenly, for the first time, I was aware of myself as an outsider. Neither at home nor at school did I quite fit in. That is one of the moments I remember with a vividness which has never faded. I was staring fixedly at the Round Hill—an ancient, tree-covered fortification from which Lismore takes its name—and I felt not at all upset by this recognition of my own apartness. Neither did I see it as anything to be smug about; but I was interested in it, because it seemed to presage numerous as yet indefinable threats and promises. Then as the train changed its tune, on the bridge across the Blackwater at Cappoquin, I changed my mood and went swaying up the corridor to join my classmates.

It was true that at school I remained always, though not obviously, an outsider. Yet that interlude away from home was immensely important to me. Lacking it, I would have grown up with my social adaptability untested and my knowledge of human nature derived mainly from books. And, as T. S. Elliot observed, 'It is simply not true that works . . . depicting . . . imaginary human beings *directly* extend our knowledge of life. Direct knowledge of life is knowledge directly in relation to ourselves, it is our knowledge of *how* people behave in general, of *what* they are like in general, in so far as that part of life in which we ourselves have participated gives us material for generalization.' What I most appreciated about school was the access it gave me to this 'direct knowledge of life'. I revelled in analysing my schoolmates' characters, observing how they reacted on each other, speculating about why they were as they were—in other words, wondering what made them tick, as Mr Eliot would not have said. To me the works of Pope were as yet a closed book but I arrived independently at one of his most celebrated conclusions:

> 'Know then thyself, presume not God to scan,
> The proper study of mankind is man.'

Academically I was backward because sheer laziness deterred me from using what was in any case a fairly limited intelligence. But my early sharing in adult problems and responsibilities had made me, emotionally, unusually mature and this 'grown-upness' prompted many of my classmates (all of whom, apart from Sally, were my seniors) to treat me as an older sister. Thus my study of mankind flourished because I received numerous confidences which enabled me to discern the reality behind various elaborate adolescent façades. Having been brought up to regard the breaking of confidences as a gross dishonour I never felt tempted to gossip about other people's secrets, even with Sally, and eventually I established quite a reputation as a restorer of damaged friendships—no doubt because my amateur psycho-analysing helped me to see where things had gone wrong though neither of those concerned might know exactly why they had quarrelled.

There were other problems, too—parents who didn't get on, delinquent brothers, family debts. (Thus I learned that the price of a yacht could be peace of mind.) And early one summer morning another thirteen-year-old came creeping into my cubicle and stood, trembling all over, by my bed. "I think I'm bleeding to death," she whispered. "My sheets are all soaked in blood—will you tell the dormitory sister? Will they put me in hospital? Will Daddy and Mummy come?" Visiting each other's cubicles was so strictly forbidden that even I had never broken this rule, but now I was too angry—with Eileen's mother—to care. I gave the semi-hysterical child a few sanitary towels and a brief lecture on menstruation and led her back to her bloody bed. She was the eighth child of a Dublin doctor and it appalled me that she should have been sent off to school unaware of the facts of puberty. I pitied her all the more when I recalled my own experience—rushing into my parents' bedroom early one morning waving a pair of bloody pyjama-trousers and yelling triumphantly, "Look! I'm a woman now!"

At least amongst my age group, sex was not in those days a popular topic. Twice I was questioned, tentatively, about my theory of the origins of babies, and on both occasions I replied shortly, "Ask your mother." This instinctive reluctance to discuss the subject marked my own growing-up. Two years earlier I would gaily have described what I knew of the whole process, from conception to delivery, to anyone who showed an interest. But now I felt—I could not have said why—that it was a special subject, needing to be treated with reticence and reverence and not suitable for schoolgirlish chatterings. Today there can be few thirteen-year-olds unaware of the facts of life; but I find it sad that this knowledge is being spread in ways that erode reticence and reverence. However wisely or foolishly modern parents treat sex-education, the sort of innocence my generation knew has by now become an emotional impossibility. This realisation disturbs me when I look at my own daughter. A time of innocence is surely a prerequisite for the total experience, in young adulthood, of the ecstasy of erotic love. What has never been possessed can never be gloriously lost.

11

Despite her little misadventure in April, Brid coped unexpectedly well with the Murphy ménage. When the holidays began in mid-June she was still worshipping my mother and had even become quite a passable cook.

Pappa's health was now causing some concern and to our sorrow he cancelled his Lismore vacation for the first time. It was then decided that I should spend July in Dublin, staying with relatives and visiting him regularly. This pleased me immensely—and not only because taking the train for Dublin alone, with my bicycle in the luggage-van, made me feel splendidly emancipated. Attached as I was to Lismore, I was very aware of being a Dubliner by heredity. Before the Emergency we had gone to Dublin every month for a long week-end and always, as we approached the city, one part of me felt that it was coming home. As an individual I belonged to Lismore, but as a social unit I belonged—and perhaps still belong—to Dublin. My relatives and their friends saw me as the cousin up from the country, a gauche and rather curious creature who dressed abominably and knew nothing about the theatre or the latest films or the feuding and gossiping of the literary world. Yet as I cycled about the city I felt completely at home. I was moving among familiar ghosts—not only those of my biological ancestors, but also those of my cultural forbears. That was what was missing in Lismore; there the ghosts were unfamiliar.

The contemporary Dublin scene never greatly interested me. What I enjoyed was cycling down Dorset Street and remembering that Richard Brinsley Sheridan was born at No. 12—and thinking of him again as I cycled up Grafton Street, where he attended 'The Seminary for the Instruction of Youth' run by Samuel Whyte, the natural son of his grand-uncle. Pedalling through the Liberties I would wonder if Swift had really been born at 7 Hoey's Court. And in Fishamble Street I remembered that James Clarence Mangan had lived there above his father's grocery-shop, just as Tom Moore lived above *his* father's grocery-shop in Aungier Street. Then there was 21 Westland Row, where Oscar Wilde—my mother's most beloved, if not most admired, writer—was born; his father and my mother's grandfather had been close friends. And Lower Sackville Street I associated with Shelley, who once lodged at No. 7 and tossed from the balcony to the street below numerous copies of his pamphlet, 'An Address to the Irish People'. At Templeogue I thought of Thackeray being entertained by Charles Lever, to whom *The Irish Sketch Book* was dedicated. And when I stayed at 3 Orwell Park, Rathgar, with my mother's eldest brother, I was living in a house very familiar to Synge; his maternal grandmother, Mrs Traill, had lived there, and when his father died of smallpox his mother moved to No. 4 with her infant son. Then, when I went on to stay with my mother's only sister, at 25 Coulson Avenue, Rathgar, I was conscious of the friendly ghost of George William Russell (A.E.). For some years after his marriage, A.E. lived in that cosy little redbrick house. And in August 1902, late one night, he came walking home to find a tall young man leaning against the railings of No. 25, waiting for him. He had never before met James Joyce, yet he at once invited him into the square, low-ceilinged sitting-room where I spent so many childhood hours; and there they talked until 4.00 am—a conversation that sparked off *Dubliners*.

All my savings were spent in the intoxicating second-hand bookshops along the quays, to which I had been introduced by Pappa even before I could read. But what gave Dublin its special significance were the scores of tiny family links, stretching back for generations, with almost every district of the South Side. (One rarely penetrated very far into the North Side, which was understood to be alien territory.) Yet Dublin was never necessary to me, as Lismore has always been. It seemed a pleasant diversion—a place where for short periods one could enjoy feeling nostalgic—but its urban attractions never exercised any magnetism. Now I rarely visit the city, which has been so degraded by developers that I could weep at every corner. But my dependence on Lismore has increased with the years. Something inside me would wither and die should circumstances ever compel me to uproot from the Blackwater Valley.

During that sunny July—it must have rained sometimes, but I recall only sunshine—I cycled out to Seapoint every day, with a covey of cousins, to bathe and play water-polo. I also saw a lot of Sally, who lived within walking distance of all my relatives' homes, and I was deeply disappointed when—ostensibly because of her mother's ill-health—she declined my invitation to spend August in Lismore. Years later she confessed that she hadn't really wanted to accept. Being an orthodox Dubliner— not a maverick like my parents—she dreaded moving too far away from the city.

For a fortnight I imagined myself to be everlastingly in love with a tall, dark, handsome cousin who claimed to be writing an epic poem and went into appropriate trances at mealtimes. The fact that he was about to enter a Jesuit seminary surrounded my passion with an aura of poignant tragedy. But I was not really made of languishing material and within days of my returning home he had been virtually forgotten.

The first three weeks of August passed very agreeably. I had dozens of newly acquired books to read and Mark was spending his vacation at home. Then Fate hit us below the belt. Suddenly the reason for Brid's mysterious contentment was revealed; she had been furtively (and fruitfully) walking out with the butcher's boy and on September 1 they were to marry. Consternation ensued. On September 10 I was to return to school, and what to do?

My parents soon came to their decision. Back to school I must go and they—always hoping for another Brid, if possible not quite so fruitful—would manage somehow. It was a brave decision, though many thought a foolish one. For my mother it involved remaining alone in the house, in bed, from 9.45 am until 1.15 pm and from 2.15 until 5.45. And she could not even switch the wireless on and off, or reach out to pick up a glass of water, or blow her nose. Moreover, she had a phobia about fire—a result of a nursery accident when she was three and a half which badly burned her eighteen-months-old brother. Since becoming an invalid she had fussed about only one thing —never being alone in the house for more than ten or fifteen minutes. Yet now, for my sake (or was it really for my father's sake?), she was prepared to overcome even this terror; and she approached the overcoming of it with characteristic common sense and resolution. No fire would be lit in her room until the evening and no heating would be left on anywhere in the house. Instead, she would sit up in bed, wrapped in layers of woollen shawls and surrounded by hot-water bottles, with only her tiny, deformed hands exposed so that by patiently manipulating two knitting needles she could turn the pages of the book poised above her knees on its specially made book-rest. Her window would be left open, whatever the weather, so that in case of fire—for instance, if one of the household's many rats gnawed through an electric wire—she could attempt to summon help. And her liquid intake would be carefully controlled in accordance with the hours when a bedpan would be available.

For my father the decision involved just as much hardship, of a different sort. In addition to his normal day's work in the library, he had to care for a complete invalid, shop on the way home, make do with a hurried snack at lunch-time (he had a vast appetite despite his slim build), cook the supper, do the washing-up and then translate demanding tomes until one or two o'clock in the morning.

All this I knew—or would have known had I stopped to think about it—yet throughout that long, cold, Christmas term of 1945 I cannot remember worrying even slightly about my parents. They wrote regularly and cheerfully and I, seeing no reason why they should not martyr themselves for my benefit, continued to enjoy life immensely.

Some of our relatives, viewing the situation from Dublin, thought it odd that my parents received no neighbourly help. They would have expected Mrs A. to run in at eleven o'clock with a cup of coffee, while Mrs B. did the shopping and Mrs C. ran in at four o'clock with a cup of tea, and Mrs D. prepared the vegetables for supper and Mrs E. perhaps took away my father's socks to wash and darn them. However, I perfectly understood why none of this happened. My parents had never tried very hard to integrate with the local community, simply because the futility of such efforts became apparent to them soon after their arrival in Lismore. They were friendly towards everybody, but in a politely distant way that did not encourage offers of neighbourly help. Both had the sort of pride with which I completely sympathised. Doubtless some people felt that no one with any sort of pride could live amidst the squalor that prevailed chez Murphy while my father was in charge. But my parents valued independence far more than comfort, convenience or 'respectability'. Having made the decision to send me back to school, they alone would deal with the consequences. Even Miss Knowles, to whom we were all devoted, and who was eager to help, was allowed to do so only in emergencies because it was not the proper function of a Jubilee nurse to care regularly for middle class patients.

Christmas came again. I was now fourteen, physically fully grown and totally self-centred. The home I returned to was in chaos, but I went to no great trouble to remedy this and for the first time my mother and I clashed seriously, as two strong-willed women. She considered it my duty to sort things out, I considered it my entitlement to spend the greater part of the school holidays doing as I pleased. A new hostility pervaded the atmosphere and deeply distressed my father, who looked ten years older after his three-month ordeal. But still it was never suggested that I should remain at home.

Eily appeared on New Year's Eve. An elderly woman, she had worked for years as housekeeper to a couple who were about to leave Lismore. She agreed to 'do for us' six days a week and even volunteered to pack my school trunk and see to my mending. But my mother grimly—and quite rightly—declared that Miss Dervla would be packing her own trunk and seeing to her own mending.

From the first, I thought Eily too good to last—and she was. Having been accustomed to comparatively luxurious working conditions, her health (or morale) broke down after a few weeks with the Murphys. By the beginning of February my parents were again on their own and even I felt shocked by my father's appearance at the start of the Easter holidays.

I knew then, with certainty, that I would never go back to school. The knowledge was deep down; it had not yet reached a level of consciousness at which I could examine it and decide how I felt about it. But it prepared me for our family conference on Good Friday evening.

My mother had an orderly mind and on occasions like this could give an impression of coldness as she suppressed her feelings to leave the way clear for logical argument. There were, she said, only three possible courses. We could struggle on as we were; we could accept the fact that I must remain formally uneducated; or she and I could rent Uncle Bob's basement flat at Orwell Park, leaving my father to live alone in Lismore. Some reliable help would surely be available in Dublin and I could attend my mother's old school in Stephen's Green as a day pupil.

We had just finished supper and I saw my father's hand shaking as he lifted his coffee cup to his lips. I stared at a new rat-hole in the wallpaper and wished the conference would end. There was too much tension in the air that I only imperfectly understood and in a muddled way I felt guilty for being the cause of it. At least, this is what I then imagined the source of my guilt to be. More likely it was based on a realisation that I had been brutally insensitive to my parents' ordeal during the past seven months and had ill-repaid their altruism by idling away my time in Waterford. It suddenly occurred to me that if I were to return to school the June examinations would reveal the extent of my ingratitude. But this was not my main reason for declaring immediately and emphatically that I was in favour of staying at home.

Both my parents looked surprised and my father's face seemed grey with unhappiness. Then my mother said firmly that while it seemed right for me to make the final decision I should do so only after careful thought. In due course she was to be severely criticised, especially by my father's family, for having put such a burden on a fourteen-year-old. But she knew me as none of her critics did. Had I been forced to accept the Dublin plan against my better judgement, much destructive turmoil might have followed. Besides, it was my future that was to be most profoundly and permanently affected and ever since I could toddle I had been insisting on the right to self-determination. My mother's shifting of the responsibility may have been partly inspired by moral cowardice, but it went with the grain of my wood.

"Go off on your own and think about it," said my mother. So I went for a long walk, through the mild spring dusk, though there was really nothing to think about. Or rather, there was a great deal to think about but nothing to be decided. I saw my decision as having been ordained by Fate, so that in fact it was no decision but merely an unavoidable reaction to a given set of circumstances. That Good Friday evening I became sharply aware, for the first time, that—'As flies to wanton boys, we are to the gods'. But this awareness was not yet tinged with any alarm or resentment.

I have never been easily moved by physical deprivation and pain, yet even as a child I shrank from mental or emotional suffering. Thus, though I had given no thought to the hardships recently endured by my parents, I could not for an instant consider inflicting on them the grief of separation from each other. Even had I longed to move to Dublin, I doubt if I would have hesitated; in this situation, I saw no scope for conflict. But of course I did not long to move to Dublin. Nor did I long to return to school, which considerably surprised myself. It had been good while it lasted and I would miss it: but not too much. Possibly I knew that I had drawn from the experience all it could give me and that the next few years would offer no more than unimportant variations on a theme.

It never occurred to me to speculate about the effects of this decision on myself at the age of eighteen, or twenty-five, or thirty. If I could have foreseen myself after the passing of another fourteen years, I would probably have refused to believe in the truth of my vision. Perhaps few fourteen-year-olds look far ahead, and even now, at forty-six, I feel foolish and futile if I try to do so. The present is enough. Attempts to control the future seem needlessly to limit its possibilities. If this view were general, anarchy would overtake the world. But one hopes there is room for a minority of non-planners.

That evening my immediate future, if far from ideal, looked quite tolerable. I would have ample time to read and write and cycle and swim. I would see Mark regularly—and he meant more to me than any number of school friends. Unlike most of my contemporaries, I had no interest in parties, clothes, films, dances, pop-stars (if such then existed) or boyfriends. In many ways, God had indeed fitted the back for the burden, in my case as well as my father's.

I returned from that walk at ten o'clock, an hour past my

usual bedtime, and announced that my original impulsive decision remained unchanged. I asserted again that, however favourable the domestic conditions, I would never have had either the ability or the will to distinguish myself as a scholar. And then my mother again dutifully went into details about the disadvantageous long-term implications of not at least having my Leaving Certificate, should the day ever come when I needed to earn my own living. But I knew that she was rejoicing in her heart and I hardly listened.

My father's feelings concerned me much more. I believed that he, too, welcomed my decision; but in the course of explaining it I had ruthlessly demolished his cherished dreams for my academic future. To me those dreams had always seemed absurd, yet suddenly I found them the more touching for that. During the past year he had proved how much they meant to him, how doggedly he was prepared to struggle to make them come true. But throughout that conference I was too constrained by the awkward adolescent barriers between my parents and myself, and too embarrassed by the emotional cross-currents in the atmosphere, to be anything other than belligerent and gruff. As usual, the very keenness of my appreciation of my father's feelings prevented me from allowing my sympathy even to be glimpsed. Harshly, I told myself that his present disappointment was nothing to do with me, that if anyone should be blamed it was he himself for ever having allowed a possibility to play the part of a certainty in his life.

My mother was no dreamer and had always tried to hold her husband's dreams in check, even if (or perhaps because) she recognised them for what they surely were—a reaching out towards compensation for a tragically imperfect marriage. Had they come true she would have been as pleased as he. But she argued that one should never have specific ambitions for any child before its potentialities can be gauged. As both my parents were reasonably intelligent, my father was justified in hoping for the best—but not, according to my mother's view, in staking his happiness on my success as a scholar. By the date of our conference my mother had probably accepted the obvious fact that I was not a budding intellectual and the even more obvious fact that whatever I did with my life I was unlikely to follow an established route. She was also helped to resign herself to the situation by her old-fashioned views on women and education; she saw no reason why the average woman should not become sufficiently cultivated and informed without ever going near a university. She had never been greatly impressed by blue-stockings: to her there was no virtue in being unable to scramble an egg or patch a shirt, even if one could read Russian novelists in the original and discern Tantric influences on the Gnostics.

Lying in bed that evening, too tired to go at once to sleep, I knew as certainly as if he had told me that for my father one dream was already being replaced by another. From now on he would look forward to seeing me succeed as a writer. There had to be a dream. And it comforted me that this was one we shared.

Many years were to pass before I perceived the real conflict inherent in that Good Friday situation. It should have been apparent at the time, but perhaps I dodged it, unconsciously/ deliberately, because any attempt to cope with it would have torn me asunder.

How had my father *really* felt? Had he wholeheartedly welcomed my decision, as I then believed? Or would part of him have preferred me to choose schooling in Dublin, even at the cost of my mother and he being separated for years? Quite likely he himself did not know the answer to that question. And it never even crossed my mind. To me my parents were a unit and their mutual love and interdependence seemed sacred, something to which one instinctively—almost compulsively— made sacrifices. It would have been psychologically impossible for me to desecrate that love by wondering if my father just might half-wish to put his daughter's welfare before his wife's. Moreover, I would not have wished either of my parents to put me first; this would have forged between us the sort of bond I dreaded—a bond woven of obligation that might never honourably be broken. As it was, my adolescent urge to detach from them was uninhibited by any feeling that either needed me on more than the practical level. Outwardly I was tied to them, inwardly I was far freer than if my formal education had been continued because to one or both *I* was the most important person in the world.

A cataclysmic row, between my mother and my father's

family, followed on that momentous occasion. This devastated my father, who was devoted to his family but felt bound to oppose them in defence of his wife. They, of course, were acting for the best, reckoning that my father needed support against an autocratic woman who had always been too strong for him and was now proposing to blight an innocent child's life to suit herself. This dramatic misinterpretation camouflaged certain complex truths that were not to become apparent to me for many years. At fourteen, I only saw my mother—whom I still adored, from behind the adolescent barriers—being unjustly attacked by people who disregarded all that she had recently gone through for my sake, misunderstood the intricacies of our family scene and had no knowledge of my personal inclinations. So I entered the arena armed with the armour of righteousness and attacked my affectionate, caring relatives in long, smug, stupid letters which my mother would never have allowed me to post had she read them.

As a result of our tribal warfare I never saw Pappa again. He and I had not quarrelled, but we were prevented from meeting by the animosity that persisted for years between the Dublin and Lismore Murphys. However, this sad and unnecessary ending to a lifetime (on my part) of love had one good effect. It taught me that quarrelling—with anybody about anything— is hideously wasteful. Argument, controversy and disagreement can be productive. But quarrelling in a bitter, negative, unforgiving way is a miserable admission of one's failure to cope with other people's viewpoints—and with oneself.

Mercifully the tie between Pappa and myself had in any case been gradually loosening. Essentially this was a *childhood* relationship and as I emerged from childhood Pappa's magic waned. By the time I went away to school he had ceased to be a central figure in my life though my affection for him never lessened. His death, at the end of December 1947, was my first experience of bereavement and it shattered me. The whole town mourned with us and many were the expressions of dismay because none of us was able to attend the funeral. On Christmas Eve my father had been immobilised by another attack of sciatica and I was looking after two invalids. This circumstance may have been a kindly gesture on Fate's part. My father, who had met none of his family since May 1946, would have been anguished by that reunion. He had no stomach for quarrels and only loyalty to his wife could ever have involved him in one.

Several years later I discovered that Mark, too, had opposed my parents at this time. He attached no great importance to formal schooling (for me) but felt that our domestic affairs could and should be arranged to suit my future as much as anyone else's. Also, he foresaw how hopelessly I could become trapped in the domestic cage once my mother—whose health was slowly but inexorably deteriorating—grew accustomed to my style of nursing.

On that Easter Monday Mark confronted my parents, while I was out cycling, and criticised them bluntly. For such a man to interfere in another family's affairs required enormous courage—generated, in this case, by powerful feelings of foreboding on my behalf. As I have already mentioned, there had never been any casual come-and-go between the Ryans and my parents, and Mark's occasional visits to our home had been very brief. This particular visit was still briefer. My parents—rigidly polite—at once made it clear that they were unprepared to discuss their plans for my future with anyone, however well disposed. "I came away with two fleas in each ear," Mark recalled cheerfully, ten years later. He never again met my mother, and when he and my father chanced to pass in the street they acknowledged each other's existence with a formality as pointed and cold as an icicle. However, this apparently uncomfortable situation suited me perfectly; to have had to share even a fraction of Mark's friendship with my parents would have deeply upset me. Although not normally possessive about people, I had always felt compelled to try to insulate this relationship from parental influences. And, as I realised much later, Mark felt exactly the same about insulating it from his own family.

We may have had this protective attitude towards our bond because it was such a curious one—of a kind that makes some people believe in reincarnation. It is, after all, not quite usual, or even proper, for a Roman Catholic priest to have as his closest friend a female, twenty-seven years his junior, who visits him in his secluded home in the country at all hours of the day and night. (As happened eventually, during various Murphy crises.) Had either of us cared about what the neighbours—or the parish priest, or the bishop—said or thought, we would probably have allowed our friendship to fade gently when I reached young womanhood. But of course we didn't care. And besides, such friendships have their own momentum and their own purpose, which is not always fully evident to the friends themselves.

Mark was a natural outsider; not for him the hearty greetings along the Main Street, the breezy first-name chatting-up of parishioners, the earnest discussions about hurling, coursing and the price of store-cattle. Some thought him too aloof, for he tried to hide an abnormal shyness behind a curt manner that could be disconcerting. Others, as the years passed, expressed surprise at the failure of so able a man to advance in his profession. But Mark's idea of clerical advancement had nothing to do with rising in the ranks. He was so devoid of respect for any Establishment, clerical or lay, that he might almost be described as a Christian anarchist. The letter of the law meant nothing to him, the spirit everything. He stealthily gave away every surplus penny he possessed and his generosity became a legend among the poor of three counties. When he died, beggars and tinkers and cattle drovers and lonely old age pensioners crowded into a remote country graveyard for his burial service.

Yet he was no stern ascetic; he drank and smoked and enjoyed golf and bridge. Amongst his few friends he was excellent company, witty, well informed and frequently irreverent with an inimitable caustic flippancy that would not have amused the average bishop (and 99 per cent of Irish bishops are dreadfully average). He read widely and wrote (anonymously) with considerable force and skill. Unlike most Irish people he thought naturally in international terms; and unlike most Irish priests he was neither scornful nor suspicious of the great non-European religions.

The only vice despised by Mark was what he called 'humbug'. Hypocrisy in any form he recognised at a glance and witheringly condemned. Otherwise, he was prepared to find endless excuses for human frailty; if he had had to choose a motto it would have been 'Judge not . . .' There was nothing lax or confused about his own standards—these were austerely high and uncompromisingly clear-cut—but his compassion was without limit. That virtue should be common enough among practising Christians, yet it is not. Too many of them are too sure that only *their* precise interpretation of God's law has any validity. They see themselves as being on the right side of the fence, from where they may benevolently extend forgiveness or pity or help to wrong-doers on the other side without ever showing true compassion—a word that implies 'fellow-feeling'. For Mark, however, there was no fence. And when I became familiar with Tibetan Buddhism I realised that the quality of his compassion was more Eastern than Western.

Mark and I were aged, respectively, thirty-two and five when our friendship was established—or, it may be, re-established. Yet it was from the beginning, in a very strange way, a friendship between equals. Of course I looked to Mark for advice—and even occasionally accepted it from him—and for the support and guidance and stability an older person could provide. But the essential nature of our relationship was not what might have been expected, given the disparity in our ages.

It is fashionable to take unusual relationships to bits, as though they were engines, and to explain and label their component parts. For instance—was Mark, to me, a father-figure, a man who made possible the sort of relationship I could not have with my own father? Or was he a hero to be worshipped because he was so kind and funny and cared so little for convention? Or was he a beloved guru, a priest whose concept of religion coincided, on the most fundamental issues, with my own? Was I, to him, a daughter-substitute? Or, later, a woman who might have become his mistress in any but an Irish context? Or, later still, a fascinating link with the wide world that was his natural habitat but from which he was isolated?

What does any of that matter? Maybe some or all of these elements formed strands in our bond, but the mysterious essence of such a rare friendship eludes analysis and makes nonsense of the trite 'father-figure' and 'daughter-substitute' labels. It matters only that for thirty-three years Mark stood steadfast at the centre of my emotional life while around the edges raged all the storms whipped up by passion, frustration, loyalty, loneliness, doubt, guilt and faithlessness. Francis Bacon can say the rest—'A principal fruit of friendship is the ease and discharge of the fulness of the heart, which passions of all kinds do cause and induce ... No receipt openeth the heart but a true friend, to whom you may impart whatsoever lieth upon the heart to oppress it, in kind of civil shrift or confession ... The second fruit of friendship is healthful and sovereign for the understanding, as the first is for the affections; for friendhips maketh indeed a fair day in the affection from storm and tempests, but it maketh daylight in the understanding, out of darkness and confusion of thoughts; neither is to be understood only of faithful counsel, which a man receiveth from his friend; but before you come to that, certain it is, that whosoever hath his mind fraught with many thoughts, his wits and understanding do clarify and break up, in the communicating and discoursing with another; he tosseth his thoughts more easily; he marshalleth them more orderly; he seeth how they look when they are turned into words; finally, he waxeth wiser than himself; and that more by an hour's discourse than by a day's meditation.'

12

My adolescent memories are of abrupt changes in outlook and unpredictable moods which must have made me more than usually trying; yet nobody seems to have regarded these developments as 'a problem'. Somehow my parents made me feel that certain of their standards were as immutable as the laws of nature and could never be abandoned without shame. But they always clearly differentiated between standards and opinions—or tastes. One had to tell the truth, pay bills promptly, consider servants (if any), avoid harmful gossip, respect confidences and remember that politeness has to do primarily with other people's feelings. However, should one chance, by some lamentable disorientation of the sensibilities, to prefer Mendelssohn to Bach, or Rupert Brooke to Milton, that was nobody's business or misfortune but one's own. This allowed ample scope for scorn and revolution, without any threat to law and order, and for many of the parental preferences I cultivated, at various stages, a vehement though seldom lasting contempt.

Perhaps the extent to which today's teenagers baffle me is partly a result of the abnormal circumstances of my own adolescence. Despite having adult responsibilities, my material dependence on my parents remained total and seemed unlikely to lessen in the foreseeable future. By the standards of most modern youngsters my activities were pathetically circumscribed, and to outsiders—like the Dublin Murphys—my whole way of life looked uneventful and dull to a degree.

Yet it was nothing of the sort. Were I asked to pin-point the most exciting period of a life that latterly has been more eventful than most, I would say—'The years from fourteen to seventeen'. But I must be careful here. How much do we romanticise youth and hope and energy, so that only their glory is remembered? Perhaps all I should say is that in retrospect those years seem to have contained much happiness and little unhappiness, despite a constant underlying irritation at having to waste so much time every day on tedious domestic chores. And despite occasional brief—but intense—moods of depression caused by personality clashes with my mother.

Yet 'happiness' is not the right word; it implies a lack of complications and a tranquillity which are uncharacteristic of adolescence. Elation would be more accurate, the elation of discovering literature and music, combined with the sheer animal pleasure of being young and healthy and very vigorous. Adolescence is supremely a time of discovery. To me Shakespeare represented not an aspect of the examination tyrant but a stimulating expanse of beauty. And music was a shared joy which drew the three of us very close, in a sort of truce-atmosphere, even when parent-child relations were at their worst. Then there was the natural beauty of West Waterford. At any season a walk or a cycle aroused almost unbearable delight. Apparently I was missing a lot; yet I desired, during those years, no more than I had.

For three months after leaving school I was unwontedly abstemious and wrote nothing; the long-drawn-out family quarrel was unnerving me more than I realised. Then an idea for a boys' adventure story came to me and I began to write frenziedly, sitting up in bed until the small hours, covering sheet after sheet of foolscap. And I discovered that my approach to writing had changed. No longer was I satisfied with verbal bulk and a hair's-breadth escape per paragraph. The hero of that story became to me a real person, instead of remaining an inhumanly tough yet sentimentally gallant Biggles/Bulldog Drummond hybrid. He still had 'keen fearless grey eyes and a firm mouth' (I quote from the typescript, recently accidentally disinterred), but his speech was credible though he retained an unfortunate tendency to strangle people with one swift movement. More important, however, was the fact that I now began to rewrite, and to find pleasure in seeing sentences improve, even if I had had to sacrifice three words of six syllables each to achieve that improvement. There is a control of language, a sense of rhythm, an intimation of style in that story—though I wrote and rewrote all 43,000 words of it in exactly three weeks.

Not until it was finished did I think of secretly sending it to a publisher—secretly because I wished to avoid parental sympathy when it was rejected. I felt very adult and earnest as I withdrew all my meagre savings from the post office, looked up the address of a suitable typist on the last but one page of the *TLS* and took down a list of possible publishers from *The Writers' and Artists' Year Book* in my father's office. I was now actively engaged in the literary world, not just daydreaming about it. The most I really hoped for were some constructive words of advice to a fourteen-year-old from kindly publishers' editors. And that is exactly what I got. I cannot remember how often that typescript was posted to England—at least half-a-dozen times—but it never came home without a positively encouraging letter accompanying the rejection slip. These letters at least confirmed that my ambition was not built on self-delusion. The literary world had taken me seriously enough to urge me on; and that, for the moment, satisfied me. I had never visualised myself as an adolescent prodigy and I came of a breed used to taking rejection slips—as it were—on the chin.

Nietzsche may have proclaimed 'the death of God' a century ago, but it took time for the news to spread and in my generation most Europeans grew up under the influence of firmly held religious beliefs, not necessarily orthodox, but involving an adherence to moral standards based on Christian ethics. Thus we are unique, for our adult world became a place where, as John Wren-Lewis has put it, 'for the first time in human history, the general climate of educated opinion has lost the religious assumptions that have hitherto been almost universal'. So we are in a position to enjoy the best of both worlds. From the old world we have inherited, if we wish to claim the legacy, a certain stability; we have something specific to move away from—and to refer back to, albeit selectively, in moments of crisis. Of course a traditional religious upbringing can also lead to innumerable irrational conflicts such as our juniors, who were 'born free', will never have to resolve. But I still feel that we are a fortunate group.

Yet for many the loss of 'religious assumptions' has—only too obviously—been demoralising and frightening. Even to consider such a loss impersonally could frighten people like my parents whose own faith was, apparently, impregnable. I remember, when I was seventeen, hearing my father gloomily quoting to my mother a prediction from Belloc—'What I think will spring out of the new filth is a new religion. I think that there will arise in whatever parts of Christendom remain, say, 200 years hence . . . a new religion, because human society cannot live on air . . . This conception of a new religion (and, therefore, an evil one) arising out of the rottenness of the grave of truth, seems today at once fantastic and unpleasant. Unpleasant I admit it is; fantastic I do not believe it to be.' My parents of course shared Belloc's view, but by then I found the notion of a new religion exhilarating.

About two years previously, however, I too would have agreed with Belloc. I had then gone through a phase of intense orthodox fervour which was altogether inconsistent with my general attitude towards religion, either before or since. This, I believe, is a common adolescent stage; and in Ireland, even today, a disquieting number of people seem to develop no further. Suddenly I began to enjoy going to church—for me a hitherto rather boring routine accepted only because it was so rigorously prescribed by one's home, school and social environment. No longer content with Sunday Mass, I now went to the convent chapel every morning at seven-thirty; and if there was an evening service (known as 'devotions') I went to that too; and I rejoiced on the first Friday of each month because then the service lasted for an hour instead of half-an-hour. I also went to confession once a week though I cannot recall committing any notable sins during this peroid. Emotionally I seemed to need the various rituals and to thrive, most improbably, on Irish Catholicism's unwholesome mush of sentimentality and superstition. But it was also important to feel that through personal prayer I was in direct touch with Christ. (The Father and the Holy Ghost introduced unnecessary complications so I left them out of it.) Had I 'got religion' a decade later, that would have been understandable enough. But by the time ritual and prayer might have served as an escape or a comfort they had ceased to have meaning for me.

My fervour lasted a year or so and then quite quickly evaporated. Meanwhile I had begun to read a little about other religions, an interest kindled by my pen-friendship with a Sikh girl. Mahn Kaur was four years my senior and lived in Kuala Lumpur, where her family had settled before she was born. Her enquiring mind and lucid, indefatigable pen did a great deal for me. Having been educated by Irish nuns, she wanted to find out as much as she could about Ireland and Europe and the various Christian Churches. In return, she told me about the Sikh religion, which inevitably made me curious about Islam and Hinduism, which eventually led on to Buddhism.

Mahn Kaur was naturally much concerned about contemporary events in India. We had begun our correspondence in September 1946, when Mark noticed a letter from Mahn Kaur in a Catholic newspaper appealing for a pen-friend 'interested in history and religion'. And this personal link with the subcontinent, slight though it was, made me feel deeply involved, emotionally, in the terrible events of 1947. These were not just another distant disaster reported in the newspapers. All Mahn Kaur's relatives lived in the Punjab.

For four or five years we wrote to each other at least once a fortnight. This correspondence, and the ripples it spread, became one of my main interests. Mahn Kaur was my only contact with an inaccessible world which I longed to experience for myself and it consoled me to feel that Fate was indirectly catering for this longing. More important, the reading she stimulated heightened my inborn awareness that all the religions of mankind are equally valid. As some modern Hindus express it, they are all fingers pointing at the moon. And it is the moon that matters. My parents would have condemned this attitude as the vague evasiveness of a lazy thinker. But to me it was the truth and having seen it I could not worry about my own religious label—or the lack of one. If certain individuals felt that they did not belong, naturally, to any religious group, what did it matter? The moon was there anyway. And worship or contemplation does not have to be restricted to churches or monasteries.

I remember one very cold January morning standing in the kitchen by the turf-range (a wartime innovation) while eagerly opening a letter from Malaya. As I slit the envelope I saw, just for an instant, the closeness of my mental relationship with Mahn Kaur as a measure of my closeness to Asia; and our whole correspondence seemed very much a preparation. Those rare moments when we apparently get a signal from the future do not effect the conduct of one's daily life. But they have their value below the level on which one feels impatient or thwarted —or even hopeless.

A few weeks later came Gandhi's assassination. I was in bed with tonsillitis and I shall never forget switching on the wireless to hear that news. During those years I was mesmerised by the writings of Gandhi and I regarded him with a rapture which has since been considerably modified.

Shakespeare, another adolescent obsession, has worn better. At school I had detested *The Merchant of Venice*, not being yet ready for Elizabethan English. (How many thirteen-year-olds are thus given an enduring distaste for great literature?) But three years later I was 'saved' when Anew McMaster's famous touring company came to Lismore. They played *Hamlet* in a huge draughty building known as the Hippodrome, which soon after fell down of its own volition. The place was packed to the door—as it would never be now, with a television set in 95 per cent of Irish homes. Most of the townsfolk were there and, tethered along the sides of the road, in both directions, stood the horses, ponies, jennets and donkeys who had provided transport for Shakespeare's rural fans. The response was tremendous at the end of every scene; in several places the floor boards collapsed beneath the hob-nailed boots of enthusiastic farm lads. It is sometimes argued that television has a unifying effect on a nation or a community because so many people watch the same programmes. But that is a very spurious unity compared to the delighted converging on the Hippodrome of most of Lismore.

I had never read *Hamlet*—or any Shakespeare, after my delivery from *The Merchant of Venice*—and presumably neither had the majority around me. Yet we were completely carried away by that performance. At the end I emerged in a fever of delight, feeling very disinclined to go home to bed. It was a wild October night. Clouds were flying before a south wind so that the full moon seemed herself in flight. Possibly that moon had something to do with my mood. I cycled up to the Vee —ten miles above Lismore—and looking down onto the silvered plain of Tipperary felt a passion of gratitude, directed towards no one in particular, because I had been born. I got home at five-fifteen—not realising, then, how lucky I was to have parents who registered no alarm at breakfast-time when their sixteen-year-old daughter explained that she had been out all night. Both regarded cycling to the Vee by moonlight as a perfectly natural reaction to one's first *Hamlet*.

Within a year of that initiation ceremony, I was not only reading and enjoying Shakespeare but studying him, seriously. All my pocket-money was being spent on esoteric volumes of Shakespeariana which my father refused to buy for the public library because they would only have a readership of one. By this time a spare room had been converted into my study, with bookshelves around two walls from floor to ceiling. It occurred to me now that I might after all have taken to university life; but I wasted no time on regrets. In my private Shakespearian studies I was at least free to please myself while flexing whatever rudimentary scholarly muscles were then demanding exercise. I had never before concentrated on anything other than writing stories. Now, though my studies sometimes became tedious, I would not allow their tedium to deter me. While writing several learned (as I supposed) essays on various Shakespearian controversies, I discovered how essential self-discipline is in any activity of this sort. It was all great fun—very much the sort of thing to which Pappa had devoted half a lifetime, though I did not then see this—and it gratified me to find that I was capable of becoming slightly knowledgeable about something.

For relaxation, during those years, I read almost all the works of all the great English novelists, from Defoe to Hardy—only skipping Walter Scott, who to me seemed insupportably dreary, and some of the minor Trollopes which numerically defeated me. For good measure I read translations of the obvious French and Russians, including *War and Peace* during a lumbago attack. When I look now at those scores of volumes—standing row upon row, fat and formidable—I marvel at my idea of relaxation some twenty-five years ago. Many I have indeed reread with increased appreciation and many others I would like to reread.

But not *all* . . . And a few I am reluctant to return to, fearing disillusion. *Middlemarch*, for instance, was amongst the most memorable experiences of my youth. Reading it seemed like watching God creating the world in miniature.

In 1948 the reopening of Lismore's Lawn Tennis Club induced me to modify slightly my solitary ways. I became a keen though never skilful member and for the next few years spent a couple of hours on the courts almost every fine summer evening. However, my interest in the club remained exclusively athletic. I got on well with all my fellow members—the majority were several years older than me—but never wished to be involved in any of their peripheral activities. Happily, this allergy to social functions was not mistaken for standoffishness. I was, I think, accepted with friendly tolerance as the inevitable freakish outcome of my parents' union.

The tennis club was our chief centre for the promotion of marriage and I attentively observed the progress of various courtships—but always with a certain detachment, as though I were studying the customs of another race. Even at sixteen, I had a strong premonition that I would never marry. Possibly the predictability of the average married life put me off; it was the antithesis of my ideal unplanned existence—travelling, writing, not knowing what was going to happen next year or next month or even next week. And I have already stated my belief that we are equipped at the start of adult life with a few pieces of basic foreknowledge—whether or not we choose to use them. This is not as fanciful as it may sound. Our lives, after all, are moulded by our temperaments even more than our temperaments are moulded by circumstances. And on the threshold of adulthood it is possible to have enough self-awareness to see the probable outline of one's future. Already I had noted the qualities needed to make a marriage work and I did not think I either possessed them or wanted, even if that were possible, to acquire them. I saw myself as a person too strong-willed, self-centred and fundamentally—if not obviously—arrogant to make a success of the married state. There is a vast difference between being a good friend—or a good mistress—and being a good wife. As long as people of my sort are free they can seem endlessly patient, understanding, cheerful—

even unselfish in a crisis. But deprive them of their freedom and everything turns sour. In my teens I could not have expressed all this: yet I knew it.

Our household had always included at least one—and often two or three—cats; but to keep a dog was not practical until my return from school. Then, just as my mother and I were debating what breed to get—my father had been badly bitten as a child and feared all breeds—I came upon Bran. A pure-bred Irish terrier, he was tied by a very short rope to the drain-pipe of an isolated cottage and looked half-starved and cowed. He had large bare patches on his back and flanks and when I went nearer I saw that these were red and raw. At first he shrank from my outstretched hand, then he sniffed it nervously, then I rubbed the roots of his ears and he wagged his tail incredulously. I reckoned that he was scarcely two years old. There was no one around the cottage, but early next morning I returned. Bran was still tied in the same spot and trembling all over; what remained of his red-gold coat was sodden and obviously he had been left to lie out on concrete during the previous night's steady rain. When I rapped sharply on the door it was opened by a shifty-looking man with blood shot eyes, a whiskey-laden breath and a week's beard. He claimed to have bought Bran from passing tinkers for £5 but offered him to me for £3 because of his 'bad skin'. This infuriated me; no such man would then spend £5 on a dog. I replied that I was not interested in buying the terrier but that I was very interested in the way he was being kept. And I added that the gardai, too, might be interested. (Privately I doubted this; cruelty to animals is rarely seen as such in countries where most of the inhabitants have for generations been 'deprived'.) However, on my mentioning the gardai the shifty eyes grew shiftier and their owner hurriedly made me a present of Bran.

We went straight to the vet, who prescribed train-oil and sulphur for Bran's eczema—a completely effective cure, though messy and protracted. After six months he had regained top condition and was acknowledged to be the most handsome dog for miles around. He slept in a corner of my bedroom—he was just too large to be a comfortable on-the-bed dog—and was respectful towards the cats who patronised him from my eiderdown. Unlike most of his breed he had a timid nature, perhaps because of puppyhood traumas. But he had no vices and despite his age proved easy to train. Eventually he could be trusted alone in a room with a shopping-basket of meat on the floor, if he had been told not to touch it. Even my father grew to love him.

Bran accompanied me on short cycles, of up to fifteen miles or so, but this meant my having to pedal slowly lest his heart might be strained. His loyalty was such that had I cycled to Dublin at eighteen miles an hour he would have tried to keep up. One of our favourite runs was to the foot of the Knockmealdowns, where I would leave my bicycle by the roadside and walk Bran over the heather and bogs. During the summer we sometimes swam in Bayl Lough, a wide lake—semi-encircled by almost sheer mountain—which always looks black and according to local legend is bottomless.

On one such walk, near the spot where I had got lost as a ten-year-old, Bran was set upon without warning by a large black and white mongrel who appeared out of nowhere. In those days one rarely saw other people or dogs on the Knockmealdowns and I felt mildly curious when a very tall, thin man with a slight limp and a shooting stick emerged from a dip in the ground. He called angrily to the mongrel, whose name was William, but was too far away to intervene. So I had to rescue Bran when it became clear that William was having much the best of it.

As William's owner approached us I saw that he had a conspicuously scarred face. He seemed genuinely distressed about Bran, who was crouching behind my legs, shivering. Meanwhile William stood a few yards away gazing at the horizon with a self-satisfied air, ignoring his master's scolding. I made polite, forgiving noises and then, as Bran had in fact been quite badly bitten on a hindleg, I turned to accompany William's owner back to the road. At seventeen I was abnormally shy, but my companion seemed even shyer. Yet he was in his mid-thirties, I judged. For once I felt at an advantage and talked almost eloquently during that half-hour walk through the bright, windy April afternoon. But we exchanged no personal information and when we parted I did not expect ever to see William's owner again.

At that time my father occasionally took over my nursing and domestic duties for a day, which left me free to enjoy a serious cycle of sixty or seventy miles. (Otherwise, I was never off duty for more than four hours at a stretch—usually from 6.00 to 10.00 pm.) So it was that I left Lismore one sunny morning towards the end of August, intending to do a round trip over the mountains and return through Cappoquin. At the Vee I paused for a swim in Bayl Lough and afterwards, as I walked up the track from the lake to the road, I saw a vaguely familiar figure strolling near my bicycle. It took me a few moments to recognise William's owner; in the four months since our first meeting I had almost forgotten him. This time he had no dog and he told me in an expressionless voice that William had been poisoned two days previously. Before I could say anything he added, very stiffly, "Would you care to motor to the sea with me?"

I hesitated, not for any conventional reason but because my few opportunities for long-distance cycling were so precious. Then I realised that a refusal would be misinterpreted—and would hurt. I also realised that though I had scarcely thought about William's owner since April we had in fact established an embryonic relationship during our first meeting. The opinions I had then formed were only now crystallising in my mind; and the chief impression was of loneliness.

When my companion held open the passenger door of the A40 I noticed a flicker of alarm in his eyes as though he were slightly taken aback by the situation our joint impetuosity had created; yet neither of us was really disconcerted by the behaviour of the other. Not until we were both in the car did he introduce himself. Then, as I was about to reciprocate that belated civility, he explained apologetically that he already knew who I was.

By the time we reached the coast, twenty-five miles away, we had exchanged potted biographies. Information that one might expect to gather from a new friend over weeks or months was given by Godfrey in moments. His need to communicate was not disguised by the precise, impersonal formality with which he told his story—almost as though he were filling in a form for *Who's Who*, carefully giving all the dates while ignoring the emotions.

Significantly, he began by explaining that he had acquired

his limp and his scars in a Japanese prison camp. That he should have referred at all to those disabilities seemed to me a tremendous compliment. And it was. He never again referred to them, or to his war experiences. I longed to question him about the latter—I had never before met an ex-POW—but plainly to do so was not on. As for his scars, they were not of the romantic sort that make a man look more manly. They were horrible. One needed the minimum of imagination to understand why he had chosen a solitary life.

Since 1947 Godfrey had been living on his army pension in an enlarged cottage not far from the Vee; the enlarging had been necessary to accommodate his books. A manservant looked after him. During the war his wife had found someone else; she was ten years his senior and he had married her while still an undergraduate. In 1947 the divorce had gone through, but it was of no use to Godfrey. As a High Anglican he did not consider himself free to remarry; his attitude here was identical to the most orthodox Irish Catholic's. To me this sad though hardly unusual story seemed a tragedy on the grand scale. I could have wept for Godfrey—especially because he had explained things so austerely, with no taint of self-pity.

I remember our getting out of the car at Goat Island—an isolated cove, even today—and facing each other for a moment in silence. Then Godfrey said, "Let's bathe!" and as he turned away my heart did something odd and I thought, 'This is absurd! I must be falling in love!' It did not, however, occur to me that Godfrey might be guilty of the same absurdity.

We separated to undress chastely behind rocks that were far apart and after our bathe—Godfrey was an excellent swimmer, I noted approvingly—we dressed equally chastely and sat on the grassy cliff top to share the picnic lunch that I had brought from home. It was meagre fare for two, but this did not matter as falling in love had quite taken away my appetite.

When we parted on the road above Bayl Lough Godfrey thanked me for a very pleasant day and I thanked him for a very pleasant day and we said good-bye without mentioning the possibility of any future meeting. But as I free-wheeled home —euphorically taking hairpin bends with my hands behind my back—I assumed that future meetings would somehow happen.

First love at seventeen soars above the practical details of time and place.

A fortnight passed without my seeing or hearing anything more of Godfrey, yet my certainty that we would meet again never wavered. I considered myself a most fortunate person and impatiently to demand more than the inner bliss I already enjoyed would have seemed greedy. In my daydreams I tried to imagine our future conversations, but I never imagined Godfrey falling in love with me. To think of being loved by this noble—almost god-like—figure would have seemed so unreasonable that it was not a fit subject even for daydreams. To love was enough. By any standards, I was an almost unbelievably naive seventeen-year-old.

Then, on a misty September evening, as I was swimming in the Blackwater a few miles upstream from Lismore, Godfrey appeared on the bank above me. He waved casually and tactfully sauntered off into the next field. I scrambled out of the water, dressed without drying and followed him. We walked until it was dusk through the dense woods on the ridge above the river. Godfrey, I now discovered, had studied archaeology and also knew a lot about Shakespeare. We had been two hours together when we came to the track where his car was parked and said good-bye. But this time Godfrey added in a matter-of-fact voice, "I expect we'll meet again quite soon." "I expect so," I agreed, dizzy with joy. And I cycled home to pursue my Shakespearian studies extra-diligently.

Even I realised that Godfrey must have deliberately sought me out by the river—a hard task, for someone unfamiliar with the countryside around Lismore. Yet still I did not think it possible that he might be interested in me as a woman. No doubt his emphasis on his permanently married state had a lot to do with this. Clearly he was not the sort of man to womanise indiscriminately and if he could not marry he would not fall in love. To me it was as simple as that. So I believed that he regarded me as a congenial friend—a nonconformist like himself—with whom he could for some reason overcome his self-consciousness about his appearance. I prided myself on my ability to conceal my own emotions and play it his way. To do otherwise, I reflected melodramatically, would be to wreck a friendship that he needed as much as I needed the hidden joy of being in love. And so I continued to think and feel for three years, during which we met perhaps once a fortnight—occasionally for a day, more usually for a few hours and always where we were unlikely to be observed.

My parents knew nothing of this new relationship. With them I had by then reached a fiercely secretive stage—the beginning of my futile rebellion against that trap foreseen by Mark when I left school. He of course was given a detailed account of the friendship with Godfrey. He listened sympathetically and wisely refrained from pointing out how improbable it was that a man of thirty-seven would remain interested only in my views on Shakespeare.

Characteristically, I never paused to wonder where this impractical love was leading me. To some those three years may seem arid, unfulfilling and wasted, but they did not seem so to me then—nor do they now. My own summing-up of the situation was ridiculously defective, yet the relationship between Godfrey and me was neither unreal nor—in any but the narrowest sense—unfulfilling. Despite the apparent artificiality of its framework, it developed and matured and grew richer as the months and the years passed. And for me it had—as I see it in retrospect—a most precious and irrecoverable beauty. For it was the fairest flower in the garden of youth: love without passion.

13

At the beginning of 1951 my mother announced that something must soon be done to get me out of Lismore, however briefly. She had always maintained—and not only, I believe, because it was a convenient conscience-soother—that for girls travel is the best form of education. Yet I was no less astonished than elated by this announcement. Gradually, over the years, my liberty had been whittled away as my mother became more dependent on my nursing. So how did she propose to organise things in my absence? I felt touched and grateful when she declared briskly that she could easily manage again for a few weeks as she had done for months while I was at school. The less obvious implications of that declaration did not strike me then, or for many years afterwards. I was much too close to what was happening to look at it.

Even now it is hard to estimate how far my mother's health had deteriorated by this time. But undoubtedly her demands for attention were already unconsciously prompted by a determination to dominate me. I might argue against scrubbing the hall floor every day and cleaning the windows every week—and indeed I flatly refused to do such chores more than once a quarter, when even by my standards they had become necessary. But I could not argue if my mother requested some attention. I could not tell her that she didn't really need to use the bedpan, or to have her position changed, or her room made warmer or cooler, or her thirst quenched. So as I became more mulish about housework and cooking she became more demanding of nursing attention.

My mulishness was not caused only by an inherent dislike for domestic chores. It is natural to be still dependent on and living with one's parents at fifteen or sixteen, but to be in exactly the same situation at nineteen felt very unnatural to me. When I compared my own situation with that of other young-sters, even factory-hands or shop-assistants seemed enviable. They were leading their own lives and earning a weekly wage—and they had whole week-ends off. More freedom was what I longed for. My lack of money mattered only because it sym-bolised being unfree; every necessity was provided by my parents and my pocket-money was adequate for the few luxuries I craved—such as *Collected Commentaries on 'Hamlet': 1650–1950.*

However, despite my bondage I was still enjoying life too much to feel more than occasional spasms of discontent. By temperament I was inclined to count my advantages rather than my disadvantages and envy of factory-hands never went far enough to make me wish that I had been born one. Pos-sibly, without Godfrey, I might have been less resigned; at that time our relationship mattered to me more than anything else. But of course it is also possible, if one is prepared to look back with cold objectivity, that this relationship developed under adverse conditions, and assumed such importance, simply because my life was so restricted. I needed the emotional excitement of being in love. And it would be rash to pretend to know whether we create what we need or whether our needs are supplied by a benevolent Fate. If, at nineteen, I had been free to travel for a year in Asia, would I have chosen instead to remain at home within reach of Godfrey? I doubt if I would.

I left Lismore on April 15, 1951, to spend three weeks cycling through Wales and Southern England—including, inevitably, five days in Stratford-upon-Avon. Some of the neighbours were aghast when they heard that I had taken off, alone, on a bicycle, to travel through what was little better than a pagan land. And they were even more aghast when they realised that my parents had encouraged me to commit this outrage.

At nineteen I had never before left Ireland, apart from one Triple Crown excursion to Twickenham. (Where, having just finished *Historic Doubts on the Life and Reign of King Richard the Third*, I deserted my fellow-fans, after the match, to search unsuccessfully for Strawberry Hill.) I was fervently nationalist and anti-partitionist and therefore, in theory, anti-British. Honour required me to see Britain as a foreign country because my school history books had taught that the British were solely responsible for all Ireland's past woes and present handicaps. Thus I was shocked to discover, as I cycled through Wales and England, that it was impossible to feel 'abroad'. Half of me seemed 'to belong' in Britain. Having been in love with a quintessential Englishman for two years may have contributed to this. Much more important, however, was the fact that I had grown up by the light of Eng. Lit. To me the British were comprehensible and congenial (to my great annoyance) because their history and literature were mine, too, with modifications and additions. At times I found them as exasperating as they can find us; but they were never baffling, as we so often are to them. One knew what made them tick. Of course the Welsh and the English differed from me, but no more than a Welshman differs from a Scotsman or a Kerryman from a Dubliner. What we had in common went deeper than what divided us. Thomas Davis made many bigoted and stupid remarks, but he was right when he said, 'A people without a language of its own is only half a nation. A nation should guard its language more than its territories—'tis a surer barrier, and more important frontier than fortress or river . . . To lose your native tongue, and learn that of an alien, is the worst badge of conquest—it is the chain on the soul. To have lost entirely the national language is death; the fetter has worn through.' In 1951, however, I was not yet ready to admit that an Ireland in every way independent of Britain could only be a mirage. It was too soon for me to analyse detachedly the Republican ideals and prejudices acquired from generations of militant Murphys. I therefore developed a form of cultural schizophrenia, with my nationalistic half resolutely remembering that Britain was 'the ancient enemy' (though already Mark and Godfrey had seen that eventually my 'literary' rather than my 'political' half would win). Indeed, the fact that the implacable nationalism inherited from my father was being threatened by the apolitical liberalism inherited from my mother made me even more aggressively Irish and proud of it. Not for many years would I be willing to recognise that Ireland's uniquely close relationship with Britain is impervious to 'constitutional rearrangements'—and that to admit this is not to be a shoneen (i.e. pro-British) but a realist.

Happily my cultural schizophrenia detracted nothing from my enjoyment of Britain. I proved that I could cycle 100 miles a day without undue effort and I cut back on food to spend wildly in second-hand bookshops, sending a postcard home almost daily to announce that another parcel of 'wonderful finds' had been despatched. Every evening I met in my Youth Hostel congenial representatives of the Great British Public and a stimulating cross-section of early fellow-tourists from Europe and America. At Stratford I actually *spoke* to Professor Dover Wilson for ten minutes after a lecture on *Richard II*—undoubtedly the highlight of the whole trip. And there too I met four undergraduates who invited me to contact them when I got to Oxford and gave me an illicit glimpse of Balliol night life. In London I rivalled the most gluttonous of American culture-vultures and packed an improbable number of concerts, ballets, operas, museums and galleries into eight days. And everywhere I found the allegedly reserved English spontaneously kind and helpful—even talkative, if the stranger was prepared to initiate the conversation.

My father never commented on the long article I wrote about Oxford on my return home, but it must have alarmed him, as a symptom of my drift away from the true-blue (or true-green) Republican tradition. In the course of it I wrote:

Oxford is a state of mind more than a place. One may enter it with reverence, or in a tolerantly amused mood—those quaint British, with their slavish adherence to tradition—or with indifference; but no one can leave it without feeling that they have been through a most exhilarating experience. Its potent, subtle charm compels recognition—seizes you with a gentle fierceness—you may resist but finally you must surrender.

Who can say what that charm is? (Perhaps all charm is merely a subjective quality and what constitutes Oxford's spell for me would mean little to another.) It is a place of paradoxes, of illogical customs often initiated in the centuries that knew Chaucer or Shakespeare, yet still revered by all if somewhat imperfectly comprehended by many. Also it is a place of the wildest unconventionality and irresponsibility. Undergraduates who seem able to discuss anything from Industrial Relations to Japanese art will in a moment turn to playing a practical joke that I would have considered infantile at twelve. Which reminds me of a cat I saw in the Garden Quad at Balliol: a plump, elderly cat she was. Anywhere else she would have sat sedately in the sun, meticulously performing her ablutions, but there she gambolled under the chestnuts and elms in an abandoned manner, as though the imperishable youthfulness which is an essential ingredient of the Oxford atmosphere had permeated her matronly body. For although the centuries have flowed over Oxford, have deposited there learning and beauty and dignity, they have not eroded her youth. How could they, when every year brings a fresh stream of undergraduates, high-spirited, enthusiastic, carefree, bearing the fragile ideals, the crazy theories, the irrepressible gaiety and optimism of the very young. They make of the ancient University of Oxford a Peter Pan among cities.

In a sense Oxford seems strangely un-British, though the cradle of so many of England's finest minds and traditions. I pondered long on this. Is it because it came into being long before what Belloc defined as the 'consciousness of nationality' developed? And so it retains a medieval attitude which allows the more important things of the spirit and the mind to predominate over political or racial conflicts or characteristics. And yet—such is the many-sidedness of the place—you feel there that you have your finger on the very pulse of England, that pulse which has beaten steadily whatever ills have afflicted the body of the nation. It is of Oxford that Englishmen may justly boast—not of Empires, or factories, of athletes or inventions—but of this quintessence of all that is best in the English, and the European, heritage.

There was an underlying sadness about my reaction to Oxford, though at the time I firmly refused to dwell upon this. I had never regretted leaving school at fourteen, but now, suddenly, I saw that university was another matter. During those few days and nights of innocent though often rule-breaking fun with my young Balliol men and their girlfriends —it was during the Eights Week—I found myself in a world where I naturally belonged. Or could have belonged, in other circumstances; as my article reveals, it would have been too late, in 1951, for me to adapt to that world even had I then been free to do so. I was only nineteen—younger than all my new friends—yet I felt considerably older than they were. I wholeheartedly enjoyed their companionship, as I still would, but they made me realise that, having never known what it was to be without adult responsibilities, I had skipped a whole stage of youthfulness.

For someone who had spent most of their nineteen years within a thirty-mile radius of Lismore, those were three seminal weeks. They also provided material for my first published writing, apart from childhood competition essays. I sold three long articles, on my impressions of Stratford, London and Oxford, to the old monthly *Hibernia*—which had nothing in common with the present-day journal of that name. Each earned me two guineas and it was most gratifying to see my work in print and to be paid sixteen weeks' pocket-money for enjoying myself. Yet the thrill was less than might have been expected. I had never wanted to be a journalist, freelance or otherwise. I was not a 100-metre, or even a 1,500-metre, writer; the marathon was my distance. And in the foreseeable future there was no possibility of my being free to do a book-length journey.

A year later I set out on a five-week continental tour, taking time-saving trains from Fishguard to Dover, *en route* for Belgium. And next day, in a First World War cemetery, on a vibrant spring afternoon, I passed one of those unforgettable hours which in retrospect are seen to have been milestones in one's development.

I was alone in the April sunshine among all those small, neat, green graves—British graves. And the sadness of that waste utterly overwhelmed me. Most had been my age, give or take a few years. Had they lived they would have been little older than my parents. But they had died—for what? For King and Country, for the defence of small nations, for the end of all warring, for a lot of platitudes. If this was nationalism in action, did it make sense? German nationalism, British nationalism, French nationalism, Irish nationalism—all decked out in flowery phrases, glorifying death, urging young men on to slaughter each other. The occupants of these graves should since have enjoyed some thirty-five years of life, as I was even then enjoying the sun and the breeze and the few white clouds in the wide blue sky above Flanders. And it didn't matter to me that they were British; I could only think of them as humanity squandered. At twenty I was tough and my blood was the blood of fighters. Yet I wept that afternoon. I could see no point in the waste and the grief and the pseudo-heroism cultivated by each country's leaders. How could any nation that claimed to be civilised fight such a war? I decided then that nationalism (as distinct from patriotism) is an affliction which humanity needs to be cured of as soon as possible

Walking back to my bicycle, I felt a sudden anguished embarrassment on my father's behalf; and a contempt for him that humiliated me because it reeked of disloyalty. He could not have reacted as I was doing to all those graves. I had grown up, but he hadn't. I was too young to understand that 'growing up', in this sense, was immeasurably harder for his generation, whatever their nationality, than for mine. At eighteen he had entered an English jail to spend three years sewing sacks for the post office, wretchedly fed and crawling with lice. And now I wonder how soon I would have 'grown up' had I endured a similar experience.

From Flanders I cycled to Bruges, Antwerp, Brussels, Luxemburg, Maastricht, Aachen, Bonn and so up the Rhine—which greatly disappointed me—to Mainz. There I spent a week-end with the Hilckmanns, whom we were to have visited in August 1939. Then on to Heidelberg, Rothenburg, Biberach, Regensburg, Creglingen (where Riemenschneider's Marienaltar excited me more than anything else on this trip), Munich, the Black Forest, Strasbourg and across central France. In Paris I spent four days feeling euphoric, except when I was kidnapped one night by White Slavers in the Place de la Concorde on my way back from the Opera to my left-bank doss-house.

It was midnight as I crossed the Place de la Concorde and when a large car pulled up just ahead of me I ignored it, assuming that some lustful male was in search of willing prey. Then a pleasant-looking woman beckoned me and, speaking in English with only a slight accent, warned me that it is very dangerous for girls to walk alone in Paris after midnight.

"Where are you staying?" she asked. "You are taking a terrible risk. My husband and I would like to take you to your hotel." I was too touched by this solicitude to point out that I *enjoyed* walking around Paris in the middle of the night. And because it would have seemed churlish to refuse such a kind offer I slipped into the back seat, explaining that I was lodging just off the Rue St Jacques.

It struck me as rather odd that my protectress left the front seat to sit beside me, but I became suspicious only as we passed Notre Dame. As I began to protest that we had missed our turning my companion switched on an electric torch and opened a large photograph album which she laid on my knee. "Look at those, my dear," she said. "We're just going to take you home for a little fun and a drink—some champagne, you would like? And then within an hour you shall be safely home in bed."

While she was speaking I had been staring at the album with a mixture of horror, terror and nausea. I had never before seen pornographic photographs—or, indeed, even heard of them. Noticing my expression, the woman's voice changed. "Look at me!" she said sharply. I looked up at her and she ordered, "Keep on looking—don't move!" Terrified, I kept on looking; she was pointing one finger directly at my eyes and gazing fixedly at me by torchlight. When I realised that she was trying to hypnotise me I swung away and groped for the door-handle—though we had crossed the river and were travelling at some 40 mph up the Boulevard de la Bastille. Her voice changed again. "You mustn't be afraid," she soothed. "We are going to have a nice party for only a little while. We are so fond of young people and we have no children for ourselves."

I sat for a moment, calculating fast. If I tried to escape at this speed I would probably be killed. If I waited for the car to stop at its destination I would certainly be overpowered by both my captors. How often had I put the hero of an adventure story into just such a dilemma! But always I provided someone to rescue him—or at least staged an earthquake for the purpose —and there was no one to rescue me, nor any likelihood of an earthquake in Paris.

There were, however, two policemen standing in the Place

de la République refereeing an argument between a taximan and his fare. As I reached again for the door-handle my 'protectress' grabbed me by the wrists. But at that age I had the strength of a young ox and very few women could have restrained me. Here we had to slow down almost to walking pace—traffic was streaming from the nearby railway stations—and when I had made it clear that I intended to escape the car stopped. As I scrambled out it half-turned and raced away down the Avenue de la République.

Had I been able to afford it I would have taken a taxi back to the Rue St Jacques because my legs felt extraordinarily wobbly. But I had just enough money left to keep me in food until I got home. So I walked, only pausing to buy a bottle of plonk for my nerves in an all-night lorry-drivers' restaurant.

My landlady—whose mother had been for three years my father's landlady—did not believe that the kidnappers were professional White Slavers. Had they been, she said, they would not have shown me 'dirty pix'—at least at that stage—and would have drugged me as soon as I entered the car. In her view they were one of the amateur gangs who had recently begun to operate to supply brothels in—of all places—Soviet Central Asia.

This was the first time I became aware of a curious personal inhibition which I have never been able to overcome. When we reached the Place de la République and I saw the policemen it would have been simpler to yell for help than to struggle to open the car door. But even had my situation been much more desperate I could not have done so. And in various other awkward situations I have experienced the same difficulty. Something very deeply rooted and stupid—I have no idea what it is—prevents me from calling out for help.

Paris inspired another long article, also published in *Hibernia*, which omitted the White Slavers but vainly tried to convey the enchantment of that city—an enchantment not at all dependent, it seemed to me, on the way its citizens treated visitors, yet potent enough to make one feel drunk on fresh air. (Which was just as well, because by the time I had got that far I could afford little else.)

This journey amazed our neighbours—mine was not a venturesome generation, as are the young of today—and it temporarily assuaged my wanderlust. Short trips to the continent were the most that could be expected of life so I derived the maximum satisfaction from the attainable and rarely, at this time, dwelt upon the unattainable. Yet down in the unconscious frustration and resentment must have been accumulating like pus. My lack of freedom inevitably galled more because I had proved how easy it was to travel very cheaply by bicycle, how little it mattered not being a linguist, how ready most people were to befriend a stranger and, above all, how well suited to wandering was my own temperament. Only domestic responsibilities stood between me and India.

While in Britain and abroad I had, out of curiosity, attended various non-Catholic services instead of going to Sunday Mass. This may not seem world-shattering, but in an Irish Catholic context it is—even now, never mind a quarter of a century ago. My omission, if known throughout Lismore, would have revealed that I was at best Losing the Faith and probably had already lost it. As of course I had, without going through any phase of violent, scornful hostility towards Christianity, even in its Irish Catholic aspect. It was then, as it still is, my instinct to respect all religions and deprecate insults to any. But from the age of eighteen or nineteen I felt no further urge to solve the insoluble, or to belong to a community with common beliefs, or to worship in traditional ways. The untroubled conscience with which I 'lost the faith' perhaps explains my lack of hostility. It was an amicable arrangement, as far as God (or whatever) and I were concerned—for me a peaceful, natural and, in a sense, unimportant development. Irish Christianity is a peculiarly hypnotising and powerful force which can make many 'deserters' feel guilty, deep down, for a lifetime. But my parents had shielded me from the Church's weapon of superstition and so, when the time came, I was free to 'desert' unscathed.

There was, however, a certain irony here. My parents, who had unwittingly shown me the easiest route out of the Church, would have been shattered to realise that I had taken it. So for a few years I continued to attend Sunday Mass in Lismore, this being the only positive action necessary to deceive—and protect—them. Going to Mass bored me but did not then represent any betrayal of my principles, as it might have done had I become a militant atheist. I would have preferred to avoid such hypocrisy, but as my motive was good my conscience for a time remained clear. Then—while in Germany, discussing Bonhoeffer in the Hilckmanns' garden—this attitude changed. I came home convinced that it was wrong to use any religious service merely as a convenience, however worthy one's motives, and I never again went to Mass in Lismore.

Instead, I continued to be hypocritical/protective by leaving the house at Mass time and going for a walk. Never having been a 'Sunday best' person, this seemed an easy deception. The neighbours would assume that I had been to an earlier Mass, or was going to a later one, and they had so few contacts with my parents that my subterfuge was unlikely to be detected. Or so I reckoned, not quite appreciating the extent of the neighbours' interest in my movements. In fact it was detected within a year, both by my parents and the neighbours—and, presumably, by the local clergy. But nobody commented on it. Concerning the clerical reaction—or lack of it—I have written elsewhere, 'When I "lapsed" a quarter of a century ago—long before such an event could be spoken about above a whisper in rural Ireland—no priest ever attempted to "get me back"; the local clergy knew perfectly well that I was not, and never had been, within their disciplinary reach. I am still living in that same little town, on good terms with the clergy of all denominations and with the nuns in the convent next door to my house. No doubt prayers are wistfully said for my salvation but nobody, clergy or lay, has ever tried to make me feel ill at ease because of my defection.' My parents were equally restrained. I was then twenty-one and though my mother sought to dominate me in other ways both she and my father had too much respect for me (and perhaps too much experience of my obstinacy) even to attempt to influence me on such a matter. This restraint must have cost them something. According to their beliefs it was a parental duty to try to persuade me to rethink, to pray for faith and repent the error of my ways. Their neglect of this duty is perhaps an indication that both had more in common with Luther than either would have cared to admit. As for the neighbours, scandalised and disapproving as they must have been, there is in the Irish an innate delicacy (or is it a form of *laissez-faire*?) which generally prevents them from ostracising those who have left the herd; unless of course the deserter flagrantly defies convention in other ways that directly offend local sensibilities.

At that time the only people with whom I discussed religion were Mark and Godfrey. Naturally it distressed Mark to realise that I was no longer doubting or wondering but had unequivocally ceased to be a Christian. Yet he was too wise a man and too genuine a priest to argue with me. And his distress was less than I had feared it might be. It now seems to me that he appreciated my real feelings about religion some fifteen years before I myself did. We referred to the matter only briefly and infrequently; in this as in other respects our understanding needed few words.

With Godfrey it was otherwise; during our first few years together religion provided the area in which we drew closest. For us both it was important, but whereas I remained undisturbed by my discovery that I could never be a sincere Christian, Godfrey needed his faith and was frightened to think of ever losing it. Characteristically, he often blamed himself for having voiced his own doubts to me, lest these might have helped to undermine my faith. Such moods of confiding in me, followed by scruples because he had confided, were typical of the dual nature of our relationship. Sometimes he treated me as a person of equal experience and maturity, sometimes his attitude was almost autocratically paternal. The first mood I regarded as an undeserved compliment, the second I meekly accepted as inevitable. To me someone approaching forty was elderly and my inherent respect for age checked any resentment I might have felt when Godfrey was at his most peremptory. Indeed, I thought his paternal moods more authentic than his 'equality' moods. These I diagnosed as symptoms of a loneliness so profound that it sometimes made my youth seem irrelevant —a diagnosis not quite fair to myself. In some ways I was of course absurdly naive. But in other ways—the ways that mattered to Godfrey—I was more percipient and tactful than many an older person. My own domestic stresses and strains had equipped me to understand the very different but no less wearing stresses and strains of Godfrey's life. He was—though I did not then see him as such—an extremely neurotic man who needed to be treated with consistent gentleness, sympathy and patience. Because I loved him, he brought these qualities out in me; and because this was so, he came to return my love.

At the end of August 1952 it was three years since our first drive to Goat Island, yet we had never once expressed our affection by even the most tentative physical contact. Then suddenly—we were sitting beside Bayl Lough, on an afternoon of sparkling water and white clouds hurrying above the hills—suddenly Godfrey turned and looked into my eyes. And then he kissed me and we made love.

The kind of love we shared from that day on would have been impossible, I believe, had physical passion always been an element in our relationship; for three years we had been laying foundations and they were deep and strong.

On our way up the rough track to the road we conversed stiltedly, like the strangers we were in these new roles. Most vividly I remember my exultant sense of kinship with everything I saw—with the sheep and the crows and the stream by the track and the rocks and the heather and the clouds in the sky. I felt that until this day I had been only half-alive, half-aware; now I had a new relationship not just with Godfrey but with all of nature. And then there was a wondering incredulity, a sensation of the impossible having become reality. And also, inevitably, there was a triumphant relishing of power—at the time unrecognised, in my romantic delirium, but already operating. For so long I had been in Godfrey's power: now at last he was equally in mine. As we stood by his car and my bicycle, at the very spot where our first drive to Goat Island had begun, I looked at him, with a strong awareness of possessing him, and asked, for the first time, "When do we meet again?"

Godfrey turned away and got into the car. "Never would be best", he said. Then he switched on the engine and added, "Tomorrow, by the river."

Free-wheeling home, I felt indifferent to Godfrey's unhappy remorse. A woman's love can be as ruthless as a man's.

Now I had exchanged innocence for understanding and that night my own aroused body told me what a marathon of self-control had ended for Godfrey by Bayl Lough. My respect for him increased accordingly—and I felt gratitude, too. Any earlier would have been too soon. As it was, that day had not been marred by any confusion, uncertainty, regret or doubt. I vaguely wished we could marry, but it mattered little that we could not. The formality of marriage seemed a mere dusty document beside the fiery jewel of our love. Godfrey of course would feel otherwise and already I was prepared to be sacrificed on the altar of his scruples. But now I felt capable of coping with any number of complex Godfrey reactions. And intuitively he must have known that at last I was ready to take the hardships as well as the joys of an adult liaison.

The following evening he first said "I love you" as we stood, towards sunset, on the river bank. Then my armour of selfishness was penetrated by the sadness behind those words. He added that really we should discuss things sensibly; but there was nothing to discuss. He meant, I knew, that we should face up to the impracticality of the situation, say good-bye and get on with life separately and rationally. Yet the idea was too preposterous even to be mentioned. To my relief he never questioned the durability of our love. This had been my only fear—that he might retreat behind a barrier of cynicism and dismiss my feelings as transient youthful emotionalism. Predictably he condemned himself, at length and bitterly, for having cultivated a friendship that was bound at some stage to complicate my future. I replied that as a woman of nearly twenty-one I could look after my own future. Godfrey well knew my views on marriage and though he disagreed with them they were now conveniently reassuring. However, he did dutifully point out that it was too soon for me to withdraw from the matrimonial stakes—if I could ever have been described as an entry—and that if I detached from him I might eventually fall for some eligible man of an appropriate age. But his tone lacked conviction; we were both conscious of an inexorability about our relationship. It didn't make sense yet it seemed to exist almost as an outside force, independent of our decisions.

Because of Godfrey's scruples about extra-marital sex I now had to excercise my share of self-control—admittedly a less difficult task for a woman, yet not easy when one's passions have just been awakened. To me these scruples were absurd, but recognising their sincerity I loyally deferred to them. It often seemed a black joke that in this relationship with a Protestant Englishman I was up against precisely the sort of inhibitions that are chiefly associated with Catholic Irishmen. Fortunately Godfrey's scruples ceased to be effective at fairly regular intervals, but my primitive delight in love-making was always overshadowed by an uneasy and faintly unflattering awareness of Godfrey's sense of sin. Had the physical bond been our strongest, this relationship would have rapidly disintegrated.

On the surface it looks like very hard luck when a woman always falls in love with 'the wrong man'. Yet in my case this apparent hard luck may be linked to that strong adolescent premonition about never marrying. Perhaps we unconsciously avoid situations for which we are ill-equipped, even if avoiding them entails an amount of immediate suffering.

Had Godfrey been free to marry, it would still have been difficult for me to leave home; so his being unfree spared me a major crisis of conscience. As things were, I took care to conceal our relationship from my parents, knowing that it would have needlessly upset them even to suspect that I was involved with a man who was still married, both by his own and their reckoning. Looking back, I doubt if my mother can have remained blind to my in-love bliss. But she never tried to pry.

Neither of my parents ever questioned me about how I spent my free time; they must have speculated, but their tact was supreme. Outwardly they got no reward for this, only an increasingly uncommunicative daughter. But indirectly they were repaid. Having been allowed, from the age of fourteen, to follow as independent a path as circumstances permitted, I carefully shielded them from all unnecessary worry on my behalf. Never once, during this period, did I even consider adding to their difficulties by staking my claim to a normal life. But to write thus gives a false impression of an heroically self-sacrificing daughter. It was not like that. I did not consider and choose and put my parents first; to do so was not in my nature. Indeed, by temperament I was peculiarly incapable of being a comfort to them. But always I was conscious of our three lives being in one sense a unit on the scales of Fate and at least I could refrain from deliberately adding to their misfortunes. I had youth and health and hope and love and an enormous capacity for enjoyment—even against the odds. To break them, in quest of further advantages, was, literally, unthinkable.

Yet there was a certain remorseless brutality in the way I went about constructing my aloof adult relationship with both parents. However useful I may have been as a daughter around the house (and I wasn't very), my failure to grow into a friend must have grieved them deeply. But I had to isolate myself mentally if I were to continue to live at home. At the time I did not weigh and calculate in this fashion; my withdrawal was instinctive though I knew what I was doing and that I was being cruel. Now I realise that by turning away from my parents at an age when exchanges of opinions could have been most rewarding, and by assuming that they would react to a given situation in a certain way, without ever testing them, I was both impoverishing myself and doing an injustice to two remarkable people. But I cannot have regrets. It was as it had to be.

14

One result of my new relationship with Godfrey was a return to 'marathon' writing, which I had sensibly abandoned for a few years to devote more time to reading. During the winter of 1952–53 I attempted my first novel. The heroine only slightly resembled myself because this was not the semi-autobiographical first effort of many aspiring novelists. Instead, it had a curiously prophetic theme—the growing-up of an illegitimate girl in a small Irish town.

It will be remembered that illegitimacy and its problems had come early to my notice. As a child I had often heard my mother arguing that the socially crippling effects of unmarried motherhood constituted an altogether disproportionate punishment for a momentary loss of self-control. At the same time it was emphasised—for my benefit—that only the 'less fortunate' sort of girl lost her self-control in this context. 'Less fortunate' was my mother's favourite euphemism when she wished to make class distinctions. Although perhaps euphemism is unfair; she was a practical Christian who used that phrase with compassion.

The illegitimate birth-rate has always been high in Ireland, among the 'less fortunate', yet until very recently the conventions demanded elaborate pretences that deceived nobody but maintained a façade of 'decent Catholic living'. Many much-loved bastards were brought up as their mother's youngest sibling (as in Brid's case) or, if this seemed biologically unconvincing, as her nephew or niece. Among the more fortunate, however, things were different—always far less civilised and frequently inhumane. A Co Cork case shocked my parents and me in 1952. The only daughter of a middle-class family—my exact contemporary—became pregnant by a married man while a student at University College Cork and was banished 'for ever' from her parents' home. Her father even discontinued her allowance and forbade her mother to contact her. In due course we heard that the wretched girl had had a nervous breakdown as a result of being forced to give up her son for adoption. And this was the too familiar tragedy behind my novel.

Despite having my own study at home, I usually worked, during my evening off-duty hours, in my father's office in the empty County Library Headquarters. Then, as now, I preferred while writing to be completely alone and beyond reach of any interruption. Besides, the domestic atmosphere was gradually becoming less conducive to concentration. Often my mother and I quarrelled during the day about some trivial point of household management and by six o'clock I was longing to escape from the very unpleasant vibes we had created between us.

I wrote this novel only because it was kicking to get out—but Godfrey, to my gratified surprise, urged me to have it typed. It was sent to some half-dozen publishers and one cautiously hinted that if I made the tragic ending a happy one they might reconsider it. But this I was not prepared to do. Although I knew that it was mediocre and mawkish it had a certain integrity and the ending, however crudely melodramatic, was—to me—inevitable and right and so could not be changed to suit the market. This failure to get into print between hard covers did not at all depress me. I had expected it and—as on my first excursion into the literary world—I considered the 'try again' remarks of various publishers a fair reward for my labours. During the following winter I wrote another novel—just for fun—but this time had enough sense not to listen to Godfrey and waste more money on typing fees.

In 1952 my father had spent his annual month's holiday at home, while I was abroad, because he no longer felt able to cope simultaneously with library and domestic duties. My mother therefore decided that in 1953 I must do a month on solo duty while my father deep-sea-fished. To this equitable arrangement I could scarcely object. Yet incipient panic threatened if I allowed myself to think about spending two years in Lismore without even an occasional day off.

When the time came I found that month an almost intolerable strain. For me my mother would make none of those concessions which she gladly made to spare my father. On his departure for West Cork in June 1953 I was condemned to a month's virtual imprisonment. My mother insisted on never being left alone in the house for more than an hour a day, which just gave me time to rush down to the Blackwater for a swim, doing the shopping on the way home. I could not go far enough afield to meet Godfrey in the sort of seclusion he demanded and Mark's daily visits to our house afforded me my only safety-valve. He always brought a bottle of dry sherry to cheer me up and we would sit drinking in the kitchen while he told me the latest dirty jokes about the Vatican. But even his visits were a qualified form of relaxation; although my mother never commented on them I knew how much she resented Mark and after each visit she obliquely punished me. Fortunately I was still very resilient and the day my father returned I recovered my equilibrium.

Soon I was eagerly planning and reading in preparation for a Spanish tour in the following spring and it was on this journey that I first fell in love with a country. My earlier tours had been immensely enjoyable and rewarding, but none of the countries visited had had the particular ingredients needed to spark me off as a travel writer. In Spain, at that time, there was an exciting sense of remoteness, both spatial and temporal. I pedalled as far off the beaten track as possible—encountering no hostility anywhere—and never before had I experienced anything like the Spanish quality of solitude and silence. The landscape, too, was dramatic—as was the climate, for in April blizzards were still blowing over the vastness of the Castilian plateau. Burgos was snow-bound and glittering under an ice-blue sky and a northerly gale made it unnecessary to pedal on the way to Salamanca.

Significantly, perhaps, two of my mother's favourite heroines were Isabella of Castile and Teresa of Avila; I had been reared on their life-stories, with Ferdinand and John of the Cross standing slightly in the background. Many small-town names therefore sounded both cosily familiar and gloriously romantic.

Again, Pappa had been a Cervantes addict—not surprisingly, given the resemblance between himself and the man from La Mancha—and his special children's copy of *Don Quixote*, from which he often read to us on those summer days in Lismore, had been edited by himself with a pencil to avert juvenile boredom. (His other, 1796 four-volume edition, published in Dublin by John Chambers 'As an Endeavour to Improve the art of Printing in Ireland', and with 'Some Account of the Author's Life by T. Smollett, M.D.', was among his most cherished possessions—and is now among mine.) However, George Borrow's *The Bible in Spain* and Walter Starkie's *Spanish Raggle-Taggle* were the books which directly inspired me to cycle around Spain. And the fact that I had done my homework so thoroughly—reading volumes of history, biography and travel, balanced by novels, plays and poems in translation—perhaps partly explains my feeling of instant affinity with the Spaniards. They seemed at once more comprehensible and more 'foreign' than the Germans or the French and I even found myself speaking a version of Spanish despite my notorious inability to learn foreign languages.

My independence of Youth Hostels also contributed to the success of this journey. None then existed in Spain, but the village *posadas* were even cheaper and got me involved with the sort of Spaniards I most wanted to meet. Occasionally, as the weather improved, I slept out in my flea-bag—once unwittingly in a graveyard which was the only level spot I could find on a pitch black night in the mountains of Aragon; I got quite a shock on waking next morning. At twenty-two I had reached my physical peak and could effortlessly cycle 120 miles a day through mountainous country on a heavy roadster laden with large panniers which were quite unnecessary for such a short trip. (It takes time to learn that a medium-sized rucksack can hold all one needs for six months.)

In Spain I kept a detailed diary for the first time, writing it up every evening, however tired I felt, and posting it to Godfrey once a week. On my return home he encouraged me to use this material and I sold a series of twelve articles to *The Irish Independent*, Irelands' most popular daily newspaper. Heartened by this success—I had for the first time earned a considerable sum of money, by Murphy standards—I began work on a travel book, writing into the small hours every night for five months. Most of my earnings were willingly spent on the typing of those 100,000 words. This book seemed to me no worse than many recently published volumes of a similar type—and better than some—so I felt very hard-done-by when four publishers rejected it. All the skill, knowledge, energy and concentration I then possessed had gone into it and I suspected that its failure was due to the subject matter rather than to technical deficiencies. An equally well- or ill-written book on somewhere more exotic would probably have proved acceptable. To write successfully on Spain, I reckoned, one would need the ability of a V. S. Pritchett or an Arland Ussher—authors with whom I knew I could never compete. Recently I skimmed through this typescript and could find no reason to change my earlier opinion. In some ways it is more polished than my first published book and its chief defect—verbosity—could have been remedied by any competent publisher's editor.

By the beginning of May 1955 I had decided to waste no more postage on my Spanish typescript. And it was at about this time that I experienced my first mood of desperation. It was only a mood—a sunny evening of agony—but its intensity frightened me. I remember lying on smooth turf near the river, beneath the new leaves of a beech tree, and looking up at the blue sky between the leaves, and feeling the torture of my seething discontent and resentment being accentuated—instead of soothed, as always before—by the beauty of the evening. The immediate cause of this desperation was my being unable to get back to Spain until the following year. At twenty-three I felt increasingly conscious of the passage of time, of my own thwarted potentialities and of being trapped in a situation from which there could be no possible escape in the foreseeable future. My ambition to cycle to India now came more often to the surface of my mind and I tormented myself with thoughts of Afghanistan and the Himalayas. It had been established that I was physically equal to such a journey; all I needed was freedom. Yet had my mother permitted another Spanish holiday that year I would have philosophically forgotten India. I was not craving the unattainable—complete freedom. My demands were reasonable and my willingness to compromise was always there had my mother chosen to take advantage of it.

However, this obvious grievance was but one of the causes of my new unhappiness. No less important was my recent literary disappointment—the first of my career, since I had never before seriously expected a typescript to be accepted. Had I been asked to choose between returning at once to Spain for three months and having my book published there is no doubt what my choice would have been. And having proved to my own satisfaction that I could write a moderately good travel book, the circumstances that prevented me from gathering saleable raw material chafed all the more.

Loyalty to Godfrey inhibited me from acknowledging—even to myself, at the time—another factor that was compounding the tension in my life. For me the constraint which he struggled to impose on our physical relationship was becoming more and more trying as the novelty of being loved wore off and the flesh ached for its due. This constraint was prompted not only by his personal code of sexual morality but by an absurd theory that the more celibate we were the more likely I would be to detach from him, emotionally. Such an attitude says a lot for his nobility of mind but very little for his perspicacity. Even had we been entirely celibate I would have loved him no less. Faithfulness is not a virtue but a trait natural to some people. Its semblance may be cultivated—and this no doubt often is a virtue—but the converse is not true. Faithfulness cannot be quenched, except by the total and final disappearance from one person's life of another.

Godfrey's notion that sexual deprivation might eventually wither my love could be misinterpreted as a measure of how little he understood me. Yet he never really doubted my constancy; at intervals, when his constraint-system broke down, he admitted this. And then he would explain that to placate his convoluted conscience he sometimes had to pretend to himself that our bond was fragile enough to be easily snapped should my future happiness seem to require this. During such introspections I used to reflect privately that a greater concern for my present happiness would be more to the point. Yet despite my no-holds-barred approach when Godfrey did let us off his moral leash, pride would never allow me deliberately to provoke him to make love. Also, his guilty aftermath was so grim, and so unnaturally prolonged, that I could not have all that mental suffering on my conscience.

During that summer Mark realised how close I was to crisis-point and how much I needed moral support of the astringent sort that does not encourage brooding. In June he urged me to confront my mother, announce that I must have a break and request her to go away to a nursing home for a month, or employ a private nurse to look after her at home in my absence. But both those ploys had been considered and rejected two years earlier. My mother argued that we could not afford either alternative; no nursing home would accept her unless she engaged special day and night nurses and no nurse would look after her at home unless we could provide someone to dance attendance on the nurse. This I knew to be true: hence my trapped feeling. I could not yet see that my mother had become alarmingly over-dependent on my father and myself and that she would have resisted such an arrangement however much money was available.

Life might have been easier for all of us had my mother allowed herself to complain openly about her sufferings. But I had no such thoughts at the time. Even after our bickering had become an almost daily event I never ceased inwardly to admire and feel proud of her stiff upper lip. There was something at once pathetic and heroic about her indestructible gaiety, her boundless enjoyment of books and music, her acute interest in politics and social problems and her indomitable dignity. It was natural that I should not think of her as an invalid, but neither did anybody else. All her life she retained her beauty and the glow of health on her cheeks. When she sat ready to receive visitors, with her chestnut hair falling in glossy waves over an embroidered silken shawl, only her motionless, unhumanly twisted hands reminded one that for half a lifetime she had been crippled. But now, behind the gallantry, the gaiety and the dignity, something was going very wrong. The tolerance and balance that had so enriched my childhood were being eroded as twenty-two years of rigorously controlled frustration took their toll.

Our domestic framework must have seemed stereotyped

enough to outsiders. In Ireland daughters are traditionally expected to be self-sacrificing and mothers are traditionally allowed to be selfish, and families endure the consequent overt or covert hostility for barren decades. But the personalities of my mother and myself made for unusually explosive complications. I did not accept that a young adult's only consideration should be his or her parents; and my mother, I can see now, was being demoralised by a growing realisation that her misfortune had cast a cold shadow upon my youth. Yet she knew that if she released me in the only way possible at this stage of her disease—by banishing herself permanently to a nursing home—anxious guilt about my separated parents' misery would have made my freedom worthless. Unhappily, however, I was now incapable of *acting*—as well as feeling—humanely. When I should have been striving to hide my discontent from my mother I flaunted it, savagely, knowing that to do so could achieve only a slight relaxation of my own tension at the expense of an increase in her suffering. Things might have been easier had she ever directly expressed some sympathy with my situation, but instead she tried to behave as though I were doing no more than my duty—and that not very well. By 1955 we were both losing our emotional grip and looking back I can see how a grim spiral developed as she sought to punish me for adding to her sufferings by exposing my own.

We had never agreed on the subject of housekeeping and it infuriated me when my mother began to try to regulate every tiny detail, though I had then been doing the job for nine years—not efficiently, I so loathed it, but adequately. This sort of thing sounds petty—even comical, in a sick sort of way —when put on paper. To me, however, it soon became a major issue. The furniture was to be waxed on Tuesdays, the silver polished on Wednesdays, the hearths blacked on Thursdays, the shopping done at this hour and the ironing at that ... There was nothing intrinsically unreasonable about the general outline—probably many housewives operate such systems— but it was not *my* way of running a home. I had my own slap-dash methods which incorporated such ingenious labour-saving devices as never cleaning a soup saucepan before using it for a stew. Therefore I violently resented my mother's humiliating post-wash-up inspections; she was treating me now as though I were a fifteen-year-old skivvy.

Yet—improbable as this may sound—we were still capable, during those two years between my Spanish tours, of genuinely enjoying each other's company. Despite the extent to which I had long since isolated myself from my parents, mentally and emotionally, and the growing mother/daughter antagonism I have just described, our strong mutual love was still there— settled, as it were, like a sediment on the bottom of our relationship, and apparent whenever it was stirred up by something that amused us. We shared an identical sense of humour which for a time preserved what remained of our sanity. And we both instinctively recognised humour's therapeutic value. At times we must have seemed strangely flippant for we used jokes to try to solve problems which, if taken seriously, might have brought us on to a collision course. My mother liked to quote Horace, as translated by Milton—'Joking decides great things / Stronger and better oft than earnest can.'

My return to Spain in 1956 was not the anticlimax it might have been. I postponed my holiday to September, to enjoy the grape harvest, and in many ways found this tour even more satisfying than the first. Writing a personal travel book about a country brings one very close to it, for reasons that even now I do not quite understand.

In England I had first learned to beware of generalisations about national characteristics ('The English are so *reserved*—no one will talk to you over there!') and in Spain this lesson was repeated. Despite the Spaniards' reputation for excluding foreigners from their homes, I was thrice invited to stay with families to whom I was a total stranger. And though all these families—in Ronda, in a village near Valencia and in Barcelona —were either very peasant or very bourgeois, the unreasonable strait-lacedness so often associated with Spain was never apparent. The young men of the household took me sight-seeing without a chaperon and with their mothers' approval. And their attitude towards me was neither salacious nor stilted.

On my way home I crossed the Pyrenees with twelve large bottles of Spanish brandy (bought for the equivalent of 25 pence each) rolled up in my sleeping bag and carefully roped to the carrier. This feat possibly constitutes a world record of some sort. But shortly afterwards Babieca's back wheel buckled irreparably so the effort may not have been the economy it seemed.

I arrived home on October 6 to find that five days previously my mother had been taken to a Cork hospital suffering from severe kidney-stones. But Mark assured me that there was no cause for alarm; she had responded well to treatment and was due home next day. My father was staying in a boarding-house near the hospital and when I telephoned him that evening he had a message from my mother: I was to have the house thoroughly spring-cleaned by the time they arrived back on the following afternoon. At which point I shocked myself by wishing vehemently that it had been necessary for my mother to spend at least one more week in hospital.

Not for an instant did I consider obeying the maternal order and devoting those uniquely precious hours of freedom to housework. Instead, I went to Godfrey's cottage for the night —the first night we had ever spent together in seven years. Even Godfrey felt that it was not an occasion for constraint. Or perhaps he was so startled by my totally unexpected arrival that he just didn't have time to put his constraint-mechanism into gear. Lying beside him after he had gone to sleep, I wondered why I did not more often ignore my mother's less reasonable commands. Then I saw that I had been able to defy her on this point only because I was beyond reach of whatever psychic—almost hypnotic—power she had over me when we were together. And having been away, leading a normal life for five weeks, also helped. As soon as I was back into the rhythm of the treadmill I would again become impotent to assert myself. For a mad moment I thought of cycling away in the morning to take a boat to England and there finding a job— any job—and freedom. But of course it would not be freedom. While my mother lived I could nowhere find freedom.

Loyalty prevented me from discussing the sordid details of our family life with anyone but Mark. Even to Godfrey I would not admit how difficult my mother made things, though it was impossible to conceal the fact that I was living under an increasing strain. Besides, he had enough problems and tensions of his own without being expected to participate in mine. And it was good for me to forget the domestic scene, in so far as I could, while we were together.

Cycling home over the heathery Vee early next morning, through crisp, bright autumn light, I wondered—'When will I again be able to enjoy the mountains in the morning?' Then my heart seemed to twist in my chest with angry despair. For years—probably—to come I would be housebound at all times, apart from my four-hour evening break, and throughout the winter months ahead I would never be out-of-doors in daylight. This deprivation I felt more acutely and continuously than any other. It truly was a form of mental torture, to be denied the most simple, and yet for me most exhilarating pleasure of roaming the countryside in all weathers, during all seasons and at all hours of the day and night. I realised then—free-wheeling down towards the silver serpent of mist that marked the Black-water—how little emotional stamina I had left. After my earlier tours I had for a few months felt cheerfully equal to anything. But this time it was not so.

The doctors had advised my mother to maintain a regular daily intake of four pints of home-made barley-water and this gave her a semi-valid excuse for making still greater demands on me; soon my off-duty hours had been reduced to three. Hitherto my father's nursing had been acceptable in a crisis, but by the end of that year my mother had decreed that only I could cope effectively. Mark tersely condemned this as a form of moral blackmail. Yet even at the time I—perhaps unfortunately—could see the invalid's point of view. Apart from the kidney-stones, which caused considerable extra pain and discomfort, her arthritis had recently entered a new phase. She was no longer able to write, or to feed herself, and turning the pages of a book demanded much dogged patience. To make her comfortable in bed or bath chair required a combination of skill, strength and gentleness that I, after a decade of almost daily practice, naturally possessed to a greater degree than anyone else. We formed a perfect team and mine was the only touch she did not dread. Indeed, she was hardly aware of it, so smooth was our team-work, and we often became absorbed in a wireless concert while going through the daily routine of washing and dressing. But the very ease with which I could accomplish these tasks—every day of the week, every week of the month, every month of the year—increased their suffocating monotony. As a civilised human being I should have rejoiced at my ability to ease my mother's burden. But I detested nursing even more than housekeeping—and detested myself for being so devoid of proper feeling—and then I came to detest my mother because her physical helplessness gave her such power over me. Undeniably she abused that power, as Mark said. But had my own attitudes and reactions been less barbarous she might not have done so—or at least not to the same extent. Yet now I can reproach neither of us for our behaviour. Even at the time I had frequent brief moments of total detachment when I seemed to be observing the Murphys, as a family, from outside. Then I saw that we were all equally to be pitied and that none of us was to be blamed. We were enmeshed in a hideous, unbreakable net, each having to play a part that denied his or her nature, each knowing that to struggle was futile and yet each incapable of not struggling.

The most astonishing thing about this period is how much I continued to enjoy life. My desperate or resentful moods became more frequent but were always brief. Human beings can adapt to almost anything and, though my adaptability was eventually to be overstrained, there was no day when I did not revel simply in existing. All my life I had felt grateful (to whom I knew not) for the gift of existence, and I felt no less so now. I discovered that one does not have to be happy, successful or fulfilled to enjoy living. Even the bitterest despair and frustration can at a deep level be relished as part of the human experience. And so is generated a basic content which survives the surface discontents provoked by everyday miseries. Thus I was for a long time fundamentally resigned to my situation; I could not otherwise have borne it. I had none of the supports that would have been available to a devout Christian yet I sensed a certain symmetry in the background. I believed, confusedly yet firmly, that Fate organises things constructively and that in some obscure way what now seemed so wrong and arid would be proved right and fruitful.

On a different (or perhaps not so different) level I had, for my weakest moments, an absurd little consolation which I mentioned not even to Mark. Although I have never been superstitious I could not help being comforted by my mother's story of a Romany woman she had met in Somerset when she was nineteen, before she knew my father. This gypsy foretold that she would marry a small, slim, dark man, and move away from her birthplace to live among many trees, and endure a very long illness—and have only one child, a daughter who would be famous. Every prediction but the last had by now come true. And though I did not in the least want to be famous, I hoped—and in my heart believed—that this fortune-teller's blanket-term covered authorship.

15

During the winter of 1956–57 the rapid and conclusive disintegration of our house coincided with the maturing of my father's life insurance policy; so we decided to build a bungalow on the outskirts of Lismore. North, the site overlooked the Blackwater valley where wooded ridges rise from the river to the foot of the mountains: south, it overlooked placid fields, bounded by fine old trees, and against the sky lay another wooded ridge, the watershed between the valleys of the Bride and the Blackwater. We were within five minutes' brisk walk of the town yet only one other building was in sight—the farm at the end of the long field that sloped down behind us to the river.

Significantly, our building activities temporarily improved the domestic atmosphere. My mother, who had architecture in her blood, designed the house herself with the aid of a local engineer. And, having found this outlet for her energies and talents, she became much easier to deal with. We drew closer than we had been for years as we discussed colour-schemes, floorings and cupboard spaces.

The decision to build delighted me. I had no grudge against the ruin that had been my home for as long as I could remember, but to own a house in Lismore would confirm my sense of belonging to the Blackwater valley. I visited the site often and, wandering through the embryonic rooms, wondered to what events they would form the background during the next half-century or so. I felt quite sure that here was my home for the rest of my life and this certainty was soothing.

On August 31, 1957, my father paid the last instalment of the builder's bill and next day we moved in. It was characteristic of my parents that the house did not seem very modern by contemporary standards. (Now it is often mistaken for a '30s dwelling.) Money was severely limited and all the emphasis was on sound basic materials. Not a shilling was left over for frills and to this day the pine floors remain uncarpeted. But in twenty years the place has needed no structural repairs and it seems unlikely to do so within my lifetime.

Our new house brought about a providential widening of my tiny social circle. While it was being built a mutual acquaintance had introduced me to an English couple who for ten years had been farming near Lismore. I found the Pearces unusually congenial but, though their invitation to call any time was plainly sincere, I felt diffident about accepting it. (My restricted life had left me a very gauche twenty-five-year old.) However, I eventually decided to use our move as an excuse to meet them again. They came to a house-warming supper, were introduced to my parents and asked me back. This time I readily accepted; I had by then realised that the Pearces were—on more than one count—in a somewhat similar situation to the Murphys. Like ourselves, they lacked an obvious social niche in West Waterford. Neither came of farming stock; Brian's father had been a business man, Daphne's an Anglican clergyman. And though they were on excellent terms with the neighbourhood, and had many friends in various parts of Ireland, they had found nobody on their own wavelength in the Lismore area. This lack was more constricting for Daphne than for Brian. He, as an indefatigable member of the National Farmers' Association, had for years been well integrated with the local community.

Daphne's interests and skills ranged from stock-breeding—at which she was outstandingly successful—to painting, literature and philosophy. She was a most unlikely person to be found farming on a remote Irish hillside and she clearly considered me an equally unlikely person to be found living in a bungalow outside Lismore. We needed each other and within a month of that supper party I was visiting the Pearces twice a week. There was no gradual process of assimilation; I had at once become a member of the family.

The Pearces, with their two children aged fifteen and five, provided a substitute for the normal family life I had never known. Yet the Pearce family could be described as normal only in contrast to the Murphy household's painfully distorted affections. I had suspected, when we first met, that they too had their problems and soon I was as immersed in those as the Pearces were in mine. For all concerned, this diversification of tensions and worries was helpful and we supported each other equally during the next gruelling year.

Daphne—my first woman friend—had entered my life at such an appropriate time that our meeting might have been stage-managed by some amiable angel. On one level we seemed to have known each other for a lifetime, so quickly did we become close. Yet, as a fresh observer of the Murphy scene, Daphne was able to provide objective insights and down-to-earth advice such as neither Mark nor Godfrey was capable of, both having been too close to my problems for too long.

During 1958 I needed every sort of moral support I could get. By Easter I had begun to worry about Godfrey's worsening smoker's cough and new irritability. But when I suggested a check-up he assured me most persuasively that he felt perfectly fit and I stopped worrying—consciously.

Meanwhile things had become almost intolerable at home. Since the onset of my mother's kidney complaint in 1956 I had not had one unbroken night's sleep. Every night I was roused once, in the small hours—and often twice, and sometimes thrice. Each break kept me up for at least an hour of torturing drowsiness and it was not possible for me to lie on in the morning because by seven-thirty my mother would once more need the bedpan.

My father, who slept on a folding divan bed in my mother's room, was also disturbed every night—needlessly—and the obvious solution was for me to give up my bedroom to him. No logical argument could be opposed to this move, yet for me it represented the erosion of the last fragment of my liberty. I had never, except at school, had to share a bedroom with anyone and the effect of this apparently trivial change in our domestic arrangements was devastating. Until then, nights had been a time of unwinding, despite the strain of being regularly awakened out of a deep sleep. If too overwrought to sleep, I could read, or write letters, into the small hours. (My concentration had been so diminished by lack of sleep that I had given up attempting to write anything more than letters.)

Above all I could feel that I was *myself*, in the solitude of my personal refuge. At the end of the day I needed, desperately, to be alone, having spent so many fraught hours in the dank shadow of my mother's inner disintegration. I often felt utterly unnerved by what then looked to me like a complete personality change though I now see it as a mere shift of emphasis. Under the pressure of steadily deteriorating health, certain traits which had always been present, but either suppressed or used constructively, were now being released and used destructively.

Mark urged me not to give up my bedroom, however unreasonable my attitude might seem, and to refuse to attend to my mother at night—thus forcing her either to reduce her barley-water intake in the evenings or to employ a night nurse. He argued that already I was near breaking-point and that for everybody's sake I should refuse to be bullied. Even from him I resented the use of 'bullied' in relation to my mother's behaviour. Yet it was justified, though her methods were so subtle that they went undetected by me.

I longed to take Mark's advice but was incapable of doing so. This was partly because my mother would have made me feel so guilty had I defied her, and partly because retaining my own room would have been so unfair on my father. Thus I allowed a routine to become established that almost destroyed me. I could no longer read in bed—or between chores, because my mother kept me so busy all day. Only by the exercise of considerable ingenuity could I get through a few chapters while preparing vegetables or washing clothes or polishing silver. (When up against it one discovers how much can be accomplished 'blind'.) Worst of all—because I had become so dependent on comforting visits from my friends—my mother developed a virulent, jealous hatred of those who were closest to me. Within five minutes, at most, of my receiving Mark or Daphne or Brian, she would summon me and demand elaborate attentions calculated to last longer than my visitor could wait. Occasionally her need was genuine, but usually it was simulated—and I knew this. Yet I could not fully accept my friends' verdict: that now her illness was not only physical. The rational part of me assented, but to act on the basis of this fact was impossible. Emotionally I resisted the thought of my mother's *mind* being diseased, though had I been able to think clearly I would have seen that the choice lay between this and a much more terrible form of spiritual corruption. So I persisted in treating her as an antagonist rather than as a patient—which proves that during those years I, too, was mentally unsound.

My mother and I were the most obvious victims of the Murphy situation, but my father must have suffered as much as either of us. While we went our tormented, obsessive ways, at least deriving some perverse relief from being active in our campaign of mutual destruction, he was a helpless, passive, sane observer, pitying us both yet unable directly to help either of us in our relationship with the other. Of course he was still helping my mother in other ways and indirectly he did help me, for I was aware of his unspoken sympathy. Our persisting inability to communicate and his loyalty to my mother prevented him from voicing this sympathy. But the older I grew the more pronounced became our strange, telepathic understanding—defying years of estrangement with the knowledge that blood has of blood.

This estrangement was now brought into my feud with my mother. For years she had accepted it sadly and tactfully, but from 1958 onwards she contemptuously upbraided me, almost every day, for my seeming indifference and ingratitude towards her beloved husband. My friends blamed my father for not intervening to free me from the maternal grip and when goaded beyond reason and justice I, too, used to condemn his pusillanimity. But this was unfair. My father, who had his own sort of moral courage and endurance, had always lacked decisiveness in his relationship with his wife. This had helped, in the past, to make their marriage the improbable success that it was; now it meant that he was no less trapped than myself. For him to appear to 'take my side' would have seemed a betrayal to my mother—though ultimately it would have been of as much benefit to her as to me—and like myself he was paralysed, at this stage, by misplaced compassion.

In my memory, August will always be the month most closely associated with Godfrey. In August 1949 we first drove to Goat Island, in August 1952 we first made love—and in August 1958 he told me that at last he was going to Peru. I did not believe him. For years he had been planning to explore Inca sites—archaeology was his subject—'When I feel better about things.' This meant when he had overcome his self-consciousness about his appearance; and I had noticed no recent improvement in that respect. We looked at each other in silence. And for an instant—it was a weird time-shift, not at all like a memory —I seemed to be back by Bayl Lough on the day when he had first looked at me with love. I knew that he knew that I did not believe him. I moved away, across the room. My heart was pounding with fear and I was shaking all over, uncontrollably. Then my fear was displaced by a desolating grief because he would not confide in me. I felt reduced again to the status of his young friend—the child whom he had to protect. Or was he protecting himself? In any case I would play it his way—as I always had. I left him ten minutes later, an hour earlier than necessary. We said good-bye casually at the gate, in full view of Jock, his manservant.

I can recall almost nothing of the next four and a half months. From London Godfrey wrote stiltedly to say that he had decided to spend some time there, bringing himself up to date on recent archaeological discoveries in Peru. He expected to be very busy, and not to have much time for letter writing. I think I tried at this point to persuade myself that he was telling the truth. But when there was no Christmas letter I came back to reality.

On January 3, 1959, Jock appeared at the back door as I was straining my mother's barley-water in the scullery. He had never before been to our house and he did not have to say anything. He gave me a small parcel, containing a letter and diaries, and explained that Godfrey had wished to be buried at sea. Neither of us showed any emotion. I did not encourage him to linger, but I felt that he understood. He, too, was a good friend.

As I carried the tray into my mother's room I felt—for the first and so far only time in my life—that I was about to faint. On the wireless Beethoven's Fifth had just begun. I put the tray by the bed and sat in an armchair out of sight of my mother. Then a curious thing happened. As I listened I could feel strength returning, and not only physical strength. This was one of the strangest experiences of my life: it is virtually impossible to describe. Physically I could *feel* the music surging through me, recharging me with every sort of energy. By the end I was completely composed and capable of continuing with the day's routine as though nothing had happened. But this was only a surface composure. Inwardly I had taken the penultimate step towards a complete mental breakdown.

Again, my memory retains few details about the appalling months that followed. Almost the only thing I can distinctly recollect is picking up a heavy chair and flinging it across my mother's room in a paroxysm of frustrated rage. Then, one July morning, I resolved to leave home for good. I cannot recall any particular 'last straw' incident. I only remember standing outside the back door, beside my loaded bicycle, and saying good-bye to my father. "I'm not coming back," I told him. He looked at me with despair in his eyes but said nothing.

Did I then believe my own words? Later it transpired that for a year or so I had been living in a fantasy world, a grim extension of the happy imaginings of childhood. Between September and December 1958 I had forged, to myself, letters from Godfrey at the rate of about two a week—and had shown them to the Pearces. Towards the end of this period, I had also forged letters from Godfrey to Brian and Daphne. And I had reported to them that Jock frequently called at Clairvaux with news of Godfrey—though at that time Jock was also in London and never once visited Ireland. Moreover, I invented friends of Godfrey who arranged secret rendezvous with me in the County Library when it was empty in the evenings. I have no recollection of all this, but long afterwards, when I had regained my balance, Daphne described to me my frantic fantasies. She also admitted that during this period, when she was driving towards Clairvaux to visit me, her predominant emotion was fear lest she might find that at last I had physically attacked my mother.

At that time I was becoming increasingly obsessed with guilt because I had broken a solemn promise to Godfrey by telling the Pearces about our relationship. This I do most vividly remember. On the secrecy issue, I can now see that Godfrey was alarmingly neurotic and had thoroughly infected me with his own neurosis—as if I hadn't enough of my own to be getting on with. The basis of his secrecy-neurosis was of course more guilt; he tortured himself with remorse about having destroyed my virtue and risked besmirching my reputation to such an extent that I would have to go through life marked as a dishonoured woman. In retrospect, it is hard to judge which of us was the more unbalanced by this stage. And I do not like to think what might have happened to me without Mark's sanity in the background.

Certainly when I left home on that July morning it was very necessary for me to believe, on the surface of my mind, that I was at last escaping. But below the surface I must still have known that no mere physical flight could free me.

I cycled straight to the Pearces' farm and spent a week there. (Mark was on holiday at the time.) During this period Daphne and Brian were doing all the giving; I could be of no help to anyone. They gave unstintingly, of understanding and affection, and greedily I took. Although they must have perceived the unreality of my fantasy plans they made no attempt to deprive me of them. Only in after years did I realise how mercilessly I then drained them, emotionally, by relentlessly forcing them to share in my own suffering. And because they loved me they did share in it, willingly.

My father telephoned—guessing where I had gone—and made a pathetically feeble attempt to persuade me to return home. I pitied him, yet knew that he knew why I could not—and should not—obey this summons. Using all the inner strength I had left, I restrained myself from thinking of my mother. To think of her would have been to pity her. And then I would have returned, dangerously abandoning my healing fantasy world.

All that week I talked feverishly of going to South America with my bicycle and cycling through the Andes. It was significant that I did not drag my real ambition—to cycle to India—into this sick morass. That belonged to a happier past—and, perhaps, to a happier future. Besides, there was nothing to prevent me from cycling to India in the morning—I could easily have borrowed the necessary small sum of money—and for my purpose I needed an impractical dream that could not possibly come true.

On August 1, having regained some outward semblance of normality, I cycled to Co Wicklow. There I spent another week—still talking of the Andes—with a family who at the time hardly knew me though they have since become close friends. Then I left for London to find, as I had convinced myself, a method of working my passage to South America. My efforts were genuine and vigorous enough—I remember visiting dozens of cargo shipping offices—but of course they failed. Meanwhile I had got a job as a canteen-hand in a home for down-and-outs in the East End. Most of my fellow workers were Irish and many of them appeared to be part-time prostitutes who, in their off-duty hours, comforted the down-and-outs for a small consideration. I liked them all, as individuals, though the crudeness of their conversation sickened me, almost literally—as it still would today, despite the changed standards of the 1970s. The home was run by a kindly woman who, when she hired me, said that I must have 'private accommodation' though the other girls slept four to a room. I protested at the time, sensing and objecting to élitism, but within twenty-four hours I felt very grateful for this privilege. (My room was a closet hardly big enough to hold a chair as well as the narrow iron bedstead.)

I spent my off-duty hours, which could be at any time of the day, visiting shipping offices, museums and picture galleries; or, when I had an evening off, going to the Old Vic or Covent Garden. To an observer, my job might have seemed dreary and arduous—dishing out steaming meals for hours on end in the heat of a London August—but to me it seemed positively relaxing. My eight-hour day left me more time to myself than I had had for many years. And—most important of all—I knew that I could sleep all night, every night. Only those who have endured long periods of interrupted and insufficient sleep can appreciate what that meant. Often, during the day, I thought with luxuriating delight of the night to come—as a drug-addict might think about his next fix.

I was of course constantly plagued by guilt. At first I ruthlessly suppressed it, but as the days passed and I unwound, and emerged from my fantasy, I allowed myself to examine it. I had certainly done a cruel thing. Although my escape had been essential it should have been effected more considerately and rationally, after alternative arrangements had been made for my mother's welfare. But she would not have consented to any such arrangements. I reasoned that it would be unfair to blame myself alone for this cruelty. It was like some poisonous vapour exhaled by a corrupting situation to which we had all three contributed. Then, for the first time, I allowed myself to look steadily and dispassionately at my mother's case. I can remember the spot where I finally reconciled myself to the fact that she had partly lost her reason. I was sitting outside St Paul's, in hot noonday sun, and my whole being seemed to be wrung by pity and anguish. The death of the mind is infinitely more terrible than the death of the body and I mourned my mother that day as I was never to mourn afterwards.

After three weeks in London I knew that I was ready to go home. I gave in my week's notice, wrote to my parents—of whom I had had news, through Mark, every other day—and positively looked forward to being back in Lismore and seeing my friends again. As I had always been wont to do, I counted my blessings, which seemed many and various when I compared my life to the lives of my workmates in the hostel. They were, indeed, free, as I had never been. But of what value was their freedom when they were so much 'less fortunate' than myself?

During that final week of liberty, while still out of my mother's emotional grip, I resolved on a campaign that would have spared us all much suffering had it been organised a few years sooner. On my return home I would, at least for a brief period, be in command. I had demonstrated not merely a reluctance but an incapacity to survive under my mother's régime; and, while she was still feeling the shock of my revolt, I would initiate my own reforms.

Arriving home, on a sunny mid-September day, I found my father in a predictable state of exhaustion and my mother in an even more amenable mood than I had hoped for. Aware of the authority conferred on me by my breakdown—the family doctor, in my presence, had bluntly said, "I told you so" to my mother—I announced quietly that I would engage a daily maid and take two hours off every morning or afternoon, in addition to four hours every evening. On alternate Saturdays and Sundays I would be out from two-thirty to ten-thirty and in April I would return to Spain. My mother meekly accepted all these reforms and was genially welcoming when I produced a cheerful, clean, intelligent, efficient sixteen-year-old who showed no alarm at the prospect of being left in charge of an invalid. (She was not of course expected to do any nursing chores, apart from helping my mother to drink her barley-water—which, incidentally, I was now rationing, to ensure my night's sleep.)

It dismayed me to find that although I had reclaimed my own bedroom, and given myself ample free time, my concentration remained unequal to reading a serious book and writing a coherent letter required a tremendous effort. Yet this was hardly surprising. The easing of my duties had not made the domestic atmosphere essentially any less tense and I was always braced for a resumption of hostilities. Outwardly my mother's attitude had changed considerably—for instance, she never now summoned me when I was talking to my friends in the sitting-room—but I could see how much she inwardly resented the extent of my victory. Despite my full awareness of her mental condition, our antagonisms had become too deeply rooted for either of us to extirpate them when we were in close daily proximity. However, for the rest of 1959 I was well able to take the strain, largely because I believed that my next year's holiday was secure.

Then, soon after Christmas, hostilities were resumed in a new and baffling way. My mother developed asthma and suffered frequent violent spasms at all hours of the night and day. This terrifying affliction was in a sense the most harrowing of all her diseases, not only for its victim but for my father and myself, who both loved her so much—though my love had long since ceased to be apparent. It of course meant that she could no longer be left in the care of a maidservant, that my bedroom again had to be sacrificed and that our nights were more broken even than hitherto. Also, before long it had been made plain that I could not reasonably expect to get away to Spain in April.

We still had Mary to do the housework and I still insisted on my alternate Saturdays and Sundays off duty. Otherwise we were back to the impasse of the previous year and by April I was again losing my grip. One symptom of this was an extreme, neurotic self-contempt. I had accepted that my mother was mentally ill, I daily witnessed her physical sufferings—yet I could feel no compassion or tenderness. I could not make myself feign sympathy during those ravaging asthmatic attacks. Worse, I now sometimes regarded my mother with a hatred that seemed to flare up like a sheet of evil fire from some diabolical inner volcano. It was her body that I hated—the body that had already destroyed the reality of *her* and was threatening to destroy my own reality. Afterwards, I understood this hatred as love gone underground. Then, I was aware of it only as a base emotion that frightened and disgusted me. I could not see deep enough within myself to discern my intense distress at my mother's agony. Had my natural reactions not been suppressed I might have disintegrated even sooner than I did. By concentrating on my own miseries, and callously ignoring my mother's, I at least remained sane enough to nurse her.

Several times, that summer, asthmatic attacks threatened my mother's life. And I did not find it necessary to conceal from myself the fact that I longed for her to die. The mother I had loved and the person I had admired was already dead. The tortured body, the tragically disordered mind and the degraded, petty emotions were a heart-breaking travesty. Yet our doctor had assured us that with the aid of modern drugs, attentive nursing and a basically ox-like constitution, my mother could live another twenty years. I dared not allow myself to dwell upon this prognosis. In twenty years' time I would be nearing fifty—a middle-aged woman, drained of physical stamina, emotionally embittered and intellectually atrophied. There were enough such dutiful unmarried daughters around Lismore for me to have a clear prevision of myself in 1980. It was about then that I switched from sherry to whiskey.

16

My father was sixty on December 16, 1960—a singularly auspicious date, my mother used to say, being also the birthday of Beethoven and Jane Austen. A few days later he went down with influenza, from which he usually recovered within forty-eight hours. But his resistance had been drastically lowered by the griefs and anxieties of the past few years and this time he spent a week in bed. While still convalescent he insisted on going to Dublin, by train, in blizzard conditions, on December 27. He had promised to lead a delegation of librarians to discuss with a government minister some—to him—vitally important point concerning the development of the library service; and he refused to back down at the eleventh hour, having had no opportunity to brief a substitute leader. My mother did all she could to check this lunacy, but on such an issue not even she could sway my father.

When he arrived home three days later, glorying in his delegation's victory over the minister, my mother and I were both shocked by his appearance. He went straight to bed and next morning was running a high temperature and too weak to stand up. At first we took this to be a not surprising influenza relapse, but by New Year's Day our doctor was suspecting nephritis. On January 3 a specialist came from Cork and explained that this well-known complication of neglected 'flu did not require hospital treatment. Given my father's medical record—apart from two attacks of sciatica, he had never in his life had any illness more serious than 'flu—it would probably right itself in a matter of weeks. I listened to these cheerful assurances with a disbelief that reminded me of Godfrey's Peruvian plans. On January 2 (the second anniversary of Godfrey's death) I had realised that my father was dying—and that he knew it.

For the next month I nursed both my parents, with the aid of twice-daily visits from the Jubilee Nurse. I lived on whiskey and cigarettes and often did not bother to undress at night when I slept on a camp-bed in my father's room. My mother now demanded far less attention. Engrossed in the suspense and horror of my father's illness, she was neglecting her barley-water treatment and had had no asthmatic attack since New Year's Eve. Her anguish, at the prospect of losing all that really mattered to her in this world, completely dissolved my hard core of unfeeling. We sat up at night over tumblers of whiskey, and my mother reverted to smoking Turkish cigarettes specially sent from Dublin—an indulgence foresworn, many years before, in the cause of economy—and we talked as adult friends, savouring the sort of relationship that should always have been ours. I marvelled then at this rebirth, in the shadow of death, of the person I had thought lost for ever.

For some three weeks my mother continued to hope, or to pretend to herself that she was hoping, yet my father's condition gave her less and less reason to do so. Meanwhile I existed in a strange state of thought-suspension, not attempting to cope intellectually with what I had never tried to evade emotionally. I only knew how thankful I was that the specialist had advised against hospital treatment. During those weeks a twenty-year-old barrier went down and the ordeal of witnessing my father's physical dissolution was eased by the fact that he was so palpably unafraid of death. Going into his room one dark afternoon at the end of January, I found him lying there, looking serenely out at the wide grey sky, with a hand on his open bible. I had thought of him, these past few years, as suffering no less than myself though in very different ways. Now I saw how wrong I had been. He wore an armour that I had not inherited.

A few days later the specialist came again and advised my father's removal to hospital. At seven o'clock an ambulance arrived and, as the stretcher was being carried past my mother's open door, my father weakly called, "Au revoir!" My mother and I both got slightly drunk that night as we listened to a Brandenberg Concerto and the Archduke Trio.

During the next week I travelled daily to Cork while kindly neighbours sat with my mother saying appropriate things in hushed tones. The nurses and doctors described my father as one of the most considerate and selfless patients they had ever met. Then, on February 9—the thirtieth anniversary of my parents' wedding—I was warned that he could not possibly live more than another two days, and that he had been told this. Yet when I went into his room he seemed no worse than previously. We looked at each other, and then spontaneously shook hands with a curious mixture of formality and tenderness. "Will Kit be able to come?" my father asked. I assured him that she would—in fact her suitcases were already packed—and within half-an-hour I had booked another hospital room and organised an ambulance in which I drove back to Lismore. Three hours later, my mother's bath chair was wheeled close to my father's bedside.

Despite the medical forecast, a few days passed, and another few days, and a week, and still my father lived on, calm and clear of mind, steady of speech, holding his wife's deformed hand for hours on end. I was entirely superfluous to both of them and spent most of the day in my mother's room across the corridor, reading P. G. Wodehouse and sipping whiskey. When I joined them at mealtimes, to feed my mother, I often found them laughing together. Sometimes my father attempted to discuss the practical problems that were looming for his widow and daughter. But my mother would dryly point out that this was an inappropriate time to change a life-long habit of concentrating on spiritual rather than monetary matters. I saw then how firmly they believed in a reunion elsewhere. To me, death was a question mark. To them, it was a temporary separation—sad beyond measure, yet not final. At that time a strange sort of gaiety possessed us as a family, artificial on one level, genuine on another. And as the days passed my father, inexplicably, continued to live. His doctors used to pace up and down the corridors in a ferment of scientific curiosity and bewilderment, muttering theories *sotto voce*. To me, however, my father's surviving was a clear case of mind over matter; he did not want to leave my mother. He himself took a keen interest in the mystery of his own continuing existence. Medical conundrums had always fascinated him and now he was not only willing but eager to consider the most grisly hypotheses with his doctors.

By this stage, inevitably, my mother had begun to hope again, though she would not admit as much. But then, on the morning of February 25, my father had a haemorrhage and became perceptibly weaker. Yet he did not lose consciousness and all that day, as we sat by his bed, he was aware of us. At twenty to seven in the evening he was still holding my mother's hand firmly with his right hand. I was holding his left hand, with a finger on the slowing pulse. So gently did he go that I realised it moments before my mother did.

The hospital staff were a little disconcerted by my mother's composure—and, indeed, by mine. Tears, one gathered, were obligatory, yet we shed not one between us. As I went to and fro, arranging what had to be arranged, I was pursued up and down corridors by perplexed nuns brandishing unwanted sleeping pills and assuring me that everybody needed sedatives after a bereavement.

My father's was the first corpse I had seen, yet it left me unmoved. It was simply an irrelevant, impermanent piece of matter. As the funeral procession travelled to Lismore I sat by my mother in the ambulance behind the hearse, more conscious of apprehension about my new responsibilities than of grief.

My father was buried in Lismore on February 27—the first of his family, for many generations, to be laid to rest outside Dublin. The town that had received him so coldly thirty years earlier closed its shops in mourning, and it comforted us that the phrases of praise and regret were uttered not only because convention prescribed them.

I stood between Daphne and Brian at the graveside, disliking my conspicuous rôle as chief mourner and feeling more embarrassed than distressed by the inescapable ritual. Many, I knew, were expecting me to break down and add a touch of drama to the occasion. The Irish have a flair for wringing from death the last drop of emotion and they do not quite understand those who react otherwise. It was a still, sunny day, the air damp and warm; birds sang their first desultory spring songs in the grassy graveyard—until alarmed by the volley of shots that rang out over the coffin of a man who had been a soldier not only in his youth.

*　　*　　*

We all enjoy drama with some part of ourselves—whatever its source—and are stimulated by it. But now suddenly the tension, the need for courage, the compulsion to consider only the dying, the will to control panic and grief, the first challenging confrontation with the vast, incomprehensible fact of Absence—all were gone. So too, on the morning after the funeral, were the visiting friends and relatives from Dublin. My mother and I faced each other, alone, in a house that felt chill and damp after two and a half weeks of emptiness. Soon it had become clear that my mother expected me to be able, by some miracle, to fill my father's place. The absurdity of this expectation both touched and enraged me. I had hoped that she and I could continue to build on our new friendship, but if my mother could not accept me as myself she would have to forgo all the support that I was then most willing to give.

I did not, of course, see the situation so plainly at the time. I only saw the maternal will to dominate reasserting itself. It was decided that Mary must go, as we could no longer afford her wages; and though I knew this to be true I also knew that the time was inopportune for such an economy. We argued, and within hours my mother had had another severe asthmatic attack. The doctor had to be summoned, Mary had to be dismissed and for precisely ten weeks from the day of my father's funeral I did not once set foot outside the garden gate.

My mother's reversion to normality during my father's illness made it harder to accept mental derangement as a valid excuse for her behaviour. True, she had just suffered the heaviest possible emotional blow. But the effect of her irrational demands was to make me insensitive to her grief and I reproved myself hourly for my cruelty while watching it drive us both into ever deepening misery. Our neighbours added to my guilt by making me feel a hypocrite. They stared at the surface, and admired it, and had no conception of the spiritual betrayal below it. I was there twenty-four hours a day and my mother's every physical need, real or imagined, was ministered to promptly and efficiently—and with a savage resentment that would have scandalised those good neighbours had they been capable of discerning it. Looking back, I find it odd that I had not learned enough from my 1959 experience to resist this latest take-over by my mother's will. But this time she had the

two new weapons of asthma and bereavement, while I w
bereft of my father's tacit moral support and practical assistanc
Also, from him I had inherited a weak soft-heartedness that w.
closer to moral cowardice than to true kindness because
fostered my mother's neuroses.

My long imprisonment, during those ten weeks of spring
completely broke my spirit. I ceased to fight, inwardly, anc
lived from day to day in a cocoon of resignation. I ate almost
nothing, smoked far too many cigarettes and drank far too much
whiskey. Yet I never got drunk; I was at the more dangerous
stage of keeping my alcohol level up twenty-four hours a day.
Finally Mark took action, when he was unable to endure any
longer the change taking place within me. I can remember no
details, but a responsible daily woman was installed, my
mother was somehow persuaded of the urgent necessity of
releasing me and on May 7—that date I have never forgotten
—I cycled down the road, feeling incredulous, with three
hours of freedom ahead of me. This was to be the routine:
Saturdays and Sundays excepted, I would be free from two to
five every afternoon.

It needed only this break in the automaton rhythm of the
past months to release a cataract of despair. I was nearly
thirty and had achieved—it then seemed—nothing. As a
daughter I was a failure, as a woman I was ageing, as a writer
I was atrophied, as a traveller I had only glimpsed possibilities.
But at least I was again reacting and feeling, even if all my
feelings were painful.

In the middle of June, when we were granted probate, the
financial facts of our new life had to be faced. For the past
decade, one of my mother's most trying phobias had been an
economy mania. Gradually she had developed an obsessional
fear of real poverty, should my father predecease her—and now
her nightmare had come true. What were we to live on? We
had our home, and a weekly income from investments of
exactly £4. 2s.—and nothing else. Should we sell Clairvaux
and buy a small cottage or rent a couple of rooms? Or let
Clairvaux while living elsewhere? Or take in lodgers? Or
convert Clairvaux into two flats and let one of them? There
could be no question of my earning anything as I was almost

221

unnaturally devoid of accomplishments—unable to drive, type, sew, cook, garden, keep accounts or even amuse children. Yet I could not take our parlous economic state seriously; my Micawber streak is too strong. I have never been able to worry about money, partly because I need so little of it to keep me happy and partly because of an unshakeable conviction that 'Something Will Turn Up'. (Something always does.)

I at first thought it healthy for us to have this immediate, concrete problem to deflect us from our psychotic personality battle; but soon the problem had become part of the battle. I was totally opposed to selling Clairvaux; in an odd way I had always thought of it as particularly *mine*. And, despite what we had each endured within the house, I loved it—less for itself than for its surroundings. My mother, however, had worked out, most logically, that it made no sense for people with such a tiny income to have so much capital tied up in their home. She therefore decided, towards the end of June, to sell Clairvaux and move to a Dublin flat—or, more likely, bed-sitter.

I resisted this plan strenuously, and not only for the sake of the house. I knew that I could not possibly cope if uprooted from Lismore and deprived of my friends' support. But I lost the first round and early in July we moved to Dublin, leaving Clairvaux on an estate agent's books.

Our poverty notwithstanding, my mother was too proud to put any relative to the inconvenience of entertaining an invalid. She settled into a nursing home, moderating her nocturnal demands to avoid having to engage a private night nurse. I stayed nearby with an aunt and did duty from 7.00 am until 11.00 pm. At intervals I was despatched to inspect flats—a task which I mitched, having made up my mind that under no circumstances would I agree to settle in Dublin.

Our unfortunate relatives, suddenly drawn into the Murphy inferno, were altogether at a loss. They gave us much well-meant, conflicting and usually irrelevant advice, which we ignored. Only in opposing my decision to take a holiday abroad were they unanimous, seeing this as no way to treat a recently bereaved invalid mother. But I was impervious to their criticisms. I knew that I must now assert myself, once and for all,

222

as an adult whose reasonable demands had to be met if my mother and I were to have any future together. Our relatives, however, being unaware of these undercurrents, could not be blamed for condemning my plans as pure selfishness. (My mother and I habitually closed ranks in the presence of outsiders and never allowed them to see just how strained was our relationship.)

Now it was my turn to blackmail. In mid-July I told my mother that I had resigned myself to the sale of Clairvaux but would never agree to leaving the Blackwater Valley. If she would return to Lismore, we could go home after my holiday and set about searching for a suitable cottage. Otherwise, I would remain abroad. Without a moment's hesitation, my mother called my bluff by refusing even to consider a return to Lismore. A few hours later, my bicycle Roz and I took the night boat from Dun Laoghaire.

This time I was not being swept away from Ireland on a wave of demented fantasy; I intended to return as soon as my mother could adjust herself to the realities of our situation. Yet this flight from duty distressed me even more than my 1959 escape. My actions were not out of control, as they had been two years previously, and I knew that my ostensibly final departure was a calculated measure designed to break the will of someone who had already had to suffer far more than her share. Therefore during the internal dialogues that took place between the two halves of myself I found it necessary to emphasise how relentlessly my mother had followed a course that must drive me away—almost, indeed, as though a part of her wished to do so, thus unloading from her conscience the burden of being my millstone.

I landed at Calais with £10 in my money-belt—enough to take me to the Hilckmanns, in Mainz. There I could be sure of a warm welcome; they had stayed with us for six weeks during the previous summer while Anton was being taught Irish—his twenty-second language—by my father. I slept out in my flea-bag each night—the weather was almost too hot for long-distance cycling—and had unwound considerably by the time I reached Mainz. There I relaxed for a week before getting work as a farm-hand in the village of Ober Saulheim, some fourteen miles further down the Rhine. I spent the next six weeks hoeing vines, scouring churns, harvesting straw, mucking out cow byres, grading eggs and corking wine. My working hours were not much shorter than at home—5.0 am to 11.0 pm with a half-day on Sundays—but I welcomed being (by Irish standards) slave-driven. It was exactly what I needed at that time. Ceaseless labour, with only four half-hour breaks for vast meals—two of them picnic-style, eaten on the job-site—left me without the energy to fret. At the centre of me a hard little knot of guilty misery remained untied and I dared not think about the future. But meanwhile constant exertion in the open air, good food, few cigarettes and unbroken nights of deep sleep were rapidly restoring my health.

Even as late as 1961, in technological Germany, one could, as a farm-labourer, feel closely in touch with the past—with the many generations of villagers who had lived in those same houses, cultivating those same hectares. The almost universal farm village is unknown in Ireland and I enjoyed the novelty of sharing in Ober Saulheim's rhythmical community life. Early each morning lines of oxcarts creaked off to the cornfields in a cloud of yellowish dust, and files of vineyard workers made for the sunny slopes above the river with hoes over their shoulders, and groups of hausfraus gathered by the communal deep-freeze in the village centre to take out great hunks of meat and containers of fruit and vegetables. At that season Ober Saulheim smelt pleasantly of fresh cow-dung and sweet hay and new milk and fermenting wine, with only an occasional discordant whiff of diesel oil from a passing tractor. The nearest autobahn was only a kilometre away, but as far as the villagers were concerned it might have been on another planet.

Although my employer's vineyard was well known, and his son and heir was a forward-looking twenty-one-year-old, the Landgraf family—like their neighbours—used few labour-saving devices. They had all the basic bits of agricultural machinery, and a simple hand-machine for milking their ten cows, but the house, outbuildings and cellars—and most of their work methods—remained exactly as they had always been. This disdain for gadgetry and the symbols of affluence greatly appealed to me, as did the whole village atmosphere.

There must have been jealousies, squabbles and gossip, as in every such community, but the general feeling was of uncomplicated serenity.

Yet that holiday confirmed what I had suspected on my first visit to Germany: that the Germans and the Irish have remarkably little in common. The Landgrafs could not have been kinder to me and I became especially fond of Frau Landgraf, who treated me like an adopted daughter. But whether in the farming world of Ober Saulheim or in the academic world of Mainz—where I spent most Sunday afternoons with the Hilckmanns—I found it impossible to establish that rapport which had come about so effortlessly in Spain. No doubt the Germans are as well able to enjoy themselves as anyone else; it was probably mere chance that in both those circles nobody seemed to have the slightest interest in anything but unsmiling hard work.

At least twice a week relatives wrote to report on my mother's state. Physically she was no worse than usual and was being well cared for by the nursing-home staff—though she herself did not think so. Mentally, however, she was suffering intensely as a result of my desertion. Then, in mid-September, came a letter saying that she was longing to return to Lismore and enclosing a Frankfurt–Dublin air-ticket. On compassionate grounds, a dismantled Roz was allowed to travel with me as baggage.

I could detect no reproach in my mother's manner when we were reunited. And I wondered then, as I had for the same reason in 1959, if, with the residue of her 'real' self, she understood all and so could forgive all.

On our first evening at home in Lismore my mother suddenly said, "I want you to take Clairvaux off the books tomorrow. All my worrying about money is silly—not necessary. You'll have your freedom quite soon." She had spoken very matter-of-factly and I thought she was probably right; with my father she had wanted to live, without him she wanted to die. But her tone had been accusing—and there is a unique horror about being accused of wishing someone to die when the accusation is true. Momentarily I was tempted to make some insincere, dutiful remark; but I chose silence. Any false protest could only degrade our relationship still further. As it was, that brief exchange of words, glances and silences had had a paradoxically companionable undercurrent.

During the following days, I noticed how much my mother had changed in my absence. My struggle to break her grip on me had been only too successful. Not merely had she lost the will to dominate me, she seemed also to have lost the will to live. If I wished to lacerate myself I could argue, plausibly, that I killed her by deserting her that August. But if this is so, I did it under the guidance of my own instinct of self-preservation. Jungle law operated. One of us had to be sacrificed and the fittest survived.

The eleven months that followed were the saddest of my life. At times I even looked back nostalgically to the era of my mother's domination; that, at least, had been an expression of her personality—however distorted. Now her dulled mind and passivity and compliance were my punishment for having so implacably opposed her in the past. She still listened to music, but she did not read, or listen to discussions on the wireless, or wish to hear what was in the *Irish Times*, or proffer any opinion about the running of the household. Only when visitors called did some ember of pride flicker into flame and she would receive them with a poignantly recognisable shadow of her old graciousness and cheerfulness. I was no longer in her consciously exercised power, yet never before had she had such power to move me.

By the beginning of August 1962 it was clear that soon my mother would die; she who had never accepted pain-killers or tranquillisers was now permanently under heavy sedation. I moved about the house in a daze. Sorrow contributed nothing to it—or nothing that I could perceive. Relief predominated, but there was also a primitive reaction of horror—altogether absent during my father's last illness—to the physical dissolution of the body that for so long I had tended. In thirty years of invalidism my mother had never once developed a bedsore, but now her body began to decompose while she still lived. I could cope no longer and the Jubilee Nurse came twice a day.

On the evening of August 24 Daphne came to sit with me through the night and at twenty-five past one in the morning my mother died—as peacefully, in the end, as had my father. She had survived him by exactly eighteen months.

As my mother drew her last breath, peace enfolded me. It was profound and healing, untinged by grief, or remorse, or guilt, or loneliness. I thought of it as a gift from my mother's spirit—and then mocked my fancy, without quite discrediting it. For long I had suffered with her, and made her suffer, and been made to suffer by her; and of late I had mourned for her. Now I could only rejoice—and in Daphne's company I did not have to disguise my joy. A great burden was gone, the double burden of another's tragedy and my own inadequacy. I stood at the threshold of an independent life and I felt, that night, my parents' blessing on it.

After a moment I left the room—my mother had not yet assumed the aspect of the dead—and in defiance of local custom I never looked on her face again. Twelve years passed before a letter from a friend, on the subject of her own mother's death, allowed me to see why I had so obstinately stayed in the sitting-room when I should have been pretending to pray with the neighbours beside my mother's corpse. I knew, without permitting the knowledge to register on my conscious mind, what the undertaker would have to do to accommodate a malformed body in a conventional coffin. And I could not bring myself to look upon that body in a normal lying posture.

It is difficult to convey my feelings when I woke next morning and realised that I was responsible to and for no one but myself—that I was free to do what I liked, when I liked, as I liked. For more than sixteen years every day had been lived in the shadow of my mother's need. Even on holidays, my movements had had to be exactly regulated so that I would unfailingly arrive home on a certain date. I remember sitting in hot sunshine in the back garden with Daphne—surrounded by that untrammelled growth of nettles and thistles which proved me to be my father's daughter—and feeling currents of an appreciation of liberty running through my body like mild electric shocks. I was exalted by the realisation of freedom. When callers came to offer sympathy, Daphne received them

227

and gave the necessary convention-soothing impression that I was too distrait to appear.

Afterwards, I discovered that some of my friends had dreaded my reaction to my mother's death; when at last the almost intolerable pressure was removed, anything, they felt, might happen. They had overlooked the fact that for months the pressure had been gradually easing, giving me an opportunity to readjust.

Again I stood between Daphne and Brian at the graveside, as my mother's coffin was lowered to lie beside my father's. Then I returned with them to Monatrim and next morning visited Clairvaux for a few hours and was alone for the first time in my own home. Unexpectedly I found myself revelling in the novel sensation of ownership; possession of a house and all it contained seemed to symbolise Freedom and Independence. It never occurred to me that I had no means of maintaining the place: possession was all. At the age of thirty I had not yet possessed anything but the minimum of clothes, the maximum of books and a bicycle.

I wandered happily from room to room. The ghosts were friendly; the misunderstandings and antagonisms and furies and resentments of the past had left no stain. I decided to convert my mother's bedroom into my study, a simple change that needed only the replacing of her bed by the dining-room table. All the other furnishings of the room were left unchanged—it had been designed as a sitting room rather than a bedroom—and unchanged they remain to this day. I write on the spot where she died.

Love leaves calm. Even when circumstances have given it the semblance of hate, this is so. In the tangled relationships between my parents and myself love was often abused, denied, misdirected, thwarted, exploited and outwardly debased. But it existed, and it left calm.

17

Two days after my mother's funeral I left Lismore to visit my Co Wicklow friends. By then I realised that despite my basic calm I was, inevitably, suffering from shock. A total lack of physical energy betrayed this condition. Feeling too exhausted to cycle the 130 miles to Wicklow, I hitch-hiked.

My friends' house was near a private beach to which they and their guests had access. There, during the first week of September, I spent long, sunny, solitary days lying on the slopes of curving sand-dunes, gazing at the blue sky through tall clumps of green-gold grass and hearing nothing but the hiss of a lazy sea on the beach below. Swiftly my strength and energy returned. And then, towards the end of the week, something odd happened to my sense of time.

So stark was the contrast between my previous bondage and my present liberty that I could scarcely conceive of them as belonging to the same existence, and the few days since my mother's death seemed as long as the many years that had gone before. Yet counterbalancing this was a powerful sense of continuity. I had briefly experienced something similar after Godfrey's death and my father's; from now on I was to be aware of it as a permanent undercurrent. For however long my new life lasted, it would be subtly conditioned, in every detail, by a past which already seemed so remote that I saw myself moving through it as a stranger. And with no part of myself could I regret that past. This was not because of any deliberate effort to accept, in retrospect, what I had so often rejected when it was a present torment. In fact, I had never quite rejected it. Usually I had been half aware, and occasionally fully aware, of the potential value to any human being of a certain degree of suffering. Had mine continued much longer, it would have destroyed me. As it was, I could feel, at the end of the ordeal, wholly without resentment.

What had so often seemed wasted years, in my many moods of bitterness, now seemed otherwise. During those September days I could not have given any reason for feeling thus. But I have since realised that events and emotions which at the time of their happening were apparently destructive and enfeebling, in their enduring results were constructive and tempering. I had learned a lesson in humility that could not have been taught to anybody of my arrogant nature by less violent means. Without my friends I could not possibly have survived; their love had borne me to safety. And I recognised that, because of my prolonged emotional dependence on them, the person I had become over the past decade was partly their creation. Had I left home at eighteen and made a successful career for myself, I would probably have gone through life as an intolerant, unsympathetic bitch—a rôle for which I had as a youngster all the necessary qualifications. But years of being confronted by my personal weaknesses, and striving to comprehend our family weaknesses, had to some extent modified these traits. At thirty, I could ignore neither my own flaws nor the endless variety of causes that can lie behind the flaws of others. The school was hard, but the knowledge was priceless.

Many hours on the sand-dunes had been spent methodically planning my journey to India. Having for the past twenty years intended to make this journey, it did not strike me as in any way an odd idea. I thought then, as I still do, that if someone enjoys cycling and wishes to go to India, the obvious thing is to cycle there. Soon, however, I realised that most people were regarding me either as a lunatic or an embryonic heroine; in 1962 Western youth's mass trek to the East had not yet begun. When I went into a cycle shop to have Roz's derailleur gears removed, and explained that I was going to India and felt they would not be suitable for Asian roads, the mechanic looked at me very strangely indeed. After that I became a trifle inhibited about discussing my plans.

Several people suggested that the trip should be sponsored, perhaps by the makers of my bicycle—or by Guinness, since their product so habitually nourished the body that was to undertake this alleged marathon. Or even by a newspaper, to which I could send back dramatic stories from improbable places. But these suggestions appalled me. Any sponsor would have made of my private journey a public stunt and the very thought of the resultant limelight made me sweat with terror. Also, sponsorship would have given a dishonest twist to the whole experience. By this stage I had had to concede that there was, objectively, something slightly peculiar about the notion of cycling to India; to have persisted in denying this would have been to argue that the rest of the world was out of step. Yet subjectively it remained true that I saw nothing peculiar in it and to have the project presented to the public as something exotic and daring would have falsified it utterly. Of course I saw it as an adventure—that had been its attraction, since my tenth birthday—but I knew it required no unusual courage or stamina. It was planned as, and it proved to be, a happy-go-lucky private voyage to enjoy some of the world in the way that best suited my temperament. And, if the publishing trade winds were blowing my way, to provide material for a book.

I can see now that this journey seemed extraordinary to many simply because I provided my own energy. When the overland trek to Asia became popular among the young, a few years later, the vast majority hitch-hiked or used local transport—though they were half a generation my juniors and should have had that much more personal energy available. This dependence on motor transport I find very disquieting, when adventure and enjoyment are the objects of the exercise and time-saving is not a consideration. It indicates that we have become more dependent on *things* than rational beings should be. In some societies this dependence is already causing people to degenerate physically. Men and women who live all their lives in centrally heated homes and offices, and go in the car to post a letter and collect the children from school, and have labour-saving devices for every conceivable purpose (including electric tooth-brushes and carving-knives)—such people have become so sensually unaware and so unresponsive to physical challenges that they are only half-alive. If they cannot soon escape from Affluence and Technology some very odd biological mutations seem likely within the next few generations. The urge to effect this escape of course underlay what was vaguely known as the Hippy Movement. But few hippies realised that their routine of quitting the rat-race, seeking a guru, going vegetarian and growing a lot of hair was no substitute for training their bodies to do what in previous generations any healthy young body could do.

The winter of 1962–63 was Europe's most severe for eighty years and I shall never forget the agonising cold of that dark January morning when I began to cycle east from Dunkirk on an ice-bound road. As I wrote to Daphne a few days later, 'To have the fulfilment of a twenty-one-year-old ambition within one's grasp is quite disconcerting. I had thought about this moment so often that when I actually found myself living through it I felt as though some favourite scene from a novel had come, incredibly, to life.'

The hardships and poverty of my youth had been a good apprenticeship for this form of travel. I had been brought up to understand that material possessions and physical comfort should never be confused with success, achievement and security. And soon I was discovering for myself that our real material needs are very few and that the extras now presented as 'needs' not only endanger true contentment but diminish our human dignity. None of the privations, hazards or unforeseen diffi-culties of that journey bothered me. To be able unrestrainedly to gratify my wanderlust, after so many years of frustration, was all that mattered.

Soon after my arrival in New Delhi, I volunteered for work in a Tibetan refugee camp in the Himalayan foothills. Some of my friends then imagined that the miseries of Asia had so moved me that I felt compelled to contribute my mite towards their alleviation. But this was too simple an explanation, as was the reason I gave myself at the time—that it was too hot to travel any further. I now suspect that I took this unpaid job, and again immersed myself in grinding hard work amidst extreme physical suffering, because some absurd puritan streak made me feel that it was my duty to do so, after six months of unrelieved self-indulgence. Of course I very soon became deeply involved, emotionally, in the whole Tibetan refugee problem. But that is another story.

232

While I was still with the Tibetans, I received a puzzling letter from a well-known English publishing house expressing interest in my 'feat' and saying that should I happen to write a book about it they would be very interested to see the typescript. The book was in fact already written, as I had kept a detailed daily diary on the way to India. I explained this, promising to send the typescript in due course. It later transpired that a garbled account of 'Miraculous Overland Cycle by Lone Irishwoman' had appeared in an Indian paper and been spotted by that publisher's New Delhi agent.

Then, shortly before my return home in March 1964, I met Penelope Betjeman in Delhi. She had come to India to collect material for a book and when I confessed to literary ambitions she said, "Of course! Marvellous journey! Marvellous book! You must send it to Jock Murray."

We were cycling together through a crowded Old Delhi bazaar—Penelope with an accident-inviting load of firewood tied to her carrier—and I yelled above the blare of rickshaw horns, "To *whom*?"

"To Jock Murray," Penelope yelled back. "You'll adore Jock—everybody adores Jock."

"Do you mean John Murray in Albemarle Street?" I asked disbelievingly.

"Yes of course," said Penelope. "Jock will love it—just his sort of thing."

I was so profoundly shocked by this irreverent suggestion that I almost ran into a sacred cow. To someone reared on the lives and works of nineteenth-century English writers the very thought of submitting a Murphy typescript to John Murray seemed blasphemous. Jane Austen, Byron, Darwin, Borrow, Livingstone, Isabella Bird, Younghusband, even Queen Victoria—these and a score of other names flashed through my mind, dazzling me. I pedalled faster to draw level with Penelope and said, "You must be mad!"

"No more than usual," she retorted. "Don't forget—do as I say."

The immediate sequel to my journey was exceedingly unpleasant. In India I had been working under the Save the

Children Fund umbrella and on visiting their London headquarters I found myself seized upon as invaluable material for a fund-raising campaign. I was to be exposed to everything I most detested: a press conference, photographers, wireless interviews and—the ultimate hell—television interviews. Obviously I could not say no; I had witnessed too much suffering in the refugee camps not to co-operate. Miserably I went through the hoops, revolted by the spurious 'heroine image' being presented to a gullible public.

Before leaving London I called on the enterprising publishers who had already written to me. Their brand-new building was many-storeyed and many-corridored; it contained an army of whizz-kids and reminded me of a factory. I was received by three of the army in a large gleaming room with angular metal furniture and not a book in sight. There was much talk of royalties and promotion and a contract lay on an ugly table awaiting my signature. After my recent experiences the word 'promotion' brought me out in goose-flesh. I edged away from the contract and said I couldn't think of signing it until they had seen the typescript. What if they didn't like it? The three closed in, effusive and reassuring. I needn't worry—I had a fascinating story to tell—they had excellent editors—all would be well if I signed just *there*. 'Excellent editors . . .' My hackles rose. I did not intend to have my 'fascinating story' told in the words of any editor, however excellent. Besides, I intensely disliked the thought of any book being processed in this aseptic wilderness. Muttering vague half-promises, I withdrew.

Meanwhile another publisher was eagerly pursuing me but, being in no mood for further premature bargaining about my first-born brain-child, I hurried home to go through the final stages of parturition. I had had little time to consider what form my book might take, but the four friends for whose benefit it had been written were unanimous that I must rewrite nothing, transpose nothing, add nothing. I must simply delete, reducing a quarter of a million words to 80,000.

Towards the end of this five-week task another publisher arrived on the scene by post and I felt rather disheartened; clearly the publishing world coveted my book for its supposedly sensational theme. However, when the manuscript had been typed I sent a copy off to each of the interested houses and